Shawn Riley
(410) 531-6120

e-Learning
and the Science of
Instruction

Proven Guidelines for Consumers and Designers of Multimedia Learning

Ruth Colvin Clark • Richard E. Mayer

Pfeiffer
A Wiley Imprint
www.pfeiffer.com

Published by Pfeiffer
An Imprint of Wiley
989 Market Street, San Francisco, CA 94103-1741 www.pfeiffer.com

Readers should be aware that Internet websites offered as citations and/or sources for further information may have changed or disappeared between when this was written and when it is read.

For additional copies/bulk purchases of this book in the U.S. please contact 800-274-4434.

Pfeiffer books and products are available through most bookstores. To contact Pfeiffer directly call our Customer Care Department within the U.S. at 800-274-4434, outside the U.S. at 317-572-3985, fax 317-572-4002, or www.pfeiffer.com.

Pfeiffer also publishes its books in a variety of electronic formats. Some content that appears in print may not be available in electronic books.

ISBN: 0-7879-6051-9

Library of Congress Cataloging-in-Publication Data

Clark, Ruth Colvin
    E-Learning and the science of instruction : proven guidelines for consumers and
designers of multimedia learning / Ruth Colvin Clark and Richard E. Mayer.
        p. cm.
    Includes bibliographical references and index.
    ISBN 0–7879–6051–9
    1. Business education—Computer-assisted instruction. I. Mayer, Richard E., 1947– II.
Title.

HF1106 .C55   2002
658.3'124'028567—dc21   2002028700

Printed in the United States of America

Printing   10   9   8   7   6

To my husband
PETE SATTIG
for his support and patience through the writing (and rewriting) of
this book and to all the educational psychology researchers without
whose work this book could not have been written. (RC)

To my wife
BEVERLY
(RM)

CONTENTS

v

10. Leveraging Examples in e-Learning 173

11. Learning Together on the Web 197

ACKNOWLEDGMENTS

WE'VE BEEN FORTUNATE to receive extensive and detailed feedback on the book before it was written. Chopeta Lyons read every chapter. Based on her extensive e-learning development experience, she helped make our examples and guidelines accurate and relevant. She also transformed our quality management e-learning examples from rough sketches into credible storyboards.

It's rare that authors can get live reader reactions during the writing of a book. Thanks to some field trials sponsored by local professional societies we had that opportunity. Specifically we thank Ron Ryan and the Los Angeles Chapter of the International Society for Performance Improvement for sponsoring a workshop that featured an early draft of the book. Chapter members gave us excellent verbal and written suggestions for making it more readable and relevant for practitioners. We got similar feedback at a workshop sponsored by the Albuquerque Chapter of the American Society for Training & Development. We put these early field trials to good use in shaping the final drafts. We also received excellent detailed feedback from reviews of draft chapters arranged by Jossey-Bass/Pfeiffer.

We are also grateful to the e-learning production organizations who generously allowed us to preview and use screen samples from their courses to illustrate our guidelines. These include: DigitalThink, Element K, Moody's Financial Investment Services, Plato Learning Inc., Smart Force, and U.S. Army Defense Ammunition Center.

Finally we thank Matt Davis for his interest in this work and Kathleen Dolan Davies for her editorial support during the writing and production of the book.

FOR ME (RUTH CLARK) this book started about five years ago at a conference presentation on e-learning. There was standing room only. Like most of the other participants, I had heard the e-learning buzz and was eager to see the reality. But the early examples we saw at that presentation were dismal. Of course, I was coming from a CD-ROM e-learning environment, where memory is plentiful and designers have the luxury of the full spectrum of media elements, including sound, animation, photographs, video, and color. The audio, the realistic graphics, the video, and the simulations had disappeared. Text on scrolling screens predominated. While Web-delivered training was revolutionary in its universal access across networks and platforms, the quality of the training seemed like a giant step backward.

After the presentation, participants asked questions about issues related to learner control, questioning techniques, and screen design. Many questions had a familiar ring. They were the same as the questions raised years ago during the pioneer computer-based training (CBT) days of the late 1970s and early 1980s. I realized we now have a new generation of CBT consumers and designers who did not have the advantage of the lessons learned from those early e-learning trials. Additionally many do not have the benefits of the last fifteen years of research on cognitive learning methods that have significantly added to our knowledge about what helps and what hinders learning.

I was a science major undergraduate and have always been interested in research. As a result, I make regular visits to the local university library to keep up on advances in the field of educational psychology. Most of the research reports are written by academic practitioners for academic readers. The articles are not readily accessible to busy corporate and government practitioners. Practitioners simply lack the time to track down and read the journals, interpret the statistics, organize the studies, and translate them into usable guidelines. Yet there have been significant advances in learning psychology during the past fifteen years that practitioners can exploit. I felt a need to bridge this gap.

I had the opportunity to meet my co-author, Richard Mayer, at an ASTD committee meeting in late 2000. I knew of his research on e-learning from his extensive publications in academic journals and from his book, *Multimedia Learning*. I knew that he had published the results of many controlled experiments focusing on basic critical issues around the design of multimedia—issues that practitioners face routinely in their e-learning work. I was delighted that he agreed to work with me on this project and that we could draw on his work as a major resource for the book.

Our goal in this book is to help you as an e-learning consumer or as part of an e-learning design team to profit from the work of the academic community. To this end we have written the chapters to focus on critical issues you face for which there are research-based recommendations. We have worked to translate empirical studies into readable guidelines and make them useful through checklists and e-learning examples. We hope that our effort will help you make better e-learning selection and design decisions that reflect research on instructional methods.

April 2002
Ruth Colvin Clark

ABOUT THIS BOOK

THIS IS A BOOK about what works in e-learning. It answers questions about what features in e-learning help people learn. Unlike many other books on multimedia training, the answers we present are not based on opinion; they are based on empirical research. In writing this book, we were guided by two fundamental assumptions: the design of e-learning courses should be based on a cognitive theory of how people learn and on scientifically valid research studies. Some of the issues we address are: What are the best ways to use text, graphics, and audio to maximize learning? When can an interesting story hurt rather than help learning? What is a learning agent and how can one best be used in e-learning? How can collaborative Internet facilities be used to maximize learning? The guidelines we present apply to all types of e-learning products, including those designed for educational purposes and personal development. However, our primary focus is to help those

selecting, designing, or developing e-learning courses that build knowledge
and skills for workers in commercial and government organizations.

In addition to presenting guidelines and examples of what works, we also
explain why specific methods work and present the research evidence. The whys
are based on how people learn. Our goal is to help you select and/or build good
e-learning courses and to be able to explain or defend your decisions to other
stakeholders. The research evidence is based on valid controlled research conducted over the past fifteen years. Our intention is to move our training profession toward an evidence-based practice. That means making decisions based
on research evidence—not just on the latest fads or common folk wisdom.

We recognize there are many issues besides learning effectiveness that
you will need to address. Whether computer delivery of training is appropriate to meet your goals and constraints, how best to select and distribute
e-learning to your audience, the technical factors that constrain e-learning
design and delivery, and how instructors need to adapt their skills to serve
as online mentors are only a few of these issues. We leave these topics to
other excellent references on e-learning so that we may focus on proven principles of e-learning design.

Overview of Chapters

Table I.1 summarizes the content of each chapter to help you find the topics
of most relevance. The first couple of chapters set the stage by defining
e-learning and describing several types of e-learning that we will address. This
is important since the term e-learning has been loosely applied to a myriad
of digital products, including Web sites of all types, electronic support systems, as well as training courses.

In Chapter One we summarize the research that tells us that it's not computers or textbooks per se that cause learning. Rather, learning results from
designing lesson materials with the right instructional methods regardless of
how the lesson will be delivered. Instructional methods are what this book
is about. To help learners acquire new knowledge and skills, instructional
methods, including media elements such as sound, text, and graphics as well
as learning aids such as examples and practice exercises, must support human
cognitive learning processes. In Chapter Two we review those learning

Table I.1. A Preview of Chapters.

Chapter	Includes
1. e-Learning: Promise and Pitfalls	• Our definition of e-learning • A description of different types of e-learning • Potential benefits and drawbacks to e-learning
2. How People Learn from e-Courses	• An overview of human learning processes and how instructional methods can support or disrupt them • A brief explanation of what makes a good research study
3. Applying the Multimedia Principle: Use Words and Graphics Rather Than Words Alone	• Evidence for the question of whether learning is improved in e-lessons that include pictures and words versus words alone • Effective and ineffective applications of the *multimedia principle* as well as the psychological basis for the results
4. Applying the Contiguity Principle: Place Corresponding Words and Graphics Near Each Other	• Evidence for the best placement of text and graphics on the screen • Effective and ineffective applications of the *contiguity principle* as well as the psychological basis for the results
5. Applying the Modality Principle: Present Words as Audio Narration Rather Than Onscreen Text	• Evidence for presenting words that describe graphics in audio rather than in text • Effective and ineffective applications of the *modality principle* as well as the psychological basis for the results
6. Applying the Redundancy Principle: Presenting Words in Both Text and Audio Narration Can Hurt Learning	• Evidence for use of audio to explain graphics rather than text and audio • Effective and ineffective applications of the *redundancy principle* as well as the psychological basis for the results

(Continued)

Table I.1. A Preview of Chapters (Continued).

Chapter	Includes
7. Applying the Coherence Principle: Adding Interesting Material Can Hurt Learning	• Evidence for *omitting* distracting graphics and stories, environmental sounds and background music, and detailed textual explanations that are included to add interest or emotional appeal to a lesson • Examples of *coherence principle* violations as well as the psychological basis for the results
8. Applying the Personalization Principle: Use Conversational Style and Virtual Coaches	• Evidence for writing scripts that use first and second person to address the learner in an informal style • Evidence for best use of computer agents to present instructional support
9. Does Practice Make Perfect?	• Evidence for use of practice exercises to improve learning • Evidence and guidelines for the type, number, and placement of practice questions in e-lessons • Effective and ineffective examples as well as the psychological basis for the guidelines
10. Leveraging Examples in e-Learning	• Evidence for the substitution of some practice with worked examples to save instructional time • Evidence and guidelines for the type and placement of worked examples • Examples of worked examples as well as the psychological basis for the guidelines
11. Learning Together on the Web	• Evidence for the benefits of collaborative learning assignments in classroom settings • Guidelines and examples of ways to adapt classroom group assignments to e-learning facilities such as chat, e-mail, and message boards

Table I.1. (Continued).

Chapter	Includes
12. Do Surfing and Learning Mix? The Effectiveness of Learner Control in e-Learning	• Evidence for when and how to use e-learning navigation options to give learners choices over what they study, their learning pace, and their selection of instructional elements such as practice
13. e-Learning to Build Problem-Solving Skills	• Evidence for ways to use e-learning to build far transfer or problem-solving skills • Discussion of the psychological basis for problem-solving • Examples of e-lessons that have used guided discovery designs to teach far transfer skills
14. Applying the Guidelines	• A brief summary of the guidelines in the book and four short e-lesson samples evaluated using the guidelines • Our projections for the future of e-learning developed to improve work performance

processes by a quick tour through human memory and the psychological events that transform words and pictures from the computer into new knowledge in the brain. Since we present research throughout the book, we also provide a short summary of what makes a research study worth paying attention to and how to interpret research results.

In Chapters Three through Eight we summarize research regarding the best use of media elements—sound, graphics, and text—research that has been demonstrated to increase the learning effectiveness of e-lessons by as much as 129 percent. Since all types of e-learning must use some combination of text, sounds, and images to teach, these chapters provide baseline guidelines of broad applicability. The chapters in this section summarize over ten years of research in multimedia design conducted by Richard Mayer at the University of California, Santa Barbara. While some of this research has been published for several years, it primarily appears in scientific journals not commonly read by practitioners. A main reason for our book is to summarize this research for you in a readable and relevant fashion.

In Chapters Nine and Ten, we provide guidelines for the best use of two very common and powerful elements in most training—practice exercises and examples. Practice in e-learning is an expensive investment. Practice takes time to design and it also adds significant time for the learner to take the training. Therefore, it's important to know which kinds of practice work best. Some of the questions we address are: What are the limits of some types of practice like Jeopardy™-style games? How often should practice be included in an e-lesson? How can you tell effective from ineffective practice? How much practice is enough? One way to save time during learning is to substitute some practice with examples. In Chapter Ten we summarize a number of recent research studies that reveal the best ways to use examples to maximize learning efficiency and effectiveness.

E-learning offers some unique features including the use of web-based collaborative tools like chat or conferencing, navigational options that can put learning into an exploratory mode, and the use of simulation for training of problem-solving skills. What do we know about the impact of these features on learning? Chapters Eleven to Thirteen summarize guidelines, examples, and research related to these questions.

Chapter Fourteen summarizes all the guidelines presented throughout the book. It includes a checklist that you can use as you evaluate or design e-learning. In Chapter Fourteen, we illustrate how we would use the checklist to assess strengths and weaknesses of four e-learning samples and end our book with a few observations about the future directions of e-learning.

Chapter Layouts Help You Find What You Need

Like most readers, you probably have interests or needs that pertain more to some topics in the book than others. For example, you may want to just learn about the guidelines for e-learning and skip the research. Or you may or may not be interested in the psychological impact of the instructional methods we present. We have organized our chapters to make surfing the book as easy as possible. Most chapters begin with a short vignette we call the *Design Dilemma*. The vignette sets the context by describing a particular decision facing either an instructional designer or a consumer evaluating e-learning alternatives. While we have disguised the names and places, all of these are drawn from real-world situations we have encountered. After the Dilemma we introduce the chapter by defining the specific instructional methods to be discussed. Next we offer several design guidelines related to the chapter topic along with some examples of how those guidelines would be applied to e-learning. We then describe the psychological reasons for the guidelines. By understanding not only what to look for, but also why a particular method works, we hope you will be able to apply the guidelines more broadly. Following the psychological basis for the guidelines, we summarize the main empirical evidence that supports the guidelines. Each of these topics is labeled so you can quickly find the sections of interest to you.

A Word About Our Examples

There is nothing more helpful than a good example to see ways that a guideline could play out in the real world. We are grateful to a number of e-learning providers who gave permission to use screenshots from their courses that illustrate one or more guidelines. We have drawn our examples from a variety of sources—created for adults delivered on CD-ROM, on the Internet, and from lessons that teach procedural skills as well as more conceptual problem-solving skills. Table I.2 provides some background about several courses from which we have used a number of screen examples.

We also wanted to show examples of e-learning that violate the guidelines. To serve this purpose, we have made up a number of screenshots for a fictitious course about application of statistical process control (SPC) techniques to improve quality in a manufacturing environment. We chose SPC because it's a real-world set of knowledge and skills that is moderately structured and lends itself well to an e-learning treatment. Keep in mind that for all our examples, the specifics of the content are not relevant. Try to avoid getting distracted by the information communicated in the screens and instead focus on the instructional method we are illustrating.

Table I.2. An Overview of Examples Used Throughout the Book.

Example	Designed to Teach	Audience	Delivery
Dreamweaver— Element K	Concepts and steps needed to create Web pages using Dreamweaver software	Computer-literate new users of Dreamweaver software	Created for Internet delivery. "Shocked" with Macromedia Shockwave for delivery of animation and sound
Commercial Bank Loan Analysis— Moody's Financial Services	Processes and decisions to research and recommend a commercial loan application	Bank loan agents with some experience	CD-ROM— Programmed in Macromedia Authorware
Introduction to Ammunition	Background facts, concepts, and processes about explosives and ammunition	Military personnel new to handling ammunition	CD-ROM— Programmed in Macromedia Authorware
Labeling of Hazardous Materials—U.S. Army	Application of regulations regarding marking and documentation of hazardous materials being transported	Anyone newly involved in transportation of hazardous materials	CD-ROM— Programmed in Macromedia Authorware
Statistical Process Control (SPC)— fictitious	Application of statistical techniques to quality management processes in product manufacturing	Workers involved in manufacturing who are new to SPC tools and concepts	N/A

About Us

We are both committed to the use of empirical evidence to inform decisions about what works best in e-learning. Richard Mayer has generated much of the evidence we report in the book through dozens of controlled research studies he and his colleagues have conducted at the University of California, Santa Barbara over the past twenty years. Ruth Clark has worked with training practitioners for more than twenty-five years and has found that most don't have access to many valuable research studies published in academic journals and reported at academic conferences. Together we wanted to summarize the research around critical decisions that must be made about e-learning and to present it in a readable format that practitioners will find useful. As time passes and more research accumulates, we anticipate our guidelines will be updated. Meanwhile, we hope that you will find useful guidance based on what is known today in the chapters to follow. Your feedback is always appreciated. You can reach us at ruth@clarktraining.com or mayer@psych.ucsb.edu.

April 15, 2002

Ruth Colvin Clark
Richard E. Mayer

CHAPTER OUTLINE

The e-Learning Bandwagon

What Is e-Learning?

e-Learning Development Process

Performance Analysis

Defining e-Learning Content

Defining the Instructional Methods and Media Elements

How Delivery Platforms Influence Instructional Methods and Media Elements

Two Types of e-Learning Goals: Inform and Perform

Near Versus Far Transfer Perform Goals

Is e-Learning Better? Media Comparison Research

What Makes e-Learning Unique?

Practice with Feedback

Collaboration in Self-Study

Use of Simulation to Accelerate Expertise

e-Learning: The Pitfalls

Pitfall One: Failure to Base e-Learning on a Job Analysis

Pitfall Two: Failure to Accommodate Human Learning Processes

Pitfall Three: e-Learning Dropout

What Is Good e-Courseware?

Training Goals

Learner Differences

Training Environment

Three Types of e-Learning

Learning as Information Acquisition

Learning as Response Strengthening

Learning as Knowledge Construction

e-Learning to Support Human Learning Processes

1

e-Learning: Promise and Pitfalls

CHAPTER PREVIEW

IN THIS CHAPTER we define e-learning as training delivered on a computer (including CD-ROM, Internet, or intranet) that is designed to support individual learning or organizational performance goals. We include e-courses developed primarily to provide information (inform courses) as well as those designed to build specific job-related skills (perform courses). Instructional methods that support rather than defeat human learning processes are an essential ingredient to all good e-learning courseware. The best methods to use will depend on the goals of the training (for example, to inform or to perform); the learner's related skills; and various environmental factors, including technological, cultural, and pragmatic constraints. We distinguish among e-learning courseware that reflect three views of learning: information acquisition (receptive), response-strengthening (directive), and knowledge construction (guided discovery).

The e-Learning Bandwagon

Will the new educational dot-coms that have proliferated over the past few years revolutionize business and government training? In 1999, Jack Welch, former chairman of General Electric, declared the Internet to be the single-most important event in the U.S. economy since the Industrial Revolution. John Chambers, Cisco Systems CEO, states that the two great equalizers in life are the Internet and education. Sensing the economic potential of marrying education and the Internet, a variety of sites have recently sprung up, offering training in everything from end-user computer skills to medical ethics. Universities also have rushed to tap into the distance learning market. Almost 90 percent of all universities with more than 10,000 students offer some form of distance learning—nearly all of which use the Internet (Svetcov, 2000). According to Gerhard Casper, outgoing president of Stanford University: "How Internet learning will shake out, I really do not know. But I am utterly convinced that over the next ten years we will see shifts from in-residence learning to on-line learning" (p. 284, Muller, 2000). In addition to Internet and university sites, corporate and government organizations that spend large amounts on employee training have developed proprietary computer-delivered courseware as a potential cost-effective alternative to classroom training.

Are the proliferating cyber courses harbingers of a new age in learning or just another overstatement of the expectations that have surrounded nearly everything associated with the World Wide Web? In spite of all the hype, since 1999, the amount of training delivered by computer in business and industry has decreased. In the year 2001, approximately 11 percent of all training was delivered via computer (including the Internet, intranets, and CD-ROM)—down from 15 percent reported in 1999 (Galvin, 2001). It remains to be seen whether in times of economic pressure and travel uncertainty the potential cost savings of desktop learning will reverse this trend.

Annual investments in training are high and growing. Every year between fifty and sixty billion dollars are spent on training workers in corporate and governmental organizations in the United States (Galvin, 2001). And these figures don't include the most expensive element of training, the salary time and lost opportunity costs of those taking training. In spite of this invest-ment, during boom times there have been shortages of trained technical staff. Does e-learning offer a potential opportunity to cost-effectively build the skills required for the knowledge-based economy of this century? Part of the answer will depend on the quality of the instruction delivered in the e-learning products you are designing, building, or selecting today.

What Is e-Learning?

We define e-learning as instruction delivered on a computer by way of CD-ROM, Internet, or intranet with the following features:

- Includes content relevant to the learning objective
- Uses instructional methods such as examples and practice to help learning
- Uses media elements such as words and pictures to deliver the content and methods
- Builds new knowledge and skills linked to individual learning goals or to improved organizational performance

As you can see, this definition has several elements concerning the what, how, and why of e-learning.

What. e-Learning courses include both content (that is, information) and instructional methods (that is, techniques) that help people learn the content.

How. e-Learning courses are delivered via computer using words in the form of spoken or printed text and pictures such as illustrations, pho-tos, animation, or video.

Why. e-Learning courses are intended to help learners reach personal learning objectives or perform their jobs in ways that improve the bot-tom line goals of the organization.

In short, the "e" in e-learning refers to the "how"—the course is digi-tized so it can be stored in electronic form. The "learning" in e-learning refers to the "what"—the course includes content and ways to help people learn it—and the "why"—that the purpose is to help individuals achieve educational goals or to help organizations build skills related to improved job performance.

Our definition indicates that the goal of e-learning is to build job-transferable knowledge and skills linked to organizational performance or to help individuals achieve personal learning goals. Although the guidelines we present throughout the book do apply to lessons designed for educational or general interest learning goals, our emphasis is on instructional programs that are built or purchased to build job-specific skills.

e-Learning Development Process

e-Learning that yields a return on investment is developed following a systematic process summarized in Figure 1.1. Since there are many good books on e-learning development, we provide only a brief overview here.

Figure 1.1. The Process of e-Learning Design to Improve Organizational Performance.

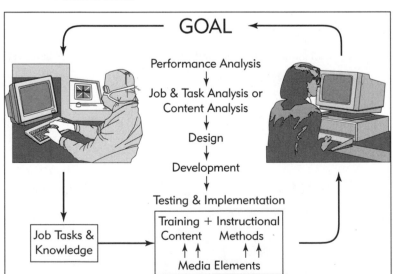

Performance Analysis

All e-learning projects should begin with a performance analysis to determine a) that training will help meet important organizational goals by filling a gap in knowledge and skills and b) that e-learning is the best delivery solution. Often training is requested to solve organizational problems that are not caused by a lack of knowledge and skills. In these cases, the root cause(s) of the problems should be defined and an expensive solution like training should be avoided. If training is needed, then the analysis should consider the tradeoffs among various delivery alternatives such as classroom, on-the-job, e-learning, or a blend of several of these.

Defining e-Learning Content

Following the performance analysis, a team begins the design of the course by defining the content needed to perform the job or achieve the educational objective. In order for training to pay off with improved job performance, an e-learning development effort must start with an analysis of the job tasks and the knowledge needed to perform these tasks. The e-learning development team observes and interviews people who are expert at a job to define the job skills and knowledge. For courseware developed for broader educational purposes, rather than a job analysis, the development team conducts a content analysis to define the major topics and related subtopics to be included. Based on either the job or content analysis, the team categorizes the content of an e-lesson into facts, concepts, processes, procedures, and principles. Table 1.1 defines these content types, which have been described in detail by Ruth Clark (1999). For example, the screen in Figure 1.2 is taken from e-learning designed to teach Dreamweaver, a software product used to build Web pages. The content being illustrated is a procedure. This screen is providing a simulation practice of the steps the user must take to effectively use the software.

At the completion of the job or content analysis, the design team will create a course blueprint that includes outlines and learning objectives. They will then begin to write the detailed course script and to select specific instructional methods to support learning.

Table 1.1. Five Types of Content in e-Learning.

Content Type	Definition	Example
Fact	Specific and unique data or instance	The company log-on screen; My password is John1
Concept	A category that includes multiple examples	Web page password
Process	A flow of events or activities	Performance appraisal process
Procedure	Task performed with step-by-step actions	How to log on
Principle	Task performed by adapting guidelines	How to close a sale

Figure 1.2. Screen from a Procedural e-Lesson on Use of Dreamweaver.
With permission from Element K.

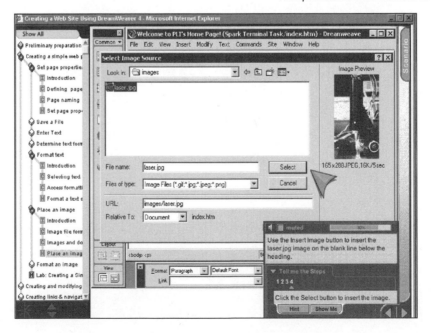

Defining the Instructional Methods and Media Elements

Instructional methods are the techniques that support the learning of the content. Instructional methods include techniques such as examples, practice exercises, and feedback. In our example screen shown in Figure 1.2 the instructional methods include a simulation practice with feedback. We define media elements as the audio and visual techniques used to present words and illustrations. Media elements include text, narration, music, still graphics, photographs, and animation. In the Dreamweaver course, audio narration presents the words of the demonstration and an animated graphic presents the actions of the demonstration. One of our fundamental tenets is that to be effective, instructional methods and the media elements that deliver them must help guide learners to effectively process and assimilate new knowledge and skills.

How Delivery Platforms Influence Instructional Methods and Media Elements

e-Learning, as we use the term, includes training delivered via CD-ROM, intranets, and the Internet. Approximately forty percent of computer-delivered training uses CD-ROM, while twenty-two percent uses the Internet and thirty percent uses intranets (Galvin, 2001). Your choice of delivery platform can influence which instructional methods and media elements can be included in the courseware. For example, limitations in bandwidth may limit the use of memory-intensive media elements (such as audio) for Internet delivery. In contrast, CD-ROM provides considerably more memory than the Internet but will be more difficult to update and disseminate to users.

Two Types of e-Learning Goals: Inform and Perform

As summarized in Table 1.2, the guidelines in this book apply to e-learning that is designed to inform as well as e-learning that is designed to improve specific job performance. We classify lessons that are designed primarily to build awareness or provide information as *inform programs*. A new employee orientation lesson that reviews the company history and describes the company organization is an example of an inform program. The information presented

Table 1.2. **Inform and Perform e-Learning Goals.**

Goal	Definition	Example
Inform	Lessons that communicate information	• Company history • New product features
Perform-Procedure	Lessons that build procedural skills (also called near transfer)	• How to log on • How to complete an expense report
Perform-Principle	Lessons that build principle-based skills (also called far transfer)	• How to close a sale • How to design a Web page

is job relevant but there are no specific expectations of new skills to be acquired. The primary goal is to share information. In contrast, we classify programs designed to build specific skills as *perform programs*. Some examples of perform e-learning are lessons on software use, marking and labeling of hazardous materials, evaluating a bank loan applicant, and use of quality control tools. Many e-courses contain both inform and perform learning objectives, while some are designed for inform only or perform only.

Near Versus Far Transfer Perform Goals

We distinguish between two types of perform goals: 1) *procedural*, also known as *near transfer*, and 2) *principle-based*, also known as *far transfer*. Procedural lessons such as the Dreamweaver example in Figure 1.2 are designed to teach step-by-step tasks, which are performed more or less the same way each time. Most computer-skills training falls into this category. This type of training is called *near transfer* because the steps learned in the training are identical or very similar to the steps required in the job environment. Thus the transfer from training to application is near. More than half of all e-learning is near transfer, devoted to teaching computer skills for end-users and for information technology professionals.

Principle-based lessons, also called *far transfer*, are designed to teach tasks that do not have only one correct approach or outcome. Thus the situations presented in the training may not be exactly the same as the situations that occur on the job. These tasks require the worker to adapt guidelines to various job situations. Typically some element of problem-solving is involved. The worker always has to use judgment in performing these tasks since there is no one right approach for all situations. Far transfer lessons include just about all soft-skill training, supervision and management courses, and sales skills. Figure 1.3 illustrates a screen from a principle-based course on selling banking products. The screen shows customer reactions to various statements of the salesperson. To apply these new skills to the job, the bank employees must adapt guidelines presented in this training to various situations they will encounter with real customers. Since the worker will always have to use judgment in applying training guidelines to the job, we say that the transfer from training to job is far.

Figure 1.3. Far Transfer Course on Selling Bank Products.

With permission from DigitalThink.

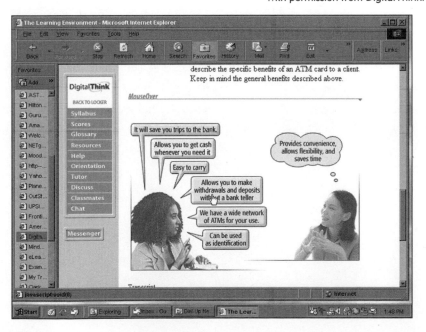

Is e-Learning Better? Media Comparison Research

Contrary to the impression left by recent reports on the use and benefits of e-learning, much of what we are seeing under the e-learning label is not new. Training delivered on a computer, known as computer-based training or CBT, has been around for more than thirty years. Early examples delivered over mainframe computers were primarily text on a screen with interspersed questions—electronic versions of behaviorist psychologist B. F. Skinner's teaching machine. The computer program evaluated answers to the multiple-choice questions and prewritten feedback was matched to the learner responses. The main application of these early e-lessons was training in the use of mainframe computer systems. As technology has evolved, acquiring greater capability to deliver true multimedia, the courseware has become more elaborate in terms of realistic graphics, audio, color, animation, and complex simulations. But as you will see, greater complexity of media does not necessarily ensure more learning.

Each new wave of instructional delivery technology (starting with film in the 1920s) spawned optimistic predictions of massive improvements in learning. For example, in 1947 the U.S. Army conducted one of the first media

THE FIRST MEDIA COMPARISON STUDY

In 1947 the U.S. Army conducted research to demonstrate that instruction delivered by film resulted in better learning outcomes than traditional classroom or paper-based versions. Three versions of a lesson on how to read a micrometer were developed. The film version included a narrated demonstration of how to read the micrometer. A second version was taught in a classroom. The instructor used the same script and included a demonstration using actual equipment along with still slide pictures. A third version was a self-study paper lesson in which the text used the same words as the film, along with pictures with arrows to indicate movement. Learners were randomly assigned to a version and after the training session they were tested to see if they could read the micrometer. Which group learned more? There were no differences in learning among the three groups (Hall and Cushing, 1947).

comparisons with the hypothesis that film teaches better than classroom instructors (see box for details). Yet after fifty years of research attempting to demonstrate that the latest media are better, the outcomes have not supported that hypothesis.

With few exceptions, the hundreds of media comparison studies have shown no differences in learning (Clark, 1994; Dillon and Gabbard, 1998). As in the Army experiment summarized in the box, the lessons delivered by various media were similar in the instructional methods they used. Therefore, the learning was the same whether the lesson was read in a book or on a computer screen. What we have learned from all the media comparison research is that it's not the medium, but rather the instructional methods that cause learning. When the instructional methods remain essentially the same, so does the learning, no matter how the instruction is delivered. Nevertheless, as we will discuss in the following sections, each medium offers unique opportunities to deliver instructional methods that other media cannot. It's a common error to design each new medium to mirror older ones. For example, some e-lessons appear to be books transferred to a screen. To exploit the media fully, the unique capabilities of the delivery media should be used in ways that effectively support human learning.

What Makes e-Learning Unique?

Can we conclude from the media comparison research that all media are equivalent? Not quite. Not all media can deliver all instructional methods. For example, the capability of a paper document to deliver animation is quite limited. Three potentially valuable instructional methods unique to e-learning are 1) practice with automated tailored feedback, 2) integration of collaboration with self-study, and 3) use of simulation to accelerate expertise.

Practice with Feedback

On the Dreamweaver screen shown in Figure 1.2 the learner has an opportunity to try a hands-on practice using a simulation of the Dreamweaver software. Prior to this hands-on practice, the learners have seen an animated, narrated demonstration of the steps required to format text in Dreamweaver.

What is special about the computer's role in learning is that the learner's actions taken in the simulation are evaluated by a program that responds with hints or feedback supporting immediate correction of errors. Chapter Nine in this book describes what to look for in effectively designed practice in e-learning.

Collaboration in Self-Study

If you take a close look at the left-hand navigation panel of the DigitalThink course (Figure 1.3), you will notice another feature that distinguishes e-learning from previous computer-delivered instruction—the ability to communicate with others. The first CBT lessons were for solo learning. There was little or no interaction with others. But the power of the Internet erases that limitation. Learners can communicate by computer in real time through chats or at different times by e-mail and discussion boards. Despite this collaborative capability, according to the 2001 Industry Report, few organizations make use of it. The vast majority of e-lessons (77 percent) are pre-programmed tutorials that involve only the learner and a computer (Galvin, 2001). One exception occurs in the academic institutions and services segment, in which 43 percent of courses build in interactions with other learners and with instructors. There is a growing research base on the benefits of learning together versus solo. Chapter Eleven specifically reviews that research and provides guidelines for ways to harness the collaborative facilities of the Internet for learning purposes.

Use of Simulation to Accelerate Expertise

Look at the screen sample in Figure 1.4 for another example of what makes e-learning unique. In this course, bank loan agents can learn an effective process to analyze and recommend funding for a commercial loan applicant. They learn by solving job-realistic cases. After receiving a new commercial loan to evaluate, the learner can access the various objects in the office such as the fax to request a credit check in this screen. They can also visit the loan applicant to conduct an interview. Once the learners have collected sufficient data, they indicate whether the loan is approved or denied. Thus, a new loan agent can experience in a short time a number of real-world loan situations in

Figure 1.4. The Learner Orders a Credit Check by Accessing the Fax Machine.

With permission from Moody's Risk Management Services.

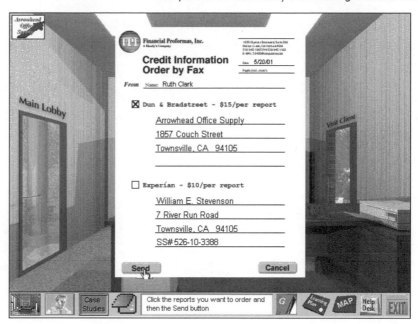

the safety of a controlled environment. The bank loan course illustrates the power of simulation in which realistic job problems are compressed into a short timeframe. We summarize what we know about using simulations to accelerate expertise in Chapter Thirteen.

Besides interactivity and simulations, computers can now deliver a diverse range of media elements to present words and graphics, including text, audio, video, and pictures. In fact, the variety and number of media elements that a lesson can deliver can easily exceed human cognitive capacity. In Chapters Three through Eight we summarize research-based guidelines for the most effective use of text, audio, and graphics to promote learning. We call these the *media elements principles* and they apply to any of the various types of e-learning designed for educational, individual, or business and industrial goals.

e-Learning: The Pitfalls

Despite these impressive capabilities of computer-delivered instruction, we see three primary barriers (summarized in Table 1.3) to the realization of the potential of online learning. These are: 1) transfer failure due to lack of job analysis, 2) failure to accommodate human learning limits and strengths, and 3) high attrition rates.

Table 1.3. Three Pitfalls of e-Learning.

Pitfall	Result
1. Failure to Define Job Knowledge and Skills	Lessons do not build knowledge and skills that transfer to the job
2. Failure to Accommodate Learning Processes	Lessons overload cognitive processes and learning is disrupted
3. Attrition	Learners do not complete their instruction

Pitfall One: Failure to Base e-Learning on a Job Analysis

To design powerful learning environments whose lessons both transfer to the workplace and improve the performance of the organization is not easy, no matter whether planned for classroom or multimedia delivery. To teach higher order problem solving skills like the one illustrated in the bank loan program (Figure 1.4), the designer must first define what those skills are. Research on expertise shows that these skills are job-specific. In other words, the knowledge base underlying a great physician is different from one that makes a master programmer. There is no one set of skills that support expertise across the diverse contemporary workforce.

Adding to the challenge of defining job-specific skills for each career field, many of the most important skills underlying knowledge-based work are cognitive skills that are not readily observable. For example, if your goal is to build training for a systems analyst, you will learn little by watching an experienced analyst at work, since the important work is going on internally. And an interview will often yield disappointing results. This is because experts typically cannot easily articulate how they accomplish mental tasks since their well-practiced skills have resulted in unconscious competence. In the case of near transfer training, visible procedural skills like the use of a new software system are relatively easy to define through observations and interviews. But even then, it is a time-consuming task to specify all the skills and knowledge needed to use a software product effectively.

In other words, whether planning for near or far transfer learning, a detailed job and task analysis is a prerequisite and a labor-intensive process. e-Lessons that bypass the job analysis process run the risk of presenting knowledge and techniques out of context. As you will see in Chapters Nine and Ten, lack of job context risks transfer failure. In the end, teaching knowledge and skills that do not result in job performance changes will not yield a return on investment.

Pitfall Two: Failure to Accommodate Human Learning Processes

Once valid skills and knowledge are defined through the job analysis, the appropriate instructional methods must be used that will both accommodate human psychological processes and exploit the capabilities of the technology. When the limits of human cognitive processes are ignored, e-learning that utilizes all of the technological capabilities to deliver text, audio, and video can actually depress learning. As you will see in Chapter Two, this is because humans have a limited capacity for the amount of information they can simultaneously process. To translate the content of the job into effective e-lessons, a range of expertise on the design team is required. This includes instructional psychology, multimedia production, graphics, programming, and interface design. Experienced multimedia developers acknowledge that it takes from ten to twenty times more labor and skill to produce good courseware for e-learning than for traditional classroom materials.

Pitfall Three: e-Learning Dropout

A third potential pitfall to the promise of e-learning is student attrition. Dropout rates have been estimated at 35 percent and above (Svetcov, 2000). It is difficult, however, to know what these statistics really mean. In many cases, a learner may only need a segment of the training and never intends to complete the full course. Dropouts give a variety of reasons that range from boring lessons to technological glitches. Unlike the classroom in which the learner is a captive audience and a live instructor can stimulate attention, an online learning environment requires individual discipline and commitment in a world full of competing alternatives for worker time and attention. To ensure successful self-directed learning, you must consider factors ranging from how you might deploy online learning in the workplace to how engaging the courseware is. Some courseware designers try to stimulate interest by adding motivational elements in the form of games or interesting graphics and stories to the training. However, as you will see in Chapters Seven and Nine, using these kinds of techniques to seduce learners may backfire and depress learning.

What Is Good e-Courseware?

A central question for our book is, "What does good courseware look like?" Throughout the book we provide specific courseware features to look for or to design into your e-learning. However, you will need to adapt our recommendations based on three main considerations—the goal of your training, the prior knowledge of your learners, and the environment in which you will deploy your training.

Training Goals

The goals or intended outcomes of your e-learning will influence which guidelines are most appropriate for you to consider. Earlier in this chapter we made distinctions among three types of training designed to inform the student, to perform procedures, and to perform principle tasks. For inform e-lessons, you should apply the guidelines in Chapters Three through Eight regarding the best use of media elements, including visuals, narration, and text to present information. To train for procedural skills, you should understand these guidelines and also apply relevant suggestions regarding the design of examples and practice sessions in Chapters Nine and Ten. If, however, your goal is to develop principle-based or far transfer skills, you will want to apply the guidelines from *all* the chapters (including Chapter Thirteen on teaching problem-solving skills).

Learner Differences

In addition to selecting or designing courseware specific to the type of outcome desired—that is, whether you wish to inform learners, develop procedural skills or support principle-based performance—effective courseware should include instructional methods appropriate to the learner's characteristics. While various individual differences such as learning styles have received the attention of the training community, research has proven that the learner's prior knowledge of the course content exerts the most influence on learning. Learners with little prior knowledge will benefit from different instructional methods than learners who are relatively experienced.

For the most part, the guidelines we provide in this book are based on research conducted with adult learners who were new to the course content. If your target audience has greater background knowledge in the course content, some of these guidelines may be less applicable. For example, Chapter Four suggests that if you integrate your text into your graphics, you reduce the mental workload required of the learner and thereby increase learning. However, if your learners are experienced regarding the skills you are teaching, overload is not as likely and they will probably learn effectively whether the text is integrated or separated.

Training Environment

A final factor that affects e-learning is the environment—including such issues as technical constraints of the delivery platform or network, cultural factors in institutions such as the acceptance of and routine familiarity with technology, and pragmatic constraints related to budget, time, and management expectations. We focus in this book on what works best from a psychological perspective, but we recognize that you will have to adapt our guidelines in response to your own unique set of environmental factors.

Three Types of e-Learning

Although all e-learning is delivered on a computer, different courses reflect different assumptions of learning. During the past one hundred years, three views of learning have evolved, and you will see each view reflected in courses available today. The three views, summarized in Table 1.4, are learning as information acquisition, learning as response strengthening, and learning as knowledge construction. The lesson designs that stem from these views are called *architectures of instruction* (Clark, 2000).

Table 1.4. Three Types of e-Learning.

Type	Builds Lessons That	Used For
Receptive: Information Acquisition	Include lots of information with limited practice opportunities	Inform Goals
Directive: Response Strengthening	Require frequent responses from learners with immediate feedback	Perform-Procedure Goals
Guided Discovery: Knowledge Construction	Provide job-realistic problems and supporting resources	Perform-Principle Goals

Learning as Information Acquisition

According to the information acquisition view (which we also call the information delivery view), learning involves adding information to one's memory. In this view, a useful instructional method is to present as much information as efficiently as possible—such as through lots of onscreen text. The instructor's job is to deliver information and the learner's job is to receive it. A common metaphor characterizes the learner as a sponge and the instruction as a jug of water. We refer to instruction designed on this premise as *receptive* instruction or show-and-tell. e-Courses built on this view often provide information in various media but may be guilty of overloading learners' cognitive systems and of not providing opportunities for learning through practice exercises. Courses of this type are common in e-learning that is designed for inform rather than perform goals.

Learning as Response Strengthening

According to the response-strengthening view, learning involves strengthening or weakening of associations between a stimulus (such as $2 + 2 = \_\_$) and a response (such as 4). In this view, a useful instructional method is *drill and practice,* in which the instructor asks a question, and then gives a reward for the correct answer or a punishment for the wrong answer. The instructor's job is to provide short content segments followed by questions accompanied by corrective feedback. The learner's job is to respond accurately to the questions and revise answers based on the feedback. We refer to this type of training as *directive* or "show-and-do" courseware. This type of instruction is characterized by small step sizes, demonstrations or examples, and frequent practice with corrective feedback. This approach is common in courses designed to teach procedures such as end-user software skills. The screen shown in Figure 1.2 is drawn from this type of courseware.

Learning as Knowledge Construction

According to the knowledge construction view, learning occurs when a learner builds a coherent mental representation. In this view, a useful instructional method is guided performance, in which a learner tries to accomplish an authentic job task (such as cross-selling banking products) with guidance from the instructor about how to process the incoming information. The instructor's job is to serve as a cognitive guide and the learner's job is to make sense of the presented material often in the context of solving a job-related problem. We call this approach to instruction *guided discovery*. This type of e-learning is most effective for far transfer performance goals, in which the guidelines presented in the training will need to be adapted to unpredictable situations on the job. Figure 1.4 is a screen drawn from this type of e-learning.

We find some merit in each view, and each seems to be best suited to support certain learning situations as summarized here. However, whichever approach to instruction is taken, we believe that knowledge construction must occur. Furthermore, for knowledge construction to occur most effectively, instructional methods must support the cognitive processes of learning.

e-Learning to Support Human Learning Processes

The challenge in e-learning, as in any learning program, is to build lessons in ways that are compatible with human learning processes. To be effective, instructional methods must support these processes. That is, they must foster the psychological events necessary for learning. While the computer technology for delivery of e-learning is upgraded weekly, the human side of the equation—the neurological infrastructure underlying the learning process—is very old and designed for change only over evolutionary time spans. In fact, technology can easily deliver more sensory data than the human nervous system can process. To the extent that audio and visual elements in a lesson interfere with human cognition, learning will be depressed.

We know a lot about how learning occurs. Over the past twenty years hundreds of research studies on cognitive learning processes and methods that support them have been published. Much of this new knowledge remains inaccessible to those who are producing or evaluating online learning because it has been distributed primarily within the research community. This book fills the gap by summarizing research-based answers to questions that multimedia producers and consumers ask about what to look for in effective e-learning.

COMING NEXT

Since instructional methods must support the psychological processes of learning, the next chapter summarizes those processes. We include an overview of our current understanding of the human learning system and the processes involved in building knowledge and skills in learners. We provide several examples of how instructional methods used in e-lessons support cognitive processes. In addition, we present some guidelines to help you understand and evaluate research evidence presented throughout the book.

Suggested Readings

Clark, R.C. (2000). Four architectures of learning. *Performance Improvement,* *39*(10), 31–37.

Clark, R.C. (1999). *Developing Technical Training.* Silver Spring, MD: International Society for Performance Improvement.

Mayer, R.E. (2001). *Multimedia Learning.* New York: Cambridge University Press.

CHAPTER OUTLINE

How Do People Learn?

How e-Lessons Affect Human Learning

Methods for Directing Selection of Important Information

Methods for Managing Limited Capacity in Working Memory

Methods for Integration

Methods for Retrieval and Transfer

Methods for Metacognitive Monitoring

Summary of Learning Processes

What Is Good Research?

Informal Studies

Controlled Studies

Clinical Trials

How Can You Identify Relevant Research?

Interpretation of Research Statistics

2

How People Learn from e-Courses

CHAPTER PREVIEW

FROM Las Vegas-style media with games and glitz at one extreme to page turners made of text on screens at the other, many e-learning courses ignore human cognitive processes and as a result do not optimize learning. In writing this book, we were guided by two fundamental assumptions: the design of e-learning courses should be based on a cognitive theory of how people learn and on scientifically valid research studies. In other words, e-learning courses should be constructed in light of how the mind learns and experimental evidence concerning e-learning features that promote best learning. In this chapter we provide an overview of cognitive learning theory by describing the memory systems and processes involved in learning. We also summarize important features of experimental studies to help you interpret the relevance and applicability of research to your work.

DESIGN DILEMMA

Suppose you are in charge of the training department at Madison Industries. Your boss, the director of human resources, asks you to develop a series of e-learning courses to be delivered via the company's employee Web site. "The Web is such a wonderful new technology for us," she says. "Let's use it to revolutionize the way we train our employees. My kids really enjoy playing games online and surfing the Web—let's try to make our training fun by using these exciting features!"

Your director of human resources is espousing what can be called a technology-centered approach to e-learning. For her, e-learning courses should take advantage of powerful, cutting-edge technologies such as video or animations available on the Web. In taking a technology-centered approach, she is basing her decisions about how to design e-learning courses on the capabilities afforded by new technologies.

Your intuition is that something is wrong with the technology-centered approach. You remember reading about the disappointing history of educational technology (Cuban, 1986). In every era, strong claims have been made for the educational value of hot new technologies, but the reality somehow has never lived up to expectations. You wonder why there have been so many failures in the field of educational technology. You conclude that it is because instructional designers took a technology-centered approach. They tried to make people adapt to the features of technology. Today, many of the same old claims about revolutionizing learning can be heard again, this time applied to Internet technology. You decide it's time to take a learner-centered approach, in which technology is adjusted to fit in with the way that people learn. It is used as a tool to extend the human mind (Norman, 1993).

You decide to do a little research and make a case to your HR director for designing the instruction to fit human needs, *not* just exploit the technology. There are many guidebooks to help you design Web-based training, so you consult some of them. They offer many suggestions for how to design your training program, but to your dismay, they offer very little scientific support. You aren't looking for another "how to" book on cool Web technologies. Instead, you seek to answer such questions as: Is there a learning theory that could guide my choices? Are there things to look for in e-learning that improve or hinder learning?

How Do People Learn?

Throughout the book, you will see many references to cognitive learning theory. Cognitive learning theory explains how mental processes transform information received by the eyes and ears into knowledge and skills in human memory. Cognitive learning theory gives us several key ideas that explain learning:

- Human memory has two channels for processing information: visual and auditory.

- Human memory has a limited capacity for processing information.

- Learning occurs by active processing in the memory system.

- New knowledge and skills must be retrieved from long-term memory for transfer to the job.

As illustrated in Figure 2.1, a lesson's visual and auditory information enters the eyes and ears, is briefly stored in a visual and auditory sensory memory, enters working memory, and is finally stored in permanent or long-term memory.

Figure 2.1. Cognitive Processes Involved in e-Learning.

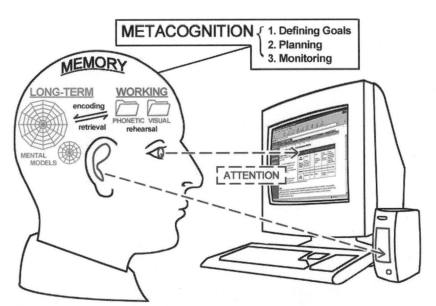

Working memory is the center of cognition since all active thinking takes place there. However, while it's a powerful processor, it's also a limited-capacity memory device. You may have heard the expression "seven plus or minus two chunks." That expression applies to the severe limits on how much information working memory can hold. Learning requires that new knowledge and skills in working memory become integrated with existing knowledge in long-term memory. The integration of new information from working memory into long-term memory is called *encoding*. Encoding requires active processing of the information in working memory. The active processing that takes place in working memory is called *rehearsal*. Finally, just getting new knowledge and skills encoded into long-term memory is not enough. Later, when back on the job, the learner must be able to retrieve those skills from long-term memory back into working memory. Without this *retrieval*, learning fails to transfer.

How e-Lessons Affect Human Learning

Instructional methods in e-lessons must guide the learner's transformation of words and pictures in the lesson through the sensory and working memories so that they get incorporated into the existing knowledge in long-term memory. This requires the following processes to occur:

1. Selection of the important information in the lesson

2. Management of the limited capacity in working memory to allow the rehearsal needed for learning

3. Integration of auditory and visual sensory information in working memory with existing knowledge in long-term memory by way of rehearsal in working memory

4. Retrieval of new knowledge and skills from long-term memory into working memory when needed later

5. Management of all of these processes via metacognitive skills

In the following sections, we elaborate on these processes and provide examples of how instructional methods can support or inhibit them.

Methods for Directing Selection of Important Information

Our cognitive systems have limited capacity. Since there are too many sources of information competing for this limited capacity, the learner must select those that best match his or her goals. We know this selection process can be guided by instructional methods that direct the learner's attention. For example, multimedia designers may use an arrow or color to draw the eye to important text or visual information, as shown in Figure 2.2. Another technique to direct attention is to list learning objectives. Most e-lessons present learning objectives in the introduction to help learners decide where to focus their efforts. Because good learning objectives clearly inform learners what they will need to do to demonstrate learning, they can direct their energy and attention to those elements in the training that support the objective.

Figure 2.2. An Arrow Is Used to Direct Attention on a Complex Application Screen.

With permission from Element K.

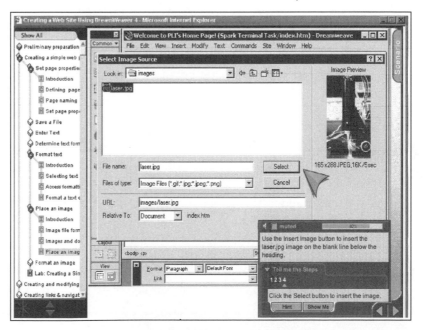

Methods for Managing Limited Capacity in Working Memory

Working memory must be free to rehearse the new information provided in the lesson. When the limited capacity of working memory becomes filled, processing gets inefficient. Learning slows and frustration grows. For example, most of us find multiplying numbers like 968 by 89 in our heads to be a challenging task. This is because we need to hold the intermediate products of our calculations in working memory storage *and* continue to multiply the next set of numbers in the working memory processor. It is very difficult for working memory to hold even limited amounts of information and process effectively at the same time.

Therefore, instructional methods that overload working memory make learning more difficult. The burden imposed on working memory in the form of information that must be held plus information that must be processed is referred to as cognitive load. Methods that reduce cognitive load foster learning by freeing working memory capacity for the rehearsal and integration processes. In the past ten years we've learned a lot about ways to reduce cognitive load in instructional materials. Many of the guidelines we present in Chapters Four through Seven work because they reduce load. For example, the *coherence principle* described in Chapter Seven states that better learning results when e-lessons minimize irrelevant visuals, omit background music and environmental sounds, and use succinct text. In other words, less is more. This is because, by using a minimalist approach that avoids overloading working memory, greater capacity is available for rehearsal processes leading to learning.

Methods for Integration

Working memory integrates the words and pictures in a lesson into a unified structure and further integrates these ideas with existing knowledge in long-term memory. The integration of words and pictures is made easier by lessons that present the verbal and visual information together rather than separated. For example, Figure 2.3 illustrates screen from a lesson on lightning formation in which the text is placed next to the graphic. This lesson resulted in better learning than a second identical version in which the text was placed under the graphic. Chapter Four summarizes the *contiguity principle* of

Figure 2.3. Integrated Text and Graphic Resulted in Better Learning.
Adapted from Mayer, 2001a.

As the air in this updraft cools, water vapor condenses into water and forms a cloud.

instruction that recommends presenting pictures and words close together on the screen.

Once the words and pictures are consolidated into a coherent structure in working memory, they must be further integrated into existing knowledge structures in long-term memory. This requires active processing in working memory. e-Lessons that include practice exercises and worked examples stimulate the integration of new knowledge into prior knowledge. For example, a practice assignment asks technical account representatives to review new product features and describe ways that their current clients might best take advantage of a product upgrade. This assignment requires active processing of the new product feature information in a way that links it with prior knowledge about their clients.

Methods for Retrieval and Transfer

It is not sufficient to simply add new knowledge to long-term memory. For success in training, those new knowledge structures must be encoded into long-term memory in a way that allows them to be easily retrieved when needed on the job. Retrieval of new skills is essential for transfer of training. Without retrieval, all the other psychological processes are meaningless since it does us little good to have knowledge stored in long-term memory that cannot be applied later.

For transfer to occur, e-lessons must incorporate the context of the job in the examples and practice exercises so the new knowledge stored in long-term memory contains good retrieval hooks. For example, one multimedia exercise asks technicians to play a Jeopardy™ game in which they recall facts about a new software system in response to clues. A better alternative exercise gives an equipment failure scenario and asks technicians to select a troubleshooting action based on facts about a new software system. The Jeopardy™ game exercise might be perceived as fun, but it risks storing the facts in memory without a job context. These facts, lacking the contextual hooks needed for retrieval, often fail to transfer. In contrast, the troubleshooting exercise asks technicians to apply the new facts to a job-realistic situation. Chapters Nine and Ten on practice and examples in e-learning provide a number of guidelines with samples of ways multimedia lessons can build transferable knowledge in long-term memory.

Methods for Metacognitive Monitoring

Just as a computer has an operating system to manage the transfer of data, so does the human processor. *Metacognition* refers to the mental management processes that oversee the information processes we summarized in the previous section. A student with effective metacognitive skills is able to set learning goals, decide on effective ways to reach those goals, monitor their progress, and make adjustments as needed. Learners with poor metacognitive skills are unable to focus their instructional efforts on the things they need to know. They typically spend a lot of time reaffirming what they already know, rather than identifying and dealing with what they don't know.

A good contrast in metacognitive skills is found by comparing the typical college freshman with the college senior. Freshmen may begin by attending classes but soon notice that roll is not taken and often there is no homework assigned. Lacking the discipline of structured assignments, the students fail to study the new knowledge presented. Weeks go by. Suddenly midterm examinations loom and the fledging students are cramming to acquire several weeks of knowledge in two or three days. Successful college seniors, however, have learned to assess the requirements of their classes and manage their study and instructional activities in a more coherent fashion. They have developed specific learning management strategies such as making up study questions, maintaining regular reading schedules, or attending study groups. They are able to recognize early when they do not understand some aspects of the class and take action to get help in those areas. All of these self-assessment and management activities grow from a well-developed metacognitive skill base.

Workers in your organization who take e-lessons may or may not have good metacognitive skills. Those lacking such skills will profit from training that provides the learners with the goal setting, monitoring, and learning support they cannot provide for themselves. For example, lesson self-checks help learners assess their knowledge and identify skill gaps. Such self-checks will be most needed by learners with poor metacognitive skills to assess their own skill acquisition. Chapter Twelve on learner control examines the topic of metacognition as it applies to how and when to allow learners to make their own selections in multimedia instruction by way of navigational options.

Summary of Learning Processes

In summary, learning from e-lessons relies on four key processes.

- First, the learner must focus on key graphics and words in the lesson to select what will be processed.

- Second, the learner must rehearse this information in working memory to organize and integrate it with existing knowledge in long-term memory. In order to do the integration work, limited working memory capacity must not be overloaded. Lessons should apply cognitive load reduction techniques, especially when learners are novices to the new knowledge and skills.

- Third, new knowledge stored in long-term memory must be retrieved back on the job. We call this process transfer of learning. To support transfer, e-lessons must provide a job context during learning that will create new memories containing the needed retrieval hooks.

- Fourth, metacognitive skills manage and adjust these processes. Learners who lack metacognitive skills will profit by lessons that include some of the management processes needed for successful learning.

All of these processes require an active learner—one who selects and processes new information effectively to achieve the learning result. The design of the e-lesson can support active processing or it can inhibit it, depending on what kinds of instructional methods are used. For example, a lesson that follows the Las Vegas assumptions of learning by including heavy doses of glitz may overload learners, making it difficult to process information in working memory. At the opposite extreme, lessons that use only text fail to exploit the use of relevant graphics, which are proven to increase learning (see Chapter Three).

The remaining chapters in this book provide specific guidelines for identifying those instructional methods that promote active learning processes. In addition, the chapters relate the psychological mechanisms overviewed here to the design guidelines in the chapters to help you adapt the guidelines to your situation and explain the basis for your decisions to others.

What Is Good Research?

We recommend that e-learning courses incorporate methods that are based on high-quality research. Certainly, it is easier to base courses on the design recommendations of experts, but it's always worthwhile to ask, "Yes, but does it work?" Until fairly recently, there was not much of a research base concerning the design of e-learning environments, but as we sit down to write this book, we are finding a useful and growing base of research (for example, Clark, 1998; Mayer, 2001a; Sweller, 1999). Our goal is not to review every e-learning study, but rather to summarize some exemplary studies that represent the best established findings. In this section, we want to help you recognize high-quality research in your role as a consumer or designer of e-learning courseware. Table 2.1 summarizes three roads to research—informal studies, controlled studies, and clinical trials.

Table 2.1. Three Types of Research.

Research Type	Definition	Example
Informal Studies	Conclusions based on feedback from and observations of students	E-lesson revisions are based on evaluation sheets completed during pilot test.
Controlled Studies	Conclusions based on outcome comparisons of randomly assigned participants to groups with different treatments	Learning from two identical lessons—one with and one without music—is compared in a laboratory setting.
Clinical Trials	Conclusions based on outcomes of lessons taken in actual learning settings	A particular e-learning program is selected based on outcomes from two hundred supervisors.

Informal Studies

Informal studies (or observational studies) involve observing people as they learn or asking them about their learning. For example, we might develop an e-learning course and ask people what they like and don't like about it. Based on this feedback, we can adjust some features of the course. The process of making changes based on learner feedback is called formative evaluation. Alternatively, we can use the feedback along with post-test learning data to summarize the positive and negative features of the course. The process of making an end-of-project evaluation is called summative evaluation. Although informal studies can play a useful role in course development, they do not meet the high scientific standards we have set for the science of instruction.

Controlled Studies

Controlled studies (or experimental studies) involve comparing the learning process and/or outcomes of two or more groups of learners. In measuring the

learning process and/or outcomes (which can be called the dependent measures), we recommend measuring how deeply people have learned. This can
be accomplished by asking them to apply what was taught to new situations
in addition to simply recalling. In setting up the groups, we recommend
keeping all the groups the same except for one variable (which can be called
the independent variable). For example, we can compare a group that receives
an e-learning course that has background music to an identical course that
lacks the music. The learners must be equivalent in the two groups—a feat
that is best ensured by randomly assigning people to the groups. This is a controlled study because all features of the learning situation are the same (that
is, controlled) except for the feature being studied (that is, the independent
variable, which in this case is background music). Large-scale application of
the experimental method to research with humans has been one of the greatest scientific achievements of the twentieth century. This is our preferred
research method for the purposes of this book.

Clinical Trials

Clinical trials (or controlled field testing) involve comparing the learning
process and outcome of people who learn from a targeted e-learning course
versus people who learn from some other venue (such as a different e-learning
course). Clinical trials use the experimental method, as described previously,
but do so by examining whether the e-learning course works in the field, that
is, in the real-world context for which it was intended. Clinical trials are useful because they evaluate outcomes in real-world contexts. However, the results
are limited by the many extraneous variables that can impact learning in the
field. Although we believe that clinical trials are an important component in
the development of effective e-learning courses, our focus in this book is on
more basic design principles that are best discovered in controlled studies.

How Can You Identify Relevant Research?

You might wonder how we selected the research we include in this book or
how you could determine whether a given research study is applicable to your
design decisions. The following list summarizes five questions to consider

when reading research studies:

1. *How similar are the learners in the research study to your learners?*
   Research conducted on children may be limited in its applicability to adult populations. More relevant studies use subjects of college age or beyond.

2. *Are the conclusions based on an experimental research design?*
   Look for subjects randomly assigned to test and control groups.

3. *Are the experimental results replicated?*
   Look for reports of research in which conclusions are drawn from a number of studies that essentially replicate the results. The *Review of Educational Research* is one good source.

4. *Is learning measured by tests that measure application?*
   Research that measures outcomes with recall tests may not apply to adult training situations in which the learning outcomes must be application, not recall, of new knowledge and skills.

5. *Does the data analysis reflect statistical significance as well as practical significance?*
   With a large sample size, even small learning differences may have statistical significance yet may not justify the expense of implementing the test method. Look for statistical significance of .05 or less and effect sizes of .5 or more.

All of these questions relate to the applicability of the research to your learning audience and desired outcomes or the confidence you can put in the results based on the validity of the study. Since experimental studies will all report the results of statistical tests, we briefly summarize how to interpret those tests in the next section.

Interpretation of Research Statistics

Suppose you read a study comparing two groups of students—a test group and a control group. The control group got a basic multimedia lesson that explains content with graphics and audio narration. We call this the no-music group. The test group received the same lesson with background music added to the narration. We call this the music group. Suppose the no-music group averaged 90 percent correct on a test of the material and the music group averaged 80 percent on the same test. Averages are also called means (for example, 90 percent versus 80 percent). Also suppose the scores were not very spread out, so most of the no-music students scored close to ninety and most of the music students scored close to eighty. Standard deviation tells you how spread out the scores are, or how much variation there is in the results. Powerful instructional methods should yield *high* averages and *low* standard deviations. In other words, high scores are achieved and nearly all learners score close to the average so that there is high consistency in outcomes among the learners.

As illustrated in Figure 2.4, let's suppose the standard deviation is ten for the no-music group and ten for the music group. Based on these means and standard deviations, can we conclude that background music hurts learning? Generally, when the difference between the score averages is high (90 percent versus 80 percent in our example) and the standard deviations are low (ten percent in our example), the difference is real. However, to accurately decide that issue requires statistical tests. Two common statistical measures

Figure 2.4. Standard Deviation and Effect Size from Two Lessons.

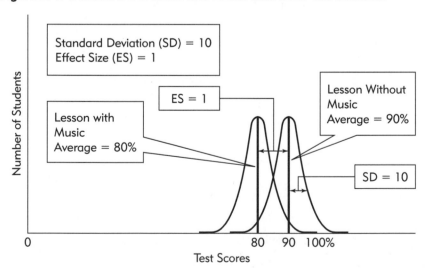

associated with research studies we present in this book are *probability* and *effect size*. As you read research, look for results in which the probability is less than .05 ($p = <.05$) and show an effect size of .5 or greater.

PROBABILITY AND EFFECT SIZE: DETAILS

Some statistical tests yield a measure of probability such as $p < .05$ (which is read, "probability less than point oh five"). In the case of our background music study, this means that there is less than a 5-percent chance that the difference between 90 percent and 80 percent does not reflect a real difference between the two groups. In other words, there is a 95-percent chance that the difference in scores is real—not just a chance result. Thus we can conclude that the difference between the groups is *statistically significant*. In general, when the probability is less than .05, researchers conclude that the difference is real, that is, statistically significant.

EFFECT SIZE: HOW BIG IS THE DIFFERENCE IN PRACTICAL TERMS?

Even if music has a statistically significant effect, we might want to know how strong the effect is in practical terms. We could just subtract one mean score from the other, yielding a difference of 10 in our music study. However, to tell whether 10 is a big difference, we can divide this number by the standard deviation of the control group (or of both groups pooled together). This tells us how many standard deviations one group is more than the other, and is called *effect size* (ES). In this case, the ES is 1, which is generally regarded as a strong effect. What this means is that an individual learner in the control group would get a 1 standard deviation increase (10 points in our example) if he or she were to study with a lesson that omitted music. If the ES had been .5 in our example, an individual learner in the control group would have a .5 standard deviation increase. When the ES is less than .2, it implies that the practical impact of the experimental treatment is a bit too small to worry about, an ES of .5 is moderate, and when it gets to .8 or above it is large enough to get very excited about.

DESIGN DILEMMA: REVISITED

A week later you stop by the HR director's office for a follow-up meeting. You explain the disappointing history of educational technology. You also show some research data proving that use of media elements like music and video stories added for dramatic effect can actually depress learning compared to a simpler approach. You end your case by saying, "You know, using the Internet for learning is not the same as using it for entertainment or reference. We really need to shape the media to our purposes, not vice versa! It's going to cost a lot to develop this training and even more for the employees to take it. Can we risk spending that money on materials that violate research-proven principles?"

Eventually, the director decides that given the investment the company is going to make, your new e-learning courses need to be scientifically sound—that is, based on a well-accepted theory of how people learn, and supported by scientifically valid research evidence. Her charge to you is to be scientific: "The courses need to be scientifically sound. You'll need to adapt your courses to how people learn and to base them on research-tested methods." You leave excited but also aware that you had better be able to explain to others in the company the rationale behind the lessons you are going to design.

WHAT TO LOOK FOR IN e-LEARNING

At the end of the remaining chapters, you will find in this section a checklist of things to look for in effective e-lessons. The checklists summarize teaching methods that support cognitive processes required for learning and have been proven to be valid through controlled research studies. In Chapter Fourteen we present a checklist that combines the guidelines from all of the chapters along with some sample e-learning course critiques.

Suggested Readings

Bransford, J.D., Brown, A.L, and Cocking, R.R. (1999). *How People Learn.* Washington, D.C.: National Academy Press.

Clark, R.C. (1998). *Building Expertise: Cognitive Methods for Training and Performance Improvement.* Silver Spring, MD: International Society for Performance Improvement.

Lambert, N.M., and McCombs, B.L. (1998). *How Students Learn.* Washington, D.C.: American Psychological Association.

Mayer, R.E. (2001). *Multimedia Learning.* New York: Cambridge University Press.

Sweller, J. (1999). *Instructional Design in Technical Areas.* Camberwell, Australia: ACER Press.

CHAPTER OUTLINE

Multimedia Principle: Include Both Words and Graphics

Some Types of Explanatory Graphics Useful for Learning

Graphics to Teach Content Types

Graphics as Topic Organizers

Graphics to Show Relationships

Graphics as Lesson Interfaces

Psychological Reasons for the Multimedia Principle

Evidence for Using Words and Pictures

3

Applying the Multimedia Principle

USE WORDS AND GRAPHICS RATHER THAN WORDS ALONE

CHAPTER PREVIEW

ADDING GRAPHICS to text in e-learning often increases the cost and production time of the training and can add to download delays in Internet-delivered training. Are these drawbacks offset by improved learning? In this chapter, we summarize the empirical evidence for learning gains that result from combining text and *relevant* graphics in e-lessons. We discuss some types of graphics that are useful in e-learning and describe the psychological basis for the improved learning that stems from a combination of text and graphics.

DESIGN DILEMMA

Suppose you work in the training department at Madison Industries, and the newly promoted vice president of quality corners you in the hallway. "I've got a simple task for you, but it's important we do it well. Our employees really need to learn this basic stuff," she says. "I need a short course that introduces our employees to our new quality management system." She hands you a few printed pages and says, "Here, I've written out a clear explanation of how the darn thing works. All you have to do is polish it up—you know—add a little color. Then put it out on our employee Web site for all to read. We don't have much time. Let me know when you've got it done."

This seems like an easy task, so to impress the VP you do a quick layout of some of her text on a storyboard as shown in Figure 3.1. But as you look at this first quick effort, your intuition is that putting pages and pages of text on a Web site may not be the best way to help people learn. Moreover, you remember something you read about the role of graphics in making text more understandable. You give her a quick

---

Figure 3.1. Storyboard for e-Lesson That Uses Only Text.

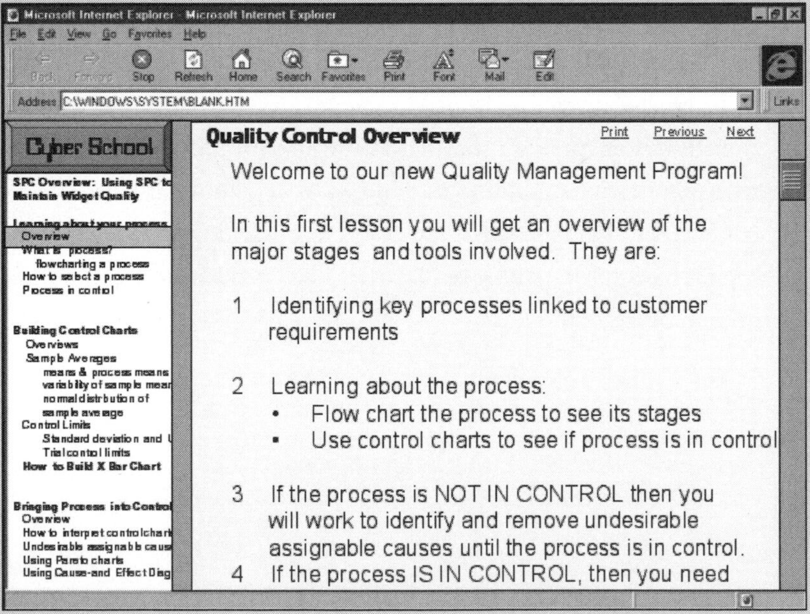

call. "I've done a mock-up of some of the content you gave me this morning. But is it OK if I try to make it a little more learner-friendly by adding some graphics?" Stung by the implied criticism, the VP says, "Well, I'm not sure what you mean. Everything they need to know is in this text. All they have to do is read it. And we don't have much time!" Sensing that a storm is brewing, you ask, "Sure, but do you mind if I try to come up with something that builds on your text? I'll show it to you next week to see what you think." The VP reluctantly agrees and you have a much larger task than you started with.

As you read the script, you think about good ways to visualize the story. Then you spend the next week finding relevant graphics—static pictures such as photos and drawings, as well as dynamic pictures such as video and animation. Finally, you lay out some storyboards that use graphics and words to deliver the message, as shown in Figure 3.2. On this introductory screen, you have interspersed some simple graphics related to the stages in the quality process and some of the tools used at each stage.

Figure 3.2. Storyboard for e-lesson That Uses Text and Graphics.

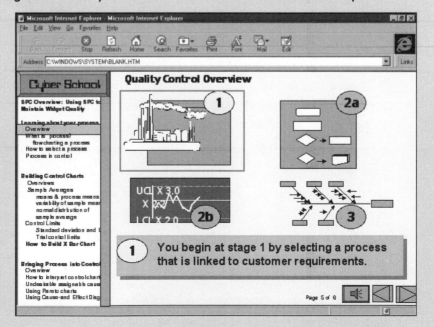

In training, it is customary to use words—either in printed or spoken form—as the main vehicle for conveying information. Words are quick and inexpensive to produce. The question is whether there is any return on investment for supplementing words with pictures—either static graphics such as drawings or photos, or dynamic graphics such as animation or video. In particular, do people learn more deeply from words and graphics than from words alone? This is the issue we want to explore with you in this chapter.

Multimedia Principle: Include Both Words and Graphics

Based on cognitive theory and research evidence, we recommend that e-learning courses include both words and graphics rather than words alone. By words, we mean printed text (that is, words printed on the screen that people read) or spoken text (that is, words presented as speech that people listen to through earphones or speakers). By graphics we mean static illustrations such as drawings, charts, graphs, maps, or photos, and dynamic graphics such as animation or video. We use the term multimedia presentation to refer to any presentation that contains both words and pictures. For example, if you are given an instructional message that is presented in words alone, we recommend you convert it into a multimedia presentation consisting of words and pictures. If you are starting your training from scratch, as you complete the job and content analysis, you should visualize how the instructional message can be communicated using both words and relevant pictures.

The rationale for our recommendation is that people are more likely to understand material when they can engage in active learning. Multimedia presentations encourage learners to engage in active learning by mentally representing the material in words and in pictures and by mentally making connections between the pictorial and verbal representations. In contrast, presenting words alone may encourage learners—especially those with less experience or expertise—to engage in shallow learning such as not connecting the words with other knowledge.

There are many examples of e-learning environments that contain window after window of text and more text. Some may even have graphics

Figure 3.3. Decorative Illustration That Does Not Improve Learning.

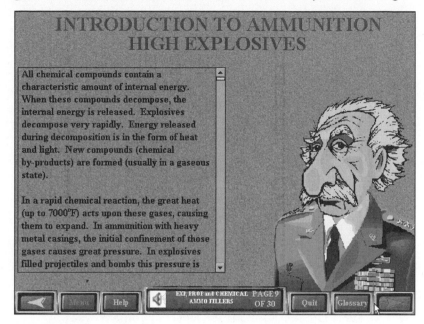

that decorate the page, but do not help you understand the text. For example, Figure 3.3 from a military course on ammunition presents scrolling text and a picture of a general as a decorative element.

Instead of presenting words alone, we recommend presenting words and pictures. Furthermore, our recommendation is not to add pictures that decorate the page (called *decorative illustrations*), but instead to add pictures that help the learner understand the material (called *explanative illustrations*). We believe that the job of an instructional designer is not just to present information—such as in a text that contains everything the learner needs to know—but rather to encourage and enable the learner to make sense out of the material. Providing relevant graphics to text is a proven method of fostering deeper cognitive processing in learners.

Some Types of Explanatory Graphics Useful for Learning

The best types of graphics to meet instructional goals is a book topic in itself. Here we offer just a few examples of the types of graphics that serve instructional rather than decorative roles.

Graphics to Teach Content Types

Graphics to use when teaching specific lesson content such as facts, concepts, processes, procedures, and principles have been described by Ruth Clark (1999) and are summarized in Table 3.1. Since over half of all computer-delivered training teaches computer procedures (Galvin, 2001), many e-learning graphics are screen captures. A screen capture is a graphic that is a replication of an actual software screen. For example, Figure 3.4 is a screen capture from a software tool called Dreamweaver. It is used as the main graphic for the demonstration of and practice on using that screen to create Web pages. Another content type that profits from graphic support is processes. Processes are flows of activity in systems, including business and mechanical systems. Process information is effectively visualized with animations. Figure 3.5 is a screen from an animated graphic comparing information flows among different elements in a Web process.

Table 3.1. Some Graphic Methods for Teaching Content Types.

Content Type	Instructional Method	Example
Fact	• Statements of fact • Pictures of specific forms, screens, or equipment	Illustration of software screen. (see Figure 3.4)
Concept	• Definitions • Examples • Non-examples • Analogies	What is a URL (see Figure 14.5)
Process	• Stage tables • Animated diagrams	Activities in a computer network. (see Figure 3.5)
Procedure	• Step-action tables • Demonstrations	How to use a software application. (see Figure 3.4)
Principle	• Guidelines • Varied context examples	How to name a link. (see Figure 14.6)

Figure 3.4. Screen Capture Graphic for Procedure Lesson.

With permission from Element K.

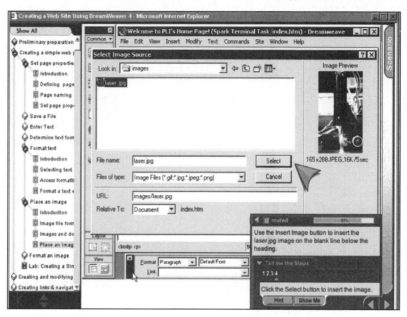

Figure 3.5. Animation to Illustrate Process Lesson.

With permission from Element K.

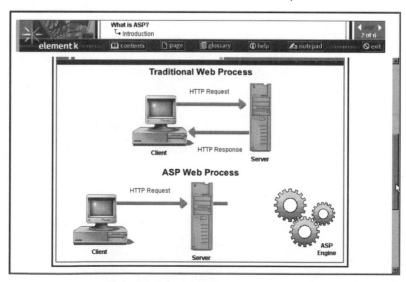

Graphics as Topic Organizers

In addition to illustrating specific content types, graphics such as topic maps can serve an organizational function by showing relationships among topics in a lesson. For example, Figure 3.6 shows a screen with a series of coaching topics mapped in the left-hand bar, including where to coach, when to coach, how long to coach, and so on. When the mouse is placed over each of the topics in the graphic organizer, a different illustration appears on the right side of the screen. In this example, the topic of formal and informal coaching sessions is reinforced with text and photographs.

Figure 3.6. Organizational Graphic for Related Concepts.

With permission from DigitalThink.

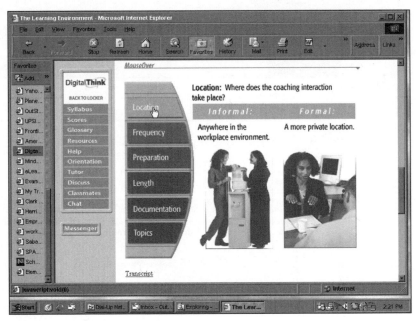

Graphics to Show Relationships

Graphics in the form of dynamic and static graphs can make invisible phenomena visible and show relationships. Imagine an e-learning lesson to teach fast-food workers safe cooking and food-handling practices. An animated line graph could be used to show what happens to bacterial growth in food cooked at different temperatures or handled in safe and unsafe ways. The lesson could include an interactive simulation in which the learner adjusts the cooking temperature and sees the impact on a dynamic line graph called a "germ meter."

Graphics as Lesson Interfaces

Finally, courses designed using a guided discovery approach often use a graphical interface as a backdrop to present case studies. For jobs that are conducted in office settings, a generic office like the one shown in Figure 3.7 provides a number of resources for the learner to use while working on a simulated job assignment. In this lesson, bank loan agents can use the computer, telephone, fax machine, and book shelf to research a commercial loan application. For additional information on the use of graphics in instruction, see the special issue of *Educational Psychology Review* (Robinson, 2002).

Figure 3.7. The Graphic Interface Provides Resources for Researching a Bank Loan Applicant.

With permission from Moody's Financial Services.

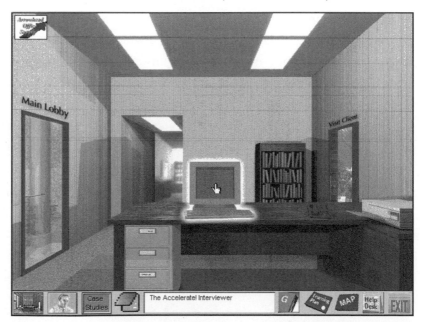

Psychological Reasons for the Multimedia Principle

Perhaps the single greatest human invention is language, and the single greatest modification of this invention is printed language. Words allow us to communicate effectively, and printed words allow us to communicate effectively across miles and years. (So does recorded speech, by the way, which is yet another modification of the great invention of language.) Therefore, it makes sense to use words when we provide training or instruction. For thousands of years, the main format for education has been words—first in spoken form and more recently in printed form. Words are also the most efficient and effective way for producing e-learning because words can convey all the necessary information and are easier to produce than graphics.

This line of thinking is based on the *information delivery theory* in which teaching consists of presenting information and learning consists of acquiring information. Information can be delivered in many forms—such as printed words, spoken words, illustrations, photos, animation, and narration. Over the years, it has become clear that words are an efficient and effective method for presenting information, so in most situations instruction should involve simply presenting words. According to the information delivery theory, the format of the information (for example, words versus pictures) does not matter, as long as the information is delivered to the learner.

In our opinion, the information delivery theory is based on an incorrect conception of how people learn. Instead, we favor a cognitive theory in which learning is seen as a process of active sense-making and teaching is seen as an attempt to foster appropriate cognitive processing in the learner. According to this theory, it's not good enough to deliver information to the learner; instructors must also enable and encourage learners to actively process the information. An important part of active processing is to mentally construct pictorial and verbal representations of the material and to mentally connect them.

This goal is more likely to be achieved with *multimedia* lessons with both words and corresponding pictures that depict the same thing. Adding relevant graphics to words is a powerful way to help learners engage in active learning.

Evidence for Using Words and Pictures

There is consistent evidence that people learn more deeply from words and pictures than from words alone, at least for some simple instructional situations. In ten different studies, researchers compared the test performance of students who learned from animation and narration versus narration alone or from text and illustrations versus text alone (Mayer, 1989b; Mayer and Anderson, 1991, 1992; Mayer, Bove, and others, 1996; Mayer and Gallini, 1990; Moreno and Mayer, in press). The lessons taught scientific and mechanical processes, including how lightning works, how a car's braking system works, how pumps work, and how electrical generators work. For example in one study students read an accurate verbal description of how a bicycle pump works, while others read the same verbal description and viewed a diagram depicting the same steps (see Figures 3.8 and 3.9).

Figure 3.8. How a Bicycle Pump Works Explained with Words Alone.
From Mayer, 2001a.

"As the rod is pulled out, air passes through the piston and fills the area between the piston and the outlet valve. As the rod is pushed in, the inlet valve closes and the piston forces air through the outlet valve."

In all ten comparisons, students who received a multimedia lesson consisting of words and pictures performed better on a subsequent transfer test than students who received the same information only in words. Across the ten studies, people who learned from words and graphics produced between 55 percent to 121 percent more correct solutions to transfer problems than people who learned from words alone. Across all studies, a median percentage gain of 89 percent was achieved with an effect size of 1.50. Recall from our discussion in Chapter Two that effect sizes over .8 are considered large. Figure 3.10 shows a result from one of these experiments. We call this finding the *multimedia effect*—people learn more deeply from words and graphics than from words alone. The multimedia effect is the starting point for our discus-

Figure 3.9. How a Bicycle Pump Works Explained with Words and Graphics

Adapted from Mayer, 2001a.

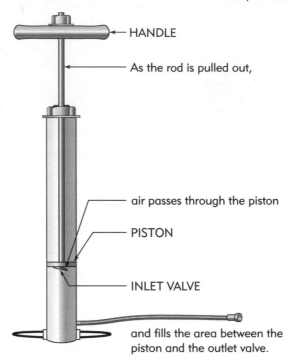

HANDLE

As the rod is pulled out,

air passes through the piston

PISTON

INLET VALVE

and fills the area between the
piston and the outlet valve.

Figure 3.10. Learning Outcomes from Words Alone and from Words and Graphics.

Adapted from Mayer, 2001a.

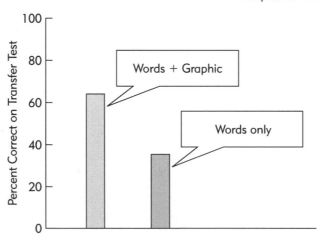

Percent Correct on Transfer Test

Words + Graphic

Words only

sion of best instructional methods for e-learning because it establishes the potential for multimedia lessons to improve human learning.

Complementary results come from research on graphic advance organizers—pictorial material presented at the start of a lesson intended to help the learner understand the material (Mayer, 1989b). For example, in one study (Mayer, 1983) students read a lesson on how radar works and then answered questions. Students performed much better on the test if they saw a graphic representation of the steps in radar (as a ball being thrown, bouncing off an object, and returning to the source) before the lesson was presented.

In a related study involving interactive multimedia, Moreno and Mayer (1999b) developed a mathematics computer game intended to teach students how to add and subtract signed numbers (such as 2--3 = __). Some students learned from drill on practice problems, whereas others worked on the same problems but as feedback also saw a bunny hop along a number line to represent each problem (such as starting at two, turning to face the left, hopping backwards three steps, and landing on five). Students learned better with symbols and graphics than from symbols alone.

DESIGN DILEMMA: RESOLUTION

Let's return to the dilemma we presented at the start of the chapter. The new vice president of quality wants you to use onscreen text for your e-learning course, but you would like to supplement the onscreen text with graphics, including animation, video, drawings, and photos. Armed with what you have learned about the multimedia principle, you can now explain to the VP that people learn more deeply when they are able to build mental connections between verbal and pictorial representations. You can also refer her to numerous studies showing that people learn more deeply from multimedia lessons than from words-only lessons. This, after all, should help get her new quality program off to a good start! Based on theory and research, you now feel very confident about the multimedia prototype storyboards you have created (as shown in Figure 3.2).

The VP listens to your plea, and with a smile says: "I guess you have done your homework. I like your presentation. Please continue with the multimedia format, but realize that the course still must be completed right away." It looks like you've won the argument and your prize is to do a lot of extra work. However, at least you know that your efforts could result in a truly powerful e-learning experience for the employees.

This chapter deals with the instructional value of multimedia, which we define as instruction involving words and pictures. Multimedia presentations may be attention-grabbing or entertaining or persuasive, but our main focus is on whether they help people learn better than simply presenting words alone. Both cognitive theory and research results encourage the *multimedia principle*, that is, the recommendation to use both words and pictures in instructional presentations. Establishing support for the multimedia principle is a crucial first step in our quest for a research-based theory upon which to base e-learning courseware. However, using just any set of pictures does not guarantee that learning will be improved. In subsequent chapters we focus on how to best use pictures in coordination with words to produce the most effective e-learning courseware. In Chapter Seven we also discuss cases in which pictures can depress learning.

WHAT TO LOOK FOR IN e-LEARNING

☐ Graphics and text are used to present instructional content.

☐ Graphics are relevant rather than decorative.

☐ Representative graphics are used to illustrate concrete facts, concepts, and their parts.

☐ Animation is used to illustrate processes, procedures, and principles.

☐ Organizational graphics are used to show relationships among ideas or lesson topics.

☐ Interpretative illustrations such as graphs are used to show relationships among variables or to make invisible phenomena visible.

☐ Graphics are used as a lesson interface for case studies.

COMING NEXT

In this chapter we have seen that learning is improved by the use of relevant graphics combined with words to present instructional content. In the next chapter, we will build upon this principle by examining the *contiguity principle* that addresses the best ways to position graphics and related text on the screen.

Suggested Readings

Clark, R. (1999). *Developing Technical Training*. Silver Spring, MD: International Society for Performance Improvement.

Mayer, R.E. (1989). Systematic Thinking Fostered by Illustrations in Scientific Text. *Journal of Educational Psychology, 81,* 240–246.

Mayer, R.E., and Anderson, R.B. (1992). The Instructive Animation: Helping Students Build Connections Between Words and Pictures in Multimedia Learning. *Journal of Educational Psychology, 84,* 444–452.

Mayer, R.E., and Anderson, R.B. (1991). Animations Need Narrations: An Experimental Test of a Dual-Processing System in Working Memory. *Journal of Educational Psychology, 90,* 312–320.

Mayer, R.E., and Gallini, J.K. (1990). When Is an Illustration Worth Ten Thousand Words? *Journal of Educational Psychology, 88,* 64–73.

Robinson, D.H. (2002). Spatial Text Adjuncts and Learning. *Educational Psychology Review, 14*(1).

CHAPTER OUTLINE

Contiguity Principle: Place Printed Words Near Corresponding Graphics

Separation of Text and Graphics on Scrolling Screens

Separation of Feedback from Questions

Covering Lesson Screens with Linked Screens

Presenting Exercise Directions Separate from the Exercise

Psychological Reasons for the Contiguity Principle

Evidence for Presenting Words at the Same Time as Corresponding Graphics

4

Applying the Contiguity Principle

PLACE CORRESPONDING WORDS AND GRAPHICS NEAR EACH OTHER

CHAPTER PREVIEW

OFTEN IN e-learning when onscreen text is used to present content and explain graphics, a scrolling screen reveals the text, followed by the graphic further down the screen. The result is a physical separation of the text and the graphic. In this chapter we summarize the empirical evidence for learning gains resulting from presenting text and graphics in an integrated fashion on the screen, compared to the same information presented separately. We illustrate some of the more common violations of this principle in misplacement of text and graphics on scrolling screens, directions and feedback to exercises, and information accessed from a lesson link. The psychological advantage of integrating text and graphics results from a reduced need to search for which parts of a graphic correspond to which words, thus allowing the user to concentrate on understanding the materials.

DESIGN DILEMMA

Suppose you've been tapped to develop a company training program that introduces employees to the new quality process to be implemented at all manufacturing plants. You begin by producing a short lesson that consists of animation with corresponding narration. After you complete the prototype, you conduct a functionality test and find that the files are too big for the level of traffic on the corporate network. The result is that the visuals appear first and the audio is considerably delayed. Since streaming technology is not an option, you decide that you will have to give up on audio narration and instead rely on text and still graphics to present the content. You revise your storyboards and use a fixed screen display that incorporates your text and graphics, such as shown in Figure 4.1.

Figure 4.1. Storyboard in Which Text Is Aligned with Figures on a Fixed Screen Display.

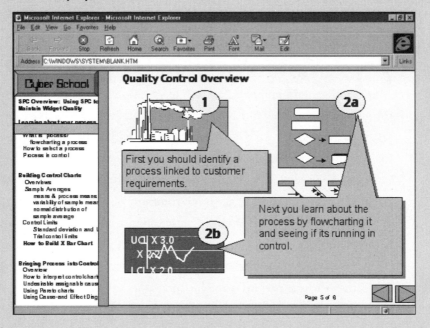

"I've looked at your storyboards," says your team leader, who is the corporate Web page designer. "Since this course will go on the intranet, we need to make efficient use of bandwidth. Let's put more on these pages and scroll them. This will reduce the number of pages learners have to hit so that we can reduce CPU usage on the server. You could put one topic on each screen and that way cut down on the number of pages you will need. Here is how I revised one of your screens" (see Figure 4.2).

Figure 4.2. Storyboard in Which Graphics Disappear as the Learner Scrolls Down to Read the Text.

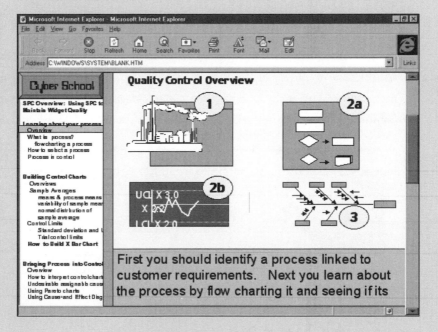

You are not sure that long scrolling screens are effective for instruction. You decide to do some research to find out the advantages and disadvantages of the layout suggested by your team leader.

Contiguity Principle: Place Printed Words Near Corresponding Graphics

In this chapter we focus on the idea that on-screen words should be placed near the parts of the on-screen graphics to which they refer. We recommend that corresponding graphics and printed words be placed near each other on the screen (that is, contiguous in space).

In designing or selecting e-learning courseware, consider how on-screen text is integrated with on-screen graphics. In particular, when printed words refer to parts of on-screen graphics, make sure the printed words are placed next to the corresponding part of a graphic to which they refer. For example, when the graphic is a diagram showing the parts of an object, the printed names of the parts should be placed near the corresponding parts of the diagram, using a pointing line to connect the name to the part. Similarly, when the text describes an action or state depicted in an illustration, the text can appear as a small pop-up message that appears when the mouse touches the graphic. This technique is called a *mouse-over* or *rollover*. For example, Figure 4.3 shows an application screen that uses the rollover technique. When

---

Figure 4.3. Use of Rollover Text to Integrate Graphics and Text.

With Permission from Element K.

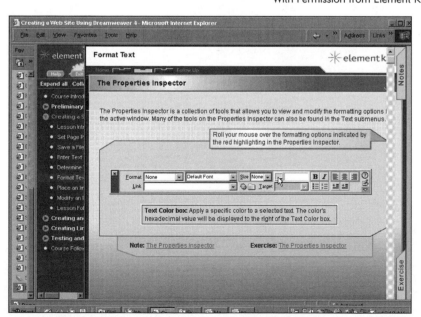

learners place their cursors over different parts of the tool bar, a small text caption appears that explains the tool.

The following list gives four common violations (although there are more) of this principle that are frequently seen in e-learning courseware:

- Visuals and explanatory text are separated, one before the other, and partially obscured because of scrolling screens.

- Feedback is displayed on a separate screen from the practice or question.

- Links leading to an onscreen reference appear in a second browser window that covers the related information on the initial screen.

- Directions to complete practice exercises are placed on a separate screen from the application screen in which the directions are to be followed.

Separation of Text and Graphics on Scrolling Screens

Figure 4.2 shows a scrolling screen in which graphics are presented first and the text describing the visuals appears further down the screen. When the user scrolls down to read the text, the graphic is no longer visible and vice versa. This is a common problem we see in many courses that use scrolling screens to present instructional content. This problem can be remedied by the use of fixed screen displays when it is important to see the text and graphic together. For example, the screen shown in Figure 4.4 is from a lesson teaching the use of Microsoft Word. The text presenting the procedural steps is placed in a box overlaid on the graphic illustrations. Another remedy to the scrolling screen problem is to use text boxes that pop up over graphics when the graphic is touched by the cursor (see Figure 4.3). Finally, you can also opt to place a reduced-size graphic next to text on a scrolling screen to avoid this problem (see Figure 4.5).

Separation of Feedback from Questions

Another common violation of the contiguity principle is when feedback is placed on a screen separate from the question itself. This requires the learner to page back and forth between the question and the feedback, adding

Figure 4.4. Text Placed Near Graphic in Procedural Lesson.

With permission from SmartForce.

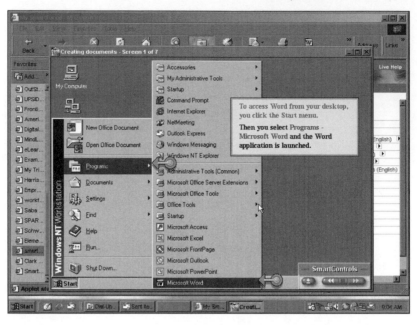

Figure 4.5. Placement of Graphic Next to Text in Scrolling Screen.

With permission from Clark Training.

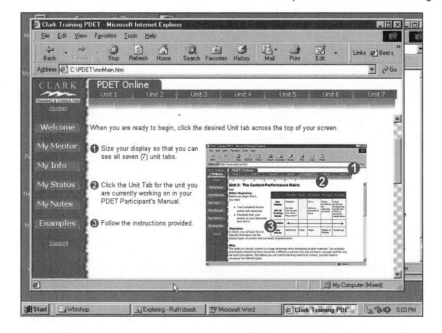

cognitive load to learning. Figure 4.6 illustrates a feedback screen from a military course on ammunition safety. A better design is shown in Figure 4.7 from a course on marking of hazardous materials. In this example, the feedback uses text, graphics, and color to inform learners about the accuracy of their answers. The feedback appears on the same screen as the question, providing learners with the opportunity to see the question, their answers, and the accuracy of their answers.

Figure 4.6. Feedback Is Separated from Question.

Covering Lesson Screens with Linked Screens

The use of links to lead to adjunct information is common in e-learning. However, when the linked information covers related information on the primary screen, this practice can create a problem. For example, Figure 4.8 shows a job aid which is accessed by clicking on a link placed on a practice question in a course on ammunition safety. Having access to reference material is a good idea for memory support. However, unfortunately,

Figure 4.7. Feedback Using Text, Graphics, and Color Appears on Question Screen.

With permission from Defense Ammunition Center.

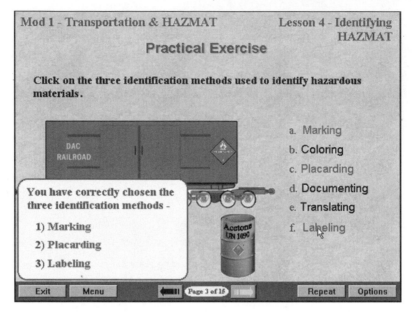

Figure 4.8. Screen in Which Reference Covers the Question.

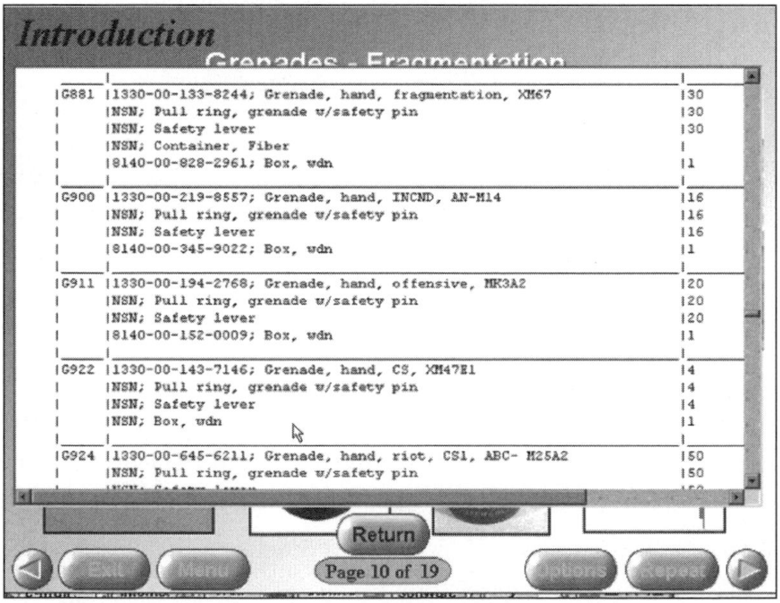

the resulting job aid covers the question. Because the question is completely obscured, the learner would need to either memorize the needed information or write it down in order to respond to the question. A better solution is shown in Figure 4.9, which presents a case study to the learner. The linked job aid shown in the left-hand window does not cover the entire screen and it can either be minimized for easy access or it can be printed for reference during the case.

Figure 4.9. Screen in which Reference Does Not Cover Question.

With Permission from DigitalThink.

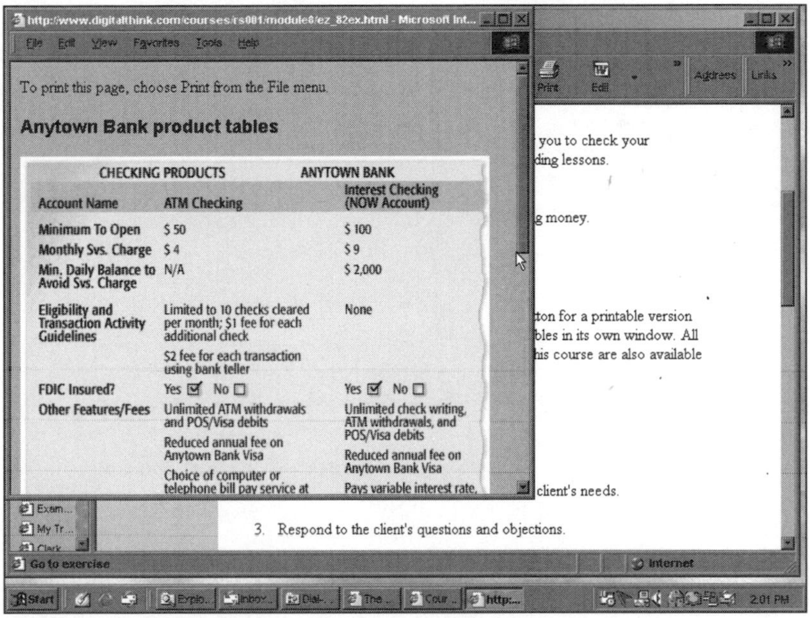

Presenting Exercise Directions Separate from the Exercise

A final common violation of the contiguity principle is the practice of including exercise directions separated from the screens on which the actions are to be taken. For example, in Figure 4.10 we see textual directions for a control chart exercise. After clicking on the "launch exercise" button, the learner no longer has access to these steps. A better alternative is to put the step-by-step directions in a box on the application screen.

Figure 4.10. Exercise Directions Separated from Activity Screen.

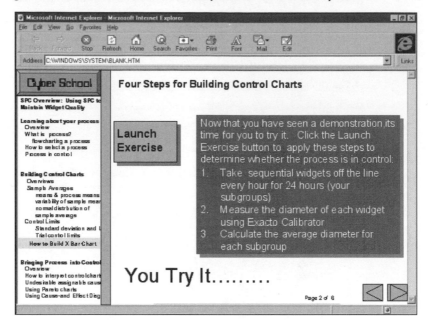

Psychological Reasons for the Contiguity Principle

As we have reviewed in the examples shown in the previous sections, it is not unusual to see text and graphics physically separated in e-lessons. The separation may occur because of vertical placement of text and graphics (one on top of the other), which separates them when the screen is scrolled, or by placing related information on separate fixed screen displays.

Some designers separate words and pictures because they haven't stopped to think about whether it's an effective way to present information. Others reason that presenting the same material in two different places on the page allows learners to choose the format that best suits their needs or even to experience the same information in two different ways. We recommend against separating words and pictures, even for environments with high traffic and low bandwidth, because it is not based on an accurate understanding of how people learn. Rather than being copy machines that record incoming information, humans are sense-makers who try to see the meaningful relations between words and pictures. When words and pictures are separated from one another on the screen, people must use their scarce cognitive resources just to match them up. Then, they have fewer cognitive resources to use to mentally organize and integrate the material. However, when words and pictures are integrated, people can hold them together in their working memories and therefore make meaningful connections between them. This act of mentally connecting corresponding words and pictures is an important part of the sense-making process that leads to meaningful learning. As we saw in Chapter Two, it is in working memory that the related incoming information is organized and integrated with existing knowledge in long-term memory. When the learner has to do the added work of integrating separated but related text and visual components, the limited capacity of working memory is taxed— leading to cognitive overload.

Evidence for Presenting Words at the Same Time as Corresponding Graphics

Our recommendation is not only based on cognitive theory, it is also based on several relevant research studies (Mayer, 1989b; Mayer, Steinhoff, Bower, and Mars, 1995; Moreno and Mayer, 1999a). In five different tests involving lessons on lightning formation and how cars' braking systems work, learners received printed text and illustrations containing several frames. For the first group of learners, text was placed near the illustration that it described (see Figure 4.11). For the second group, the full text was placed under the illustration, such as shown in Figure 4.12. Although both groups were exposed to identical text and illustrations, in five out of five studies, the integrated group performed better on problem-solving transfer tests than the separated group. Overall, the integrated group produced between 43 and 89 percent more solutions than the separated group. The median gain across all the studies was 68 percent for an effect size of 1.12, which, as mentioned in Chapter Two, is a large effect. Figure 4.13 summarizes the results from one of the experiments.

Figure 4.11. Screen from Experimental Lesson on Lightning Formation with Integrated Text and Graphics.

Adapted from Mayer, 2001a.

Figure 4.12. Experimental Lesson with Separated Text and Graphics.

Adapted from Mayer, 2001a.

As the air in this updraft cools, water vapor condenses into water droplets and forms a cloud.

Figure 4.13. Learning Outcomes from Integrated and Separated Versions.

Adapted from Mayer, 2001a.

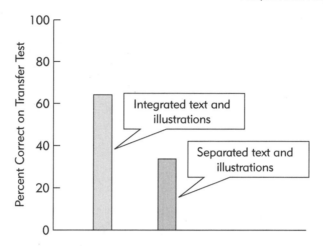

Similar results have been found with training programs for technical tasks (Chandler and Sweller, 1991; Paas and Van Merrienboer, 1994b; Sweller and Chandler, 1994; Sweller, Chandler, Tierney, and Cooper, 1990). Additional evidence comes from eye movement studies involving text and corresponding diagrams. Successful learners tended to read a portion of the text, then search the diagram for the object being described in the text, then read the next portion of text and search the diagram for the object being described, and so on (Hegarty, Carpenter, and Just, 1996). It seems reasonable that we can simplify this process for all learners by breaking text into chunks, and by placing text near the part of the graphic that it describes. Overall, there are numerous studies that support our recommendation.

DESIGN DILEMMA: RESOLUTION

Now that you have found some research on the negative impact that separating words and pictures has on learning, you feel better prepared to defend your storyboard to your team leader. Keeping in mind his perspective as the corporate Web master, you offer the following response: "The corporate Web standards have really helped make our sites much more consistent and readable. But keep in mind that they were developed primarily for the purpose of reference. We will need to revisit those standards when we are using our intranet for instructional purposes. For example, scrolling screens may be great for reference. But when their use in e-learning separates text and visuals, we know that learning is depressed. The reason is that learners are forced to use limited working memory resources to mentally integrate the information that we have physically separated. Fortunately, I think we can come up with a design that meets both our objectives. We can still use scrolling screens as long as we place the graphics near the text. I've reworked the storyboards to show you an example."

WHAT TO LOOK FOR IN e-LEARNING

☐ Screens that place explanatory text adjacent to the graphic they describe.

☐ Feedback that appears on the same screen as the question.

☐ Procedural directions that appear on the same screen in which the steps are to be applied in an exercise.

☐ Linked information that does not cover related information on the primary screen.

☐ Use of techniques such as pop-up text and reduced graphics that support integration of text and graphics.

COMING NEXT

In this chapter, we have seen the importance of the onscreen layout of text and graphics. Next we will consider the benefits of presenting words in audio narration rather than in onscreen text. We know that audio adds considerably to file sizes and can be slow to download when bandwidth or traffic constrains delivery over the Internet. Does the use of audio add anything to learning? In the next chapter we examine the *modality principle* which addresses this issue.

Suggested Readings

Mayer, R.E. (1989b). Systematic Thinking Fostered by Illustrations in Scientific Text. *Journal of Educational Psychology, 81,* 240–246.

Mayer, R.E., Steinhoff, K., Bower, G., and Mars, R. (1995). A Generative Theory of Textbook Design: Using Annotated Illustrations to Foster Meaningful Learning of Science Text. *Educational Technology Research and Development, 43,* 31–43.

Moreno, R., and Mayer, R.E. (1999). Cognitive Principles of Multimedia Learning: The Role of Modality and Contiguity. *Journal of Educational Psychology, 91,* 358–368.

CHAPTER OUTLINE

Modality Principle: Present Words as Speech Rather Than Onscreen Text

Psychological Reasons for the Modality Principle

Evidence for Using Spoken Rather Than Printed Text

5

Applying the Modality Principle

PRESENT WORDS AS AUDIO NARRATION RATHER THAN ONSCREEN TEXT

CHAPTER PREVIEW

Technical constraints on the use of audio in e-learning may lead consumers or designers of e-learning to rely on text to present content and describe visuals. However, when it's feasible to use audio, there is considerable evidence that presenting words in audio rather than onscreen text results in significant learning gains. In this chapter we summarize the empirical evidence for learning gains that result from using audio rather than onscreen text to describe graphics. To moderate this guideline, we also describe a number of situations in which memory limitations require the use of text rather than audio.

The psychological advantage of using audio presentation is a result of the incoming information being split across two separate cognitive channels—words in the auditory channel and pictures in the visual channel—rather than concentrating both words and pictures in the visual channel.

DESIGN DILEMMA

Congratulations! You have been asked by the human resources director of your company to oversee the production of a Web-based training program to teach the use of quality process control tools and techniques. One of the early lessons provides an overview of how all the quality tools will be applied in the process. You decide to build a prototype of your course. The product of your efforts is a four-minute lesson that can be accessed over the Web. It includes a narrated animation that presents a step-by-step overview of the process (as shown in Figure 5.1), followed by a series of narrated screens in which each quality tool, such as control charts, is briefly explained in narrated words. Justly proud of your prototype lesson, you set up a demonstration for the project sponsor, the director of corporate quality.

Although she seems to like the course, she offers some blunt suggestions: "You've got to get rid of all that audio. Our budget is limited. Just put the words on

Figure 5.1. Words Are Presented as Narration.

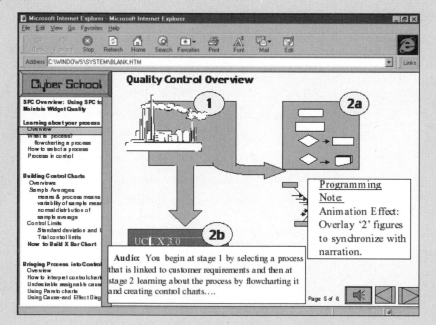

the screen in print. Onscreen text is cheaper to produce and easier to update, and besides, it conveys the same information as speech." She has a point, you think, especially about some of the technical problems with speech. However, your intuition is that people may get more from the animation if you use spoken words rather than onscreen printed words. "Let me look into it," you offer, and the director gives a half-hearted nod.

The storyboard shown in Figure 5.2 illustrates a screen that reflects what the director requested—an animation described by onscreen text. As you can see Figure 5.1 and Figure 5.2 present the same animation and the same words; only the presentation mode of the words has changed from spoken text (in Figure 5.1) to printed text (in Figure 5.2). "Let me look into it" keeps echoing in your head, so you decide to see what theory and research have to say about your dilemma.

Figure 5.2. Words Are Presented as Onscreen Text.

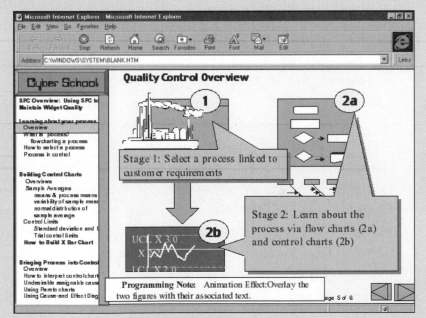

Modality Principle: Present Words as Speech Rather Than Onscreen Text

Suppose you are presenting a verbal explanation along with an animation or series of still frames. Does it matter whether the words in your multimedia presentation are represented as printed text (that is, as onscreen text) or as spoken text (that is, as narration)? What does cognitive theory and research evidence have to say about the modality of words in multimedia presentations? You'll get the answer to these questions in the next few sections of this chapter.

Based on cognitive theory and research evidence, we recommend that you put words in spoken form rather than printed form whenever the graphic or animation is the focus of the words and both are presented simultaneously. Thus, we recommend that you avoid e-learning courses that contain crucial multimedia presentations where the words are in printed rather than spoken form.

The rationale for our recommendation is that learners may experience an overload of their visual/pictorial channel when they must simultaneously process graphics and the printed words that refer to them. If their eyes must attend to the printed words, they cannot fully attend to the animation or graphics—especially when the words and pictures are presented concurrently and at a rapid pace. Since being able to attend to relevant words and pictures is a crucial first step in learning, e-learning courses should be designed to minimize the chances of overloading learners' visual/pictorial channel.

Figure 5.3 illustrates a multimedia course delivered on CD-ROM that effectively applies the *modality principle.* In this section of the lesson, a demonstration of how to use a new automated telephone management system is being given. As the animation demonstrates the steps taken on the computer screen, the audio describes the actions of the user. Another good example is seen in Figure 5.4 from a CD-ROM lesson on proper identification of hazardous materials. Audio is used to summarize what hazardous materials identifiers such as codes and names must appear on the shipping papers. During the audio summary, animation is used to highlight the identifiers in a government reference table and move them from the table to the shipping materials.

When simultaneously presenting words and the graphics explained by the words, use spoken rather than printed text as a way of reducing the

Figure 5.3. Audio Explains the Animated Demonstration of the Telephone System.

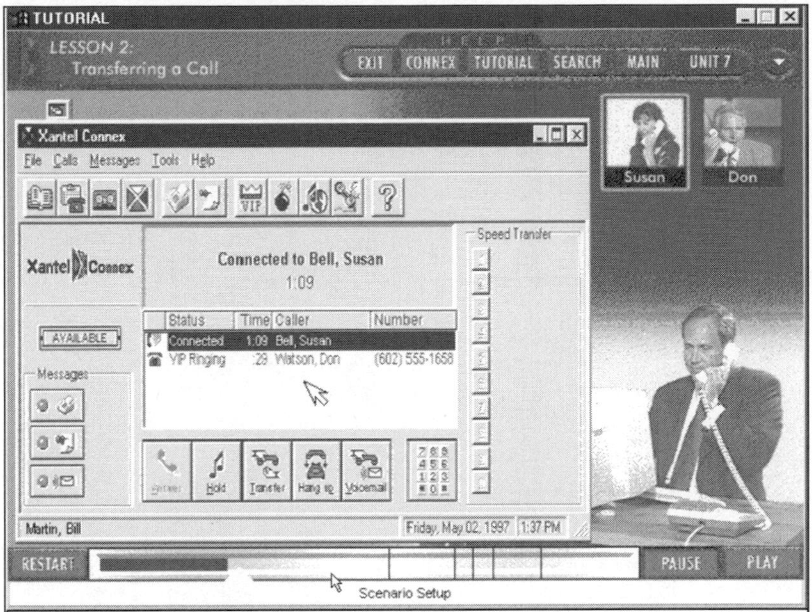

Audio: While Bill is talking to Don, Julie calls with a question. Bill knows that Julie needs to talk to Shelly in the Art Department and decides to transfer her while he is talking to Don.

demands on visual processing. We recognize that in some cases it may not be practical to implement the modality principle, because the creation of sound may involve technical demands that the learning environment cannot meet (such as bandwidth, sound cards, headsets, and so on). Using sound also may add unreasonable expense or may make it more difficult to update rapidly changing information. We also recognize the recommendation is limited to those situations in which the words and graphics are simultaneously presented, and thus does not apply when words are presented without any concurrent picture or other visual input.

Additionally, there are times when the words should remain available to the learner for memory support. For example, a mathematical formula may be part of an audio explanation of an animated demonstration, but because of its complexity, it should remain visible as onscreen text. Key words that identify the

Figure 5.4. Audio Explains Hazardous Materials Identifiers.

With permission from Defense Ammunition Center.

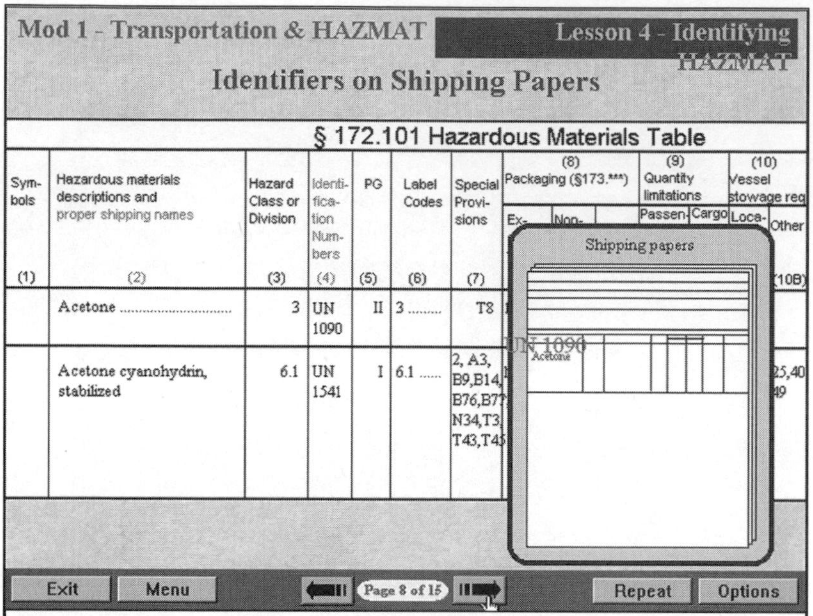

Audio: The proper shipping name is placed on the shipping paper for identification of the item. The ID code is also placed on the shipping paper in close proximity to the shipping name.

steps of a procedure may be presented by onscreen text and highlighted (thus used as an organizer) as each step is illustrated in the animation and discussed in the audio. Another common example involves the directions to a practice exercise. Thus we see in Figure 5.5 (from a hazardous materials course) that the audio used throughout most of the program is suspended when the learner comes to the practice screen. Instead, the directions to the practice remain in text for reference as the learner completes the exercise.

Psychological Reasons for the Modality Principle

If the purpose of the instructional program is to present information as efficiently as possible, then it does not matter whether you present graphics with printed text or graphics with spoken text. In both cases, identical pictures and words are presented, so it does not matter if the words are presented as

Figure 5.5. Directions to Practice Exercise as Onscreen Text for Memory Support.

With permission from Defense Ammunition Center.

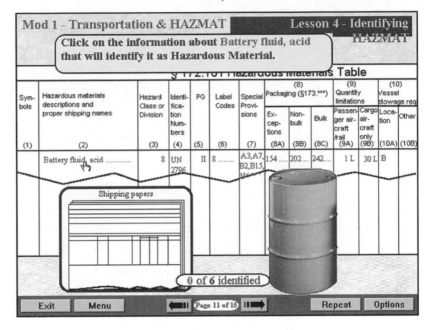

printed text or spoken text. This is the design principle suggested by the information delivery view of learning—the idea that the instructor's job is to present information and the learner's job is to acquire information. Following this view, the rationale for using onscreen text is that it is generally easier to produce printed text rather than spoken text and it accomplishes the same job—that is, it presents the same information.

We believe the rationale to present words as onscreen text in multimedia presentations conflicts with the way the human mind works. According to the cognitive theory of learning—which we use as the basis for our recommendations—people have separate information processing channels for visual/pictorial processing and for auditory/verbal processing. When learners are given concurrent graphics and onscreen text, both must be processed initially in the visual/pictorial channel. The capacity of each channel is limited, so the graphics and their explanatory onscreen text must compete for the same limited visual attention. When the eyes are engaged with onscreen text, they cannot simultaneously be looking at the graphics; when the eyes are engaged with the graphics, they cannot be looking at the onscreen text. Thus, even though the information is presented, learners may not be able to adequately attend to all of it because their visual channel becomes overloaded.

In contrast, we can reduce this load on the visual channel by presenting the verbal explanation as speech. Thus, the verbal material enters the cognitive system through the ears and is processed in the auditory/verbal channel. At the same time, the graphics enter the cognitive system through the eyes and are processed in the visual/pictorial channel. In this way neither channel is overloaded but both words and pictures are processed.

The case for presenting verbal explanations of graphics as speech is summarized in Figures 5.6 and 5.7. Figure 5.6 shows how graphics and onscreen text can overwhelm the visual channel, and Figure 5.7 shows how graphics and speech can distribute the processing between the visual and auditory channels. This analysis also explains why the case for presenting words as speech only applies to situations in which words and pictures are presented simultaneously. As you can see in Figure 5.6, there would be no overload in the visual channel if words were presented as onscreen text but there were no concurrent graphics that required the learner's simultaneous attention.

Figure 5.6. Overloading of Visual Channels with Presentation of Written Text and Graphics.

Adapted from Mayer, 2001a.

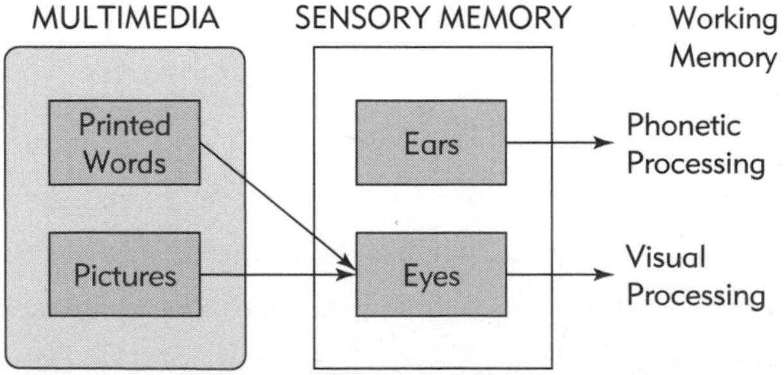

Figure 5.7. Access of Visual and Auditory Channels with Presentation of Narration and Graphics.

Adapted from Mayer, 2001a.

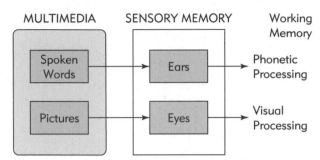

Evidence for Using Spoken Rather Than Printed Text

Do students learn more deeply from graphics with speech (for example, narrated animation) than from graphics with onscreen text (for example, animation with onscreen text blocks), as suggested by cognitive theory? Researchers have examined this question in several different ways, and the results consistently support our recommendation. Let's focus on several recent studies that compare multimedia lessons containing animation with concurrent narration versus animation with concurrent onscreen text, in which the words in the narration and onscreen text are identical and are presented at the same point in the animation. Some of the multimedia lessons present an explanation on how lightning forms or how a car's braking system works (Mayer and Moreno, 1998; Moreno and Mayer, 1999a). Others are embedded in an interactive game intended to teach botany (Moreno, Mayer, Spires, and Lester, 2001), and a final set are part of a virtual reality training episode concerning the operation of an aircraft fuel system (O'Neil, Mayer, Herl, Niemi, Olin, and Thurman, 2000). For example, as shown in Figure 5.8, in one study students viewed an animation depicting the steps in lightning formation. As you can see in Version A, the words are presented as onscreen text, whereas in Version B the words are presented as narration.

In each of the seven comparisons, students who received animation with concurrent narration generated more solutions on a subsequent problem-solving transfer test than students who received animation with concurrent

Figure 5.8. Graphics Described by Onscreen Text (Version A) or by Narration (Version B).

Adapted from Mayer, 2001a.

Version A

As the air in the updraft cools, water vapor condenses into water droplets and forms a cloud.

Version B

"As the air in the updraft cools, water vapor condenses into water droplets and forms a cloud."

onscreen text. Specifically, the animation and narration group generated between 41 to 114 percent more solutions than the animation and onscreen text group, even though both groups received identical animation and words. Figure 5.9 shows the results from one of these studies. The mean percent gain of all the studies was 80 percent, with an effect size of 1.17, which is considered to be large. We refer to this finding as the *modality effect*—people learn more deeply from multimedia lessons when words explaining concurrent animations or graphics are presented as speech rather than as onscreen text.

Figure 5.9. Learning Outcomes: Graphics Narrated Versus Graphics Described by Onscreen Text.

Adapted from Mayer, 2001a.

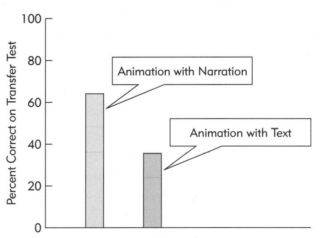

In a related study on the modality effect, Mousavi, Low, and Sweller (1995) presented worked-out examples of geometry problems along with a concurrent oral explanation or along with the same explanation printed on the page. When the words were spoken rather than printed, students performed much better on subsequent problem-solving tests involving geometry problems. Based on the growing evidence for the modality effect, we feel confident in recommending the use of spoken rather than printed words in multimedia messages containing graphics with related descriptive words.

DESIGN DILEMMA RESOLUTION

Using what you have learned both about cognitive theory and research evidence, let's return to the dilemma we outlined at the start of the chapter. The quality director wanted you to use onscreen text rather than speech in your e-learning course on quality management, but you said you'd look into it and get back to her. Based on what you have learned about the modality principle, you are ready for that follow-up meeting. You calmly explain that the visual system of learners will be overloaded if you present both on-screen text and on-screen animation at the same time. Next, you show how you can eliminate the overload on the visual system by presenting the words as speech—which can be processed through the ears in the auditory channel. Finally, you summarize how study after study showed that people learn more deeply from animation with speech rather than animation with on-screen text. You feel confident that this proven argument supports your position.

Your quality director is impressed, and reluctantly concedes: "OK, so stick with the audio, but I still think it's more work for you than if you just used text on the screen." With a smile you reply, "Yes, you're right about that, but in this case the extra work seems worth the effort."

Does the modality principle mean that you should never use printed text? Of course not. We do not intend for you to use our recommendations as unbending rules that must be rigidly applied in all situations. Instead, we encourage you to apply our principles in ways that are consistent with the way that the human mind works—that is, consistent with the cognitive theory of multimedia learning rather than the information delivery theory. As noted earlier, the *modality principle* applies only in situations in which you present graphics and their verbal commentary at the same time. As we noted previously, in some cases words should remain available to the learner over time. When you present technical terms, list key steps in a procedure, or are giving directions to a practice exercise, it is important to present words in writing for reference support. Further, if you present only words on the screen, or the graphic is not being explained, then the modality principle does not apply. Finally, in some situations people may learn better when you present both printed and spoken words. We describe these situations in the next chapter on the redundancy principle.

WHAT TO LOOK FOR IN e-LEARNING

☐ Use of audio narration to explain onscreen graphics or animations.

☐ Use of text for information that learners will need as reference, such as directions to practice exercises.

COMING NEXT

In this chapter we have seen that learning is improved when graphics or animations presented in e-lessons are explained using audio narration rather than onscreen text. What would be the impact of including both text and narration? In other words, would learning be improved if narration was used to read onscreen text? We will address this issue in the next chapter.

Suggested Readings

Mayer, R.E., and Moreno, R. (1998). A Split-Attention Effect in Multimedia Learning: Evidence for Dual Processing Systems in Working Memory. *Journal of Educational Psychology, 90,* 312–320.

Moreno, R., and Mayer, R.E. (1999). Cognitive Principles of Multimedia Learning: The Role of Modality and Contiguity. *Journal of Educational Psychology, 91,* 358–368.

Mousavi, S., Low, R., and Sweller, J. (1995). Reducing Cognitive Load by Mixing Auditory and Visual Presentation Modes. *Journal of Educational Psychology, 87,* 319–334.

CHAPTER OUTLINE

Redundancy Principle One: Avoid Presenting Words as Narration and Identical Text in the Presence of Graphics

Psychological Reasons for the Redundancy Principle

Evidence for Omitting Redundant Onscreen Text

Redundancy Principle Two: Consider the Narration of Onscreen Text in Special Situations

Psychological Reasons for Exceptions to Redundancy Principle

Evidence for Including Redundant Onscreen Text

6

Applying the Redundancy Principle

PRESENTING WORDS IN BOTH TEXT AND AUDIO NARRATION CAN HURT LEARNING

CHAPTER PREVIEW

SOME e-**LEARNING** describes graphics using words in both onscreen text and audio narration in which the audio repeats the text. We call this technique *redundant onscreen text*. In this chapter, we summarize empirical evidence that graphics explained by *audio alone* rather than graphics explained by *audio and redundant onscreen text* gets better learning results. The psychological advantage of presenting words in audio alone is that you avoid overloading the visual channel of working memory. There are also certain situations that benefit from the use of redundant on-screen text. We describe those here as well.

DESIGN DILEMMA

In response to a request from the quality director of Madison Industries, you have created the perfect multimedia presentation for a company training program. As described in the previous chapter, your introductory lesson gives an overview of the quality control tools as part of the overall company quality process. As shown in Figure 6.1, it contains a short animation coupled with concurrent narration and is consistent with many of the design principles advocated in this book. In spite of your valiant efforts, the director says, "We need to accommodate different learning styles. I read somewhere that some people are visual learners and others are auditory learners. You need to add text to the screen for those who learn better from reading. I think you should add text to the presentation so people can have the choice of listening or reading."

Figure 6.1. A Storyboard in Which Visuals Are Explained with Narration.

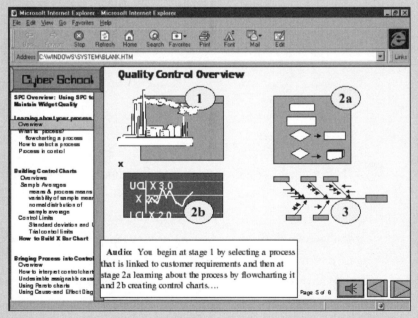

You sense that the director is serious about this request so you create a new version of your multimedia presentation by adding textual information that appears at the bottom of the screen. The textual information presents the same sentences simultaneously as they are spoken in the narration; thus, they fit the definition of *redundant onscreen text*. Figure 6.2 shows frames from your newly revised e-learning program, with redundant onscreen text added to the bottom of

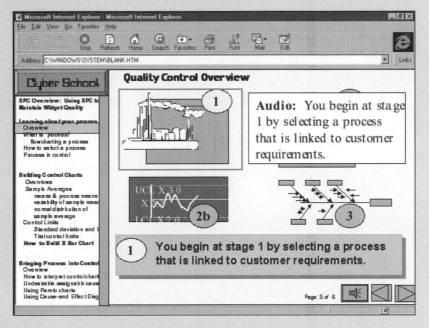

Figure 6.2. A Storyboard in Which Visuals Are Explained with Narration and Identical Text.

the screen. Although you have complied with the director's request, you are not convinced about the learning styles idea and you find that the text crowds your screens. So you decide to investigate the effectiveness of adding onscreen text to a multimedia presentation.

Redundancy Principle One: Avoid Presenting Words as Narration and Identical Text in the Presence of Graphics

If you are planning a multimedia program consisting of graphics (such as animation, video, or even static pictures or photos) explained by narration, should you also include onscreen text that duplicates the audio? We explore this question in this section.

Based on research and theory in cognitive psychology, we recommend that you avoid e-learning courses that contain redundant on-screen text presented at the same time as on-screen graphics. Our reason is that learners might pay so much attention to the printed words that they pay less attention to the accompanying graphics. When their eyes are on the printed words, learners cannot be looking at the on-screen graphics. For example, Figure 6.3 shows a screen from a lesson on ammunition safety that uses video to illustrate an explosion. Note that the explanatory narration is the same as the on-screen text. In contrast, Figure 6.4 illustrates an animated demonstration of how to use a new computerized telephone system that is narrated with audio. Note the absence of on-screen text that duplicates the narration.

**Figure 6.3. The Graphics Are Explained Using Same Words in Audio
Narration and in Text.**

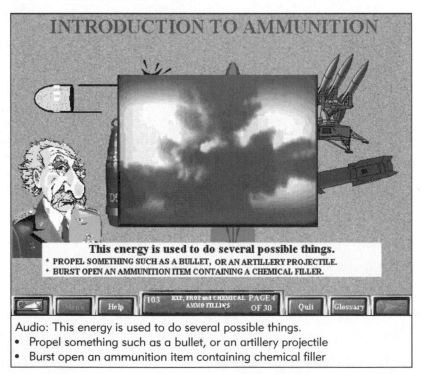

Figure 6.4. The Graphics Are Explained Using Audio Narration.

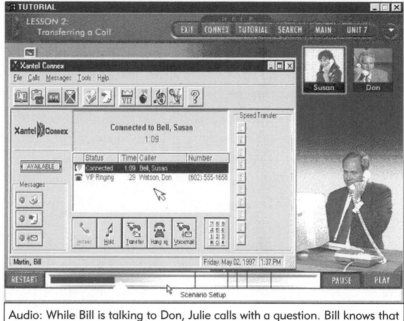

Audio: While Bill is talking to Don, Julie calls with a question. Bill knows that Julie needs to talk to Shelly in the Art Department and decides to transfer her while he is talking to Don.

Psychological Reasons for the Redundancy Principle

There is a common belief that some people have visual learning styles while others have auditory learning styles. Therefore, words should always be presented in both spoken and printed form so learners can choose the presentation format that best matches their learning preference. We call this idea the *learning styles hypothesis* because it plays on the common sense argument that instruction should be flexible enough to support different learning styles. Accommodating different learning styles may seem appealing to e-learning designers who are fed up with the "one-size-fits-all" approach and to clients who intuitively believe there are visual and auditory learners.

The learning styles hypothesis is based on the *information delivery theory* of multimedia learning, which holds that learning consists of receiving information. In our Design Dilemma, the multimedia lesson illustrated in Figure 6.1 provides two delivery routes for information—by pictures (in the animation) and by spoken words (in the narration). However, you create a third route when you add printed words (in the onscreen text) as in Figure 6.2. According to the information delivery theory, three ways of delivering the same information is better than two, especially if one or two of the routes does not work well for some learners. Therefore, the information delivery theory predicts that students will learn more deeply from multimedia presentations when redundant onscreen text is included rather than excluded.

The learning styles view—and the information delivery theory upon which it is built—seem to make sense, but let's look a little deeper. What's wrong with the information delivery theory? Our major criticism is that it makes unwarranted assumptions about how people learn. For example, it assumes that people learn by adding information to memory, as if the mind were an empty vessel that needs to be filled with incoming information. In contrast, the cognitive theory of multimedia learning is based on the assumptions that (a) all people have separate channels for processing verbal and pictorial material, (b) each channel is limited in the amount of processing that can take place at one time, and (c) learners actively attempt to build pictorial and verbal models from the presented material and build connections between them. These assumptions are consistent with theory and research in cognitive science, and represent a consensus view of how people learn.

According to the cognitive theory of multimedia, adding redundant onscreen text to a multimedia presentation could overload the visual channel. For example, Figure 6.5 summarizes the cognitive activities that occur for a presentation containing animation, narration, and concurrent onscreen text. As you can see, the animation enters the learner's cognitive system through the eyes and is processed in the visual/pictorial channel, whereas the narration enters the learner's cognitive system through the ears and is processed in the auditory/verbal channel. However, the onscreen text also enters through the eyes and must be processed (at least initially) in the visual/pictorial channel. Thus, the limited cognitive resources in the visual channel must be used to process both the animation and the printed text. If

Figure 6.5. Overloading of Visual Channels Two Visual Media Elements.
Adapted from Mayer, 2001a.

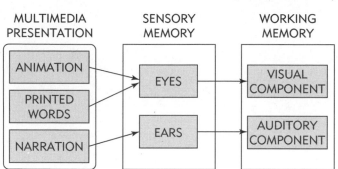

the pace of presentation is fast and learners are unfamiliar with the material, learners may experience cognitive overload in the visual/pictorial channel. As a result, some important aspects of the animation may not be selected and organized into a mental representation.

Now, consider what happens when only narration and animation are presented. The animation enters through the eyes and is processed in the visual/pictorial channel, whereas the narration enters through the ears and is processed in the auditory/verbal channel. The chances for overload are minimized, so the learner is more able to engage in appropriate cognitive processing. Thus, the cognitive theory of multimedia learning predicts that learners will learn more deeply from multimedia presentations in which redundant on-screen text is excluded rather than included.

Evidence for Omitting Redundant Onscreen Text

Several researchers have put these two competing predictions to a test. In a recent set of studies (Mayer, Heiser, and Lonn, 2001; Moreno and Mayer, 2002), some students (non-redundant group) viewed an animation and listened to a concurrent narration explaining the formation of lightning. Other students (redundant group) received the same multimedia presentation, but with concurrent, redundant onscreen text. In a series of four comparisons, students in the non-redundant group produced more solutions (ranging

Figure 6.6. Better Learning When Animations Are Described by
    Narration Alone.

Adapted from Mayer, 2001a.

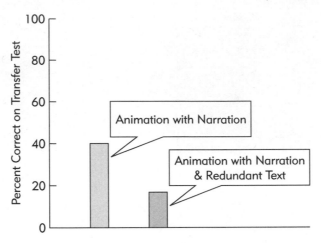

between 43 to 69 percent more) on a problem-solving transfer test than did
students in the redundant group. The median percentage gain was 79 percent with an effect size of 1.24, which is considered to be large. Figure 6.6
shows the results from one of these studies.

Kalyuga, Chandler, and Sweller (1999) provide complementary evidence.
One group (non-redundant) received training in soldering (that is, techniques
for joining metals) through the use of static diagrams presented on a computer
screen along with accompanying speech, whereas another group (redundant
group) received the same training along with onscreen printed text duplicat-
ing the same words as the audio. On a problem-solving transfer test involving
troubleshooting, the non-redundant group outperformed the redundant
group—scoring 64 percent better when redundant text was excluded rather
than included.

These kinds of results support the conclusion that in some cases, less is
more. Because of the limited capacity of the human information processing
system, it can be better to present less material (graphics with corresponding
narration) than more material (graphics with corresponding narration and
printed text).

Redundancy Principle Two: Consider the Narration of Onscreen Text in Special Situations

Are there any situations in which e-learning courses would be improved by adding redundant onscreen text? Although we recommend omitting redundant on-screen text in most e-learning programs, consider using it in special situations that will not overload the learner's visual information processing system, such as when:

- There is no pictorial presentation (for example, when the screen contains no animation, video, photos, graphics, illustrations, and so on)

- There is ample opportunity to process the pictorial presentation (for example, when the onscreen text and corresponding graphics are presented sequentially or when the pace of presentation is sufficiently slow)

- The learner must exert much greater cognitive effort to comprehend spoken text than printed text (for example, for learners who are not native speakers or who have specific learning disabilities, or when the verbal material is long and complex or contains unfamiliar key words).

REDUNDANT ONSCREEN TEXT: WHEN TO LOSE IT AND WHEN TO USE IT

Avoid narrating onscreen text when:

Words and pictures are presented simultaneously at a fast pace

Consider narrating onscreen text when:

There are no pictures

The learner has ample time to process the pictures and words

The learner is likely to have difficulty processing spoken words

---

For example, Figure 6.7 is an introductory screen that presents the learning objectives of a multimedia lesson. Since there are no graphic illustrations, narration of the objectives presented in text on the screen should not depress learning. As described in Chapter Five, situations in which learners need to

Figure 6.7. Use of Audio to Narrate Onscreen Text in Absence of Graphics.

With Permission from Defense Ammunition Center.

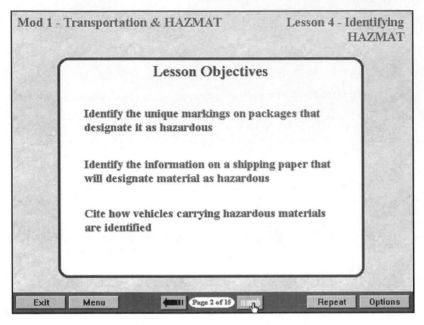

refer to information over time (such as directions to exercises) are best presented as text alone.

Psychological Reasons for Exceptions to Redundancy Principle

The major exceptions to the redundancy principle occur in special situations in which onscreen text either does not add to the learner's processing demands or actually diminishes them. For example, consider the situation in which an instructional presentation is solely spoken words with no graphics—such as in an audiotaped lesson. In this case, information enters through the ears so the verbal channel is active, but the visual channel is not active. Now, consider what happens in the learner's cognitive system when you use redundant onscreen text, for example, presented as text on a computer screen using the same words as the narration. In this case, spoken words enter through the ears and text words enter through the eyes, so neither channel is overloaded. Using dual modes of presentation can be helpful when the spoken material may be hard to process, or if seeing and hearing the words provides a benefit (such as learning a technical subject with its jargon or a foreign language).

Evidence for Including Redundant Onscreen Text

In the previous section, we summarized research in which people learned less about the process of lightning formation when the presentation included animation with redundant onscreen text than when the presentation included animation with concurrent narration alone. In this section, we explore special situations in which adding redundant onscreen text has been shown to help learning.

Research shows that in certain situations learners generate approximately three times as many correct answers on a problem-solving transfer test from presentations containing concurrent spoken and printed text than from spoken text alone (Moreno and Mayer, 2002). In these studies there were no graphics on the screen and thus the visual system was not overloaded. In another study, the animation presentation was broken into a series of sixteen short animation clips, with each clip preceded by a corresponding sentence. Thus, the learner sees and hears a sentence, then views ten seconds of animation corresponding to it, then sees and hears the next sentence, then views ten seconds of corresponding animation, and so on. In this way, the learner can view the animation without any interference from printed text. In this situation, learners who received redundant onscreen text and spoken text generated an average of 79 percent more correct answers on a problem solving test than learners who received only spoken text (Moreno and Mayer, 2002). Of course, this choppy sequential presentation is somewhat unusual and therefore is not likely to be applicable to most e-learning situations.

Based on the research and theory presented in this chapter, we offer the *redundancy principle*. When the instructional message includes graphics, explain the graphics with narration alone. Do not add redundant onscreen text. When there is limited graphic information on the screen or when the words are technical or the audience has language difficulties, consider the use of redundant onscreen text. As described in Chapter Five, use onscreen text without narration to present information that needs to be referenced over time, such as directions to complete a practice exercise.

Overall, the theme of this chapter is that e-learning should not add redundant onscreen text (that is, the same words that are being spoken) when attending to the text could distract the learner from viewing important graphics that are being presented at the same time. However, when spoken text is presented alone (that is, without concurrent graphics), you can help the learner process the words by providing concurrent printed text.

DESIGN DILEMMA: RESOLUTION

Given your familiarity with this new design principle, you are now in a better position to respond to the quality director. You can explain that you don't think it's a good idea to duplicate with onscreen text the audio you've developed to overview the quality control process. To illustrate why not, you show the director the revised version she requested (in Figure 6.2) and explain how it violates Redundancy Principle One. Redundant onscreen text is presented at the same time as onscreen animation, causing additional cognitive processing for the student.

When you discuss your plans, however, she might accuse you of being insensitive to individual differences in learning styles. You can respond by explaining how easy it is to overload people's information processing systems. To illustrate, you explain what happens when learners must look at two things at the same time—the printed words and the animation. If learners pay attention to the printed words, they are likely to miss some of the important information in the animation that is presented at the same time. Thus, as long as your e-learning lesson consists of a narrated animation, it does not pay to add redundant onscreen text that could interfere with the learner's processing of the animation.

However, if the spoken words are hard to understand—for example, because the learners are not native English speakers or the material contains many unfamiliar words—then adding redundant text might make more sense. You can stress that when learners are working on exercises in the course, text will remain on the screen in order to support learners' needs to see directions as they complete the exercises.

> ## WHAT TO LOOK FOR IN e-LEARNING
>
> ☐ Graphics are described by words presented in the form of audio narration, not by narration and redundant text.
>
> ☐ Onscreen text can be narrated when the screens do not include graphics.
>
> ☐ When language is challenging, onscreen text is narrated.

COMING NEXT

In the previous four chapters we have described a number of principles for best use of text, audio, and graphics in e-learning. We have seen that the appropriate use of these media elements can improve learning. However, there are circumstances when these elements can actually depress learning. In the next chapter we review how to apply the *coherence principle* to your e-learning decisions.

Suggested Readings

Mayer, R.E., Heiser, J., and Lonn, S. (2001). Cognitive Constraints on Multimedia Learning: When Presenting More Material Results in Less Understanding. *Journal of Educational Psychology, 93,* 187–198.

Moreno, R., and Mayer, R.E. (2002). Verbal Redundancy in Multimedia Learning: When Reading Helps Listening. *Journal of Educational Psychology, 94,* 151–163.

CHAPTER OUTLINE

Coherence Principle One: Avoid e-Lessons with Extraneous Sounds

Psychological Reasons to Avoid Extraneous Sounds

Evidence for Omitting Extraneous Sounds

Coherence Principle Two: Avoid e-Lessons with Extraneous Pictures

Psychological Reasons to Avoid Interesting but Extraneous Graphics

Evidence for Omitting Extraneous Graphics

Coherence Principle Three: Avoid e-Lessons with Extraneous Words

Psychological Reasons to Minimize Words in e-Learning

Evidence for Omitting Extraneous Words

7

Applying the Coherence Principle

ADDING INTERESTING MATERIAL CAN HURT
LEARNING

CHAPTER PREVIEW

IN ORDER TO counter high e-learning drop-out rates, some designers
attempt to spice up their materials by adding entertaining or motivational
elements such as dramatic stories or background music. In this chapter we
summarize the empirical evidence *for excluding rather than including* extraneous information in the form of

1. Entertaining stories related but not essential to the instructional
   objective

2. Background music and sounds added for motivation

3. Detailed textual descriptions

Adding interesting but unnecessary material to e-learning can harm the
learning process in several ways:

Distraction—by guiding the learner's limited attention away from the relevant material and towards the irrelevant material

Disruption—by preventing the learner from building appropriate links among pieces of relevant material because pieces of irrelevant material are in the way

Seduction—by priming inappropriate existing knowledge that is used for organizing the incoming material

DESIGNER'S DILEMMA

Suppose the director of quality of Madison Industries asks you to create a short online module to teach the operators how to apply basic statistical quality principles as part of the new quality management program. You create a one-minute narrated animation that reviews the quality process in words (narration) and depicts the major steps in pictures (animation). Figure 7.1 shows a storyboard from your multimedia presentation along with the corresponding narration. You designed the presentation to be consistent with several of the principles described in this book: the presentation consists of words and pictures rather than words alone (*multimedia principle*), and the words are presented as speech rather than as onscreen text

Figure 7.1. A Storyboard Using Narration to Describe Graphics.

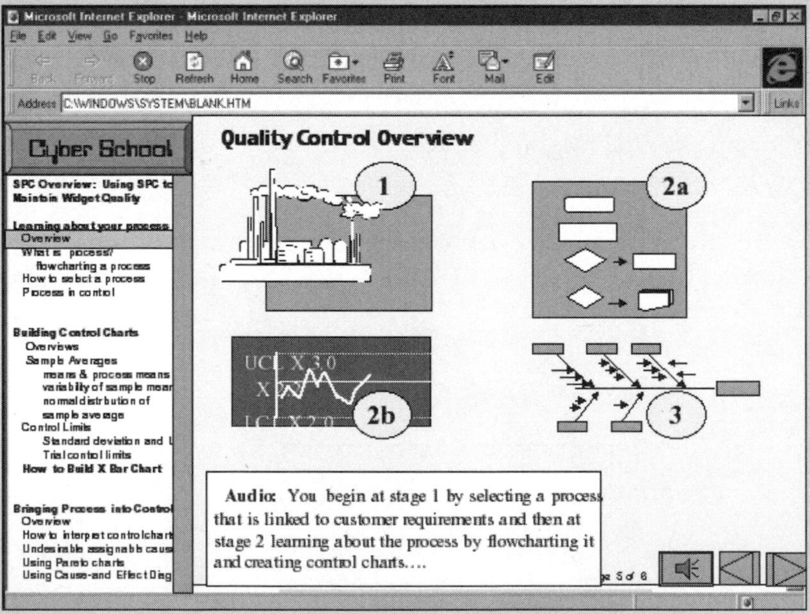

(*modality principle*). To apply the *redundancy principle*, you use narration to augment graphics, *not* to echo onscreen text.

"That's a nice first version," the director says, "but it seems a little dry. Can you spice it up a bit? You know, make it more interesting?" Seeking to please, you go ahead and redesign the multimedia presentation, creating several new versions for further testing. First, you create a sound-enhanced version by adding background music and sounds (see Figure 7.2). The music is a simple instrumental loop and the sounds are appropriate to the situation being depicted—the sound of a conveyor belt, beeps, and sounds of graphs being charted as products off the line are measured and graphed on control charts. Second, you create a graphics-enhanced version by interspersing several short video clips throughout the narrated animation (for example, ten seconds of disaster scenes that have occurred due to faulty products in various industries along with statistics about product failures). Figure 7.3 shows one of these. Third, you create a words-enhanced version like the one in Figure 7.4 by interspersing several short comments throughout the narrated

---

Figure 7.2. A Storyboard with Background Music and Environmental Sounds Added to the Narration.

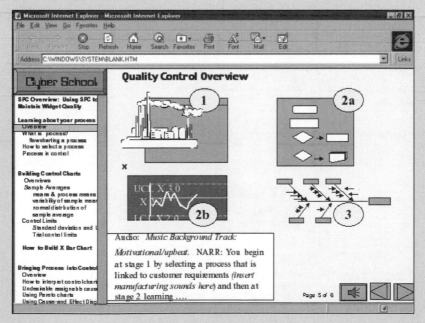

Figure 7.3. Factual Details Added to Stimulate Learner Interest.

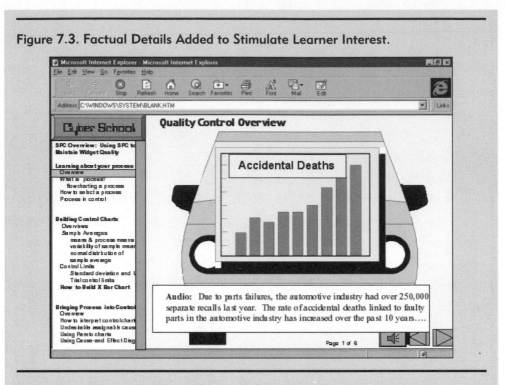

Figure 7.4. Interesting Textual Facts Added to the Narration to Stimulate Interest.

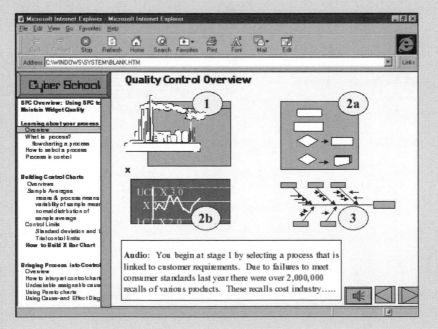

animation (for example, a ten-second description of the number of recalls that occurred last year, another ten-second description of how an injured consumer sued a company that produced a faulty product). In each case, the material you added is related to the general theme of quality control but irrelevant to the central goal of overviewing how a quality control system works.

As you review the three new versions you have created, you wonder whether or not they are improvements over the original narrated animation in Figure 7.1.

The added sounds, graphics, and words in Figures 7.2–7.4 are examples of *seductive details,* interesting but irrelevant material added to a multimedia presentation in an effort to spice it up (Garner, Gillingham, and White, 1989). The following three sections explore the merits of adding extra sounds, pictures, and words to help make multimedia environments more interesting to the learner.

Coherence Principle One: Avoid e-Lessons with Extraneous Sounds

First, consider the addition of background music and sounds to the narrated animation shown in Figure 7.2. Is there any theoretical rationale for adding or not adding music and sounds, and is there any research evidence? These questions are addressed in this section.

Based on the psychology of learning and the research evidence summarized in the following paragraphs, we recommend that you avoid e-learning courseware that includes extraneous sounds in the form of background music or environmental sounds. Like all recommendations in this book, this one is limited. Recommendations should be applied based on an understanding of how people learn from words and pictures rather than a blind application of rules in all situations. Background music and sounds may overload working memory, so they are most dangerous in situations in which the learner may experience heavy cognitive load, for example, when the material is unfamiliar, when the material is presented at a rapid rate, or when the rate of presentation is not under learner control. More research is needed to determine whether there are some situations in which the advantages of extraneous sounds outweigh the disadvantages. At this point, our recommendation is to avoid adding extraneous sounds, especially in situations in which the learner is likely to experience heavy cognitive processing demands. For example, Figure 7.5 shows a screen from a military multimedia lesson on ammunition. As the lesson illustrates the different types of ammunition that workers may encounter, background sounds such as bullets flying, bombs exploding, and tanks firing are included. These sounds are extraneous to the points being presented and are likely to prove distracting. Figure 7.6 shows a screen from the same program that invites the learners to select the type of background music they want to hear during the practice exercises. Again, the addition of extra sounds in the form of music is likely to depress learning.

Figure 7.5. Sounds of Explosions and Bullets Added to Narration of Onscreen Text.

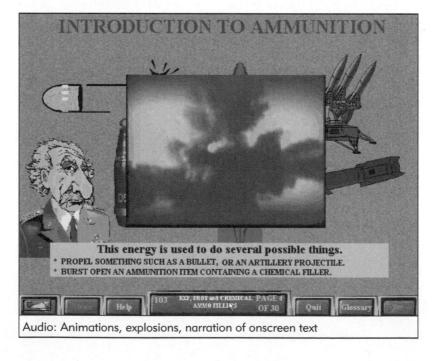

Figure 7.6. Learners Can Select Music During Practice.

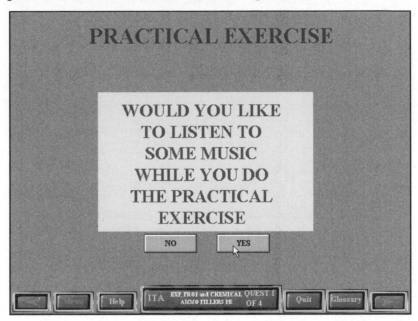

Psychological Reasons to Avoid Extraneous Sounds

e-Learning can seem boring and reports claim high drop-out rates (Svetcov, 2000). Therefore, developers may feel compelled to spice up their materials to arouse the learner's interest. Similarly, consumers may feel that a "jazzier" product will hold the learner's interest better. This is the premise underlying *arousal theory,* the idea that entertaining and interesting embedded effects cause learners to become more emotionally aroused and therefore they work harder to learn the material. In short, the premise is that emotion (for example, arousal caused by emotion-grabbing elements) affects cognition (for example, higher cognitive engagement). Arousal theory predicts that students will learn more from multimedia presentations that contain interesting sounds and music than from multimedia presentations without interesting sounds and music.

Arousal theory seems to make sense, so is there anything wrong with it? As early as 1913, Dewey argued that adding interesting adjuncts to an otherwise boring lesson will not promote deep learning: "When things have to be made interesting, it is because interest itself is wanting. Moreover, the phrase is a misnomer. The thing, the object, is no more interesting than it was before" (pp.11–12). The theoretical rationale against adding music and sounds to multimedia presentations is based on the cognitive theory of multimedia learning, which assumes that working memory capacity is highly limited. Background sounds can overload and disrupt the cognitive system, so the narration and the extraneous sounds must compete for limited cognitive resources in the auditory channel. When learners pay attention to sounds and music, they are less able to pay attention to the narration describing the relevant steps in the explanation. The cognitive theory of multimedia learning predicts that students will learn more deeply from multimedia presentations that *do not* contain interesting but extraneous sounds and music than from multimedia presentations that do.

Evidence for Omitting Extraneous Sounds

Can we point to any research that examines extraneous sounds in a multimedia presentation? Moreno and Mayer (2000a) began with a three-minute narrated animation explaining the process of lightning formation and a forty-five-second narrated animation explaining how hydraulic braking systems work. They created a music version of each by adding a musical loop to the background. The music was an unobtrusive instrumental piece, played at low volume that did not mask the narration nor make it less perceptually discernable. Students who received the narrated animation remembered more of the presented material and scored higher on solving transfer problems than students who received the same narrated animation along with background music. The differences were substantial—ranging from 20 to 67 percent better scores without music—and consistent for both the lightning and brakes presentations. Clearly, adding background music did not improve learning, and in fact, substantially hurt learning.

Moreno and Mayer (2000a) also created a background sound version of the lightning and brakes presentations by adding environmental sounds. In the lightning presentation, the environmental sounds included the sound of a gentle wind (presented when the animation depicted air moving from the ocean to the land), a clinking sound (when the animation depicted the top portion of cloud forming ice crystals), and a crackling sound (when the animation depicted charges traveling between ground and cloud). In the brakes presentation, the environmental sounds included mechanical noises (when the animation depicted the piston moving forward in the master cylinder) and grinding sounds (when the animation depicted the brake shoe pressing against the brake drum). On the lightning presentation, students who received the narrated animation without environmental sounds performed as well on retention and transfer as students who received the narrated animation with environmental sounds; on the brakes presentation, students who received narrated animation performed better on retention and transfer than students who received the narrated animation with environmental sounds.

For both lightning and brakes presentations, when students received both background music and environmental sounds their retention and transfer performance was much worse than when students received neither—ranging between 61 to 149 percent better performance without the extraneous sounds and music. The average percentage gain from all the studies was 105 percent with a very high effect size of 1.66. Figure 7.7 shows a result from one of these studies.

Figure 7.7. Better Learning When Sounds and Music Are Excluded.
Adapted from Mayer, 2001a.

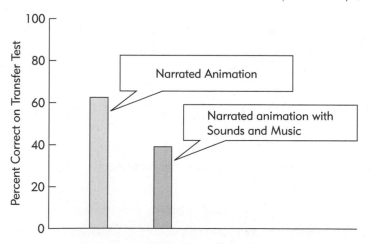

Coherence Principle Two: Avoid e-Lessons with Extraneous Pictures

The previous section shows that learning is depressed when we add extraneous sounds to a multimedia presentation, so perhaps we should try another way to spice up the narrated animation in Figure 7.1, namely interspersing interesting video clips. Figure 7.3 illustrates a storyboard from one of several short video clips that you decide to insert at various points within the presentation to dramatize the quality issues and add interest to the program. What is the learning impact of adding related but not directly relevant pictures and video clips to e-learning lessons?

Based on what we know about human learning and the evidence we summarize next, we offer a second version of the *coherence principle:* Avoid adding extraneous pictures. This recommendation does not mean that interesting graphics are harmful in all situations. Rather, they are harmful to the extent that they can interfere with the learner's attempts to make sense of the presented material. Extraneous graphics can be distracting and disruptive of the learning process. In recent reviews of science and mathematics books, most illustrations were found to be irrelevant to the main theme of the accompanying lesson (Mayer, 1993; Mayer, Sims, and Tajika, 1995). In short, when pictures are used only to decorate the page or screen, they are not likely to improve learning. As an example of irrelevant graphics, Figure 7.8 shows a screen from a lesson on ammunition safety that includes extensive video about the history of ammunition. Some of the information is quite interesting but not related to the tasks involved in handling ammunition. We recommend excluding this type of information.

Psychological Reasons to Avoid Interesting but Extraneous Graphics

Pictures—including color photos and action video clips—can make a multimedia experience more interesting. This assertion flows from arousal theory—the idea that students learn better when they are emotionally aroused. In this case, photos or video segments are intended to evoke

Figure 7.8. Interesting but Unrelated Historical Information.

emotional responses in learners, which in turn are intended to increase their level of cognitive engagement in the learning task. Thus, pictures and video are emotion-grabbing devices that make the learner more emotionally aroused, and therefore more actively involved in learning the presented material. Arousal theory predicts that adding interesting but extraneous pictures will promote better learning.

What's wrong with this justification? The problem—outlined in the previous section—is that interest cannot be added to an otherwise boring lesson like some kind of seasoning (Dewey, 1913). According to the cognitive theory of multimedia learning, the learner is actively seeking to make sense of the presented material. If the learner is successful in building a coherent mental representation of the presented material, the learner experiences enjoyment. However, adding extraneous pictures can interfere with the process of sense-making because learners have a limited cognitive capacity for processing incoming material. As we mention in the introduction to this chapter, extraneous pictures can interfere with learning in three ways:

Distraction—by guiding the learner's limited attention away from the relevant material and towards the irrelevant material

Disruption—by preventing the learner from building appropriate links among pieces of relevant material because pieces of irrelevant material are in the way

Seduction—by priming inappropriate existing knowledge (suggested by the added pictures), which is then used to organize the incoming material.

The cognitive theory of multimedia learning, therefore, predicts that students will learn more deeply from multimedia presentations that do not contain interesting but extraneous graphics and video.

Evidence for Omitting Extraneous Graphics

What happens when entertaining but irrelevant video clips are placed within a narrated animation? Mayer, Heiser, and Lonn (2001) asked students to view a three-minute narrated animation on lightning formation, like the one described in the previous section. For some students, the narrated animation contained six ten-second video clips intended to make the presentation more entertaining, yielding a total presentation lasting four minutes. For example, one video clip showed trees bending against strong winds, lightning striking into the trees, an ambulance arriving along a path near the trees, and a victim being carried in a stretcher to the ambulance near a crowd of onlookers. At the same time, the narrator said: "Statistics show that more people are injured by lightning each year than by tornadoes and hurricanes combined."

The video clip and corresponding narration were inserted right after the narrated animation describing a stepped leader of negative charges moving toward the ground. Thus, the narrated video was related to the general topic of lightning strikes but was not intended to help explain the cause-and-effect chain in lightning formation. Students who received the lightning presentation *without* the inserted video clips performed better on solving transfer problems than students who received the lightning presentation with inserted video clips—producing about 30 percent more solutions. Mayer, Heiser, and Lonn (2001, p. 187) note that this result is an example of "when presenting more material results in less understanding."

Harp and Mayer (1997) found a similar pattern of results using a paper-based medium. Some students were asked to read a 550-word, six-paragraph passage containing six captioned illustrations. The passage described the cause-and-effect sequence leading to lightning formation, and the captioned illustrations depicted the main steps (with captions that repeated the key events from the passage). Each illustration was placed to the left of the paragraph it depicted. Other students read the same illustrated passage, along with six color pictures intended to spice up the presentation. Each picture was captioned and was placed to the right of a paragraph to which it was related. For example, next to the paragraph about warm moist air rising, there was a color photo of an airplane being hit by lightning accompanied by the following text: "Metal airplanes conduct lightning very well, but they sustain little damage because the bolt, meeting no resistance, passes right through" (see Figure 7.9). Students who received the lightning passage

---

Figure 7.9. Lesson on Lightning Formation with Extraneous Details Added.

Adapted from Harp and Mayer, 1998.

When flying through updrafts, an airplane ride can become bumpy. Metal airplanes conduct lightning very well, but they sustain little damage because the bolt, meeting no resistance, passes right through.

without added color photos performed better on retention and transfer tests than students who received the lightning passage with color photos—producing about 73 percent more of the explanation on the retention test and generating about 52 percent more solutions on the transfer test. This is another example of how adding interesting but irrelevant graphics can result in less learning from a multimedia presentation.

Coherence Principle Three: Avoid e-Lessons with Extraneous Words

So far we have tried and failed twice to improve a narrated animation by adding a few pieces of interesting material such as sounds or pictures. In this, our third and final attempt, we seek to add some interesting sentences to help spice up an otherwise dry presentation about quality management. Figure 7.4 shows one of the narration segments that you decide to add to the overview of the presentation summarized in Figure 7.1. What is the learning impact of adding extra words to a presentation? We answer this question in this section.

Our third version of the coherence principle recommends that you should avoid adding extraneous words to lessons. When the goal is to promote learning of the target material—such as the workings of a cause-and-effect system—adding interesting but extraneous words may result in poorer learning. Cute little stories and interesting pieces of trivia may seem like harmless embellishments, but the research reviewed in this chapter shows that such devices may not produce the intended effects.

This guideline is helpful when limited screen real estate and bandwidth suggest shorter rather than longer narrations. Rather than fully embellished textual or narrative descriptions, stick to basic and concise descriptions of the content. Figure 7.10 shows a screen that includes a great deal of text along with an irrelevant graphic placed in the program to be entertaining. Compare this treatment with the screen shown in Figure 7.11, which limits words to the essential points and uses links to present additional details.

Figure 7.10. Detailed Textual Descriptions and Irrelevant Graphics May Depress Learning.

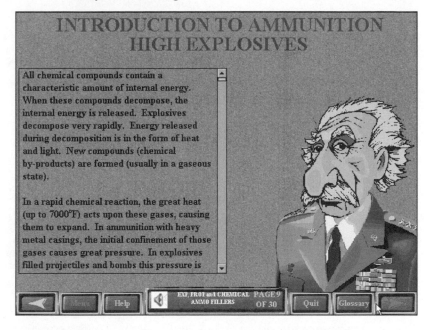

Figure 7.11. Concise Text and Relevant Graphics Increase Learning.

With permission from Element K.

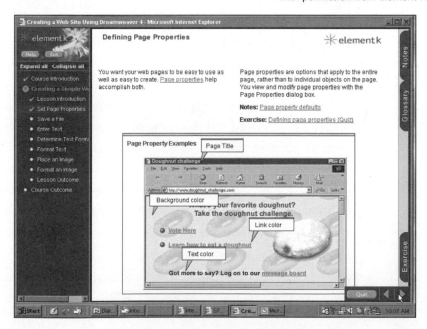

Psychological Reasons to Minimize Words in e-Learning

For the same reasons that extraneous sounds and graphics can be distracting, adding extra words can interfere with the learning process. Such added words may stimulate the learner to organize the material around the exciting themes in the added words rather than the cause-and-effect explanation in the target material.

Evidence for Omitting Extraneous Words

Do students learn more deeply from a narrated animation when interesting verbal information is added to the narration? To address this question, Mayer, Heiser, and Lonn (2001) asked some students to view a three-minute narrated animation about lightning formation, like the one described in the previous section. Other students viewed the same three-minute presentation, but with six additional narration segments inserted at various points. The narration segments were short and fit within the three-minute presentation at points that otherwise were silent. For example, after saying that water vapor forms a cloud, the narrator added: "On a warm cloudy day, swimmers are sitting ducks for lightning." Similarly, after saying that electrical charges build in a cloud, the narrator added: "Golfers are vulnerable targets because they hold metal clubs, which are excellent conductors of electrical charge." As shown in Figure 7.12, students who received the lightning presentation *without additional narration segments* performed better on transfer tests than students who received the lightning presentation with added narration segments—recalling about 35 percent more of the explanation on the retention test and generating about 30 percent more solutions on the transfer test. Again, these results show that adding interesting but irrelevant material does not help learning, and in this case even hurts learning.

In a more extreme version of this research (Mayer, Bove, Bryman, Mars, and Tapangco, 1996), students read the standard lightning passage like the one described above (that is, with six hundred words and five captioned illustrations) or a summary consisting of five captioned illustrations. The

Figure 7.12. Better Learning When Non-Essential Text is Excluded.
Adapted from Mayer, 2001a.

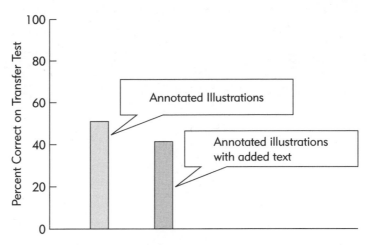

captions described the main steps in the lightning formation and the corresponding illustrations depicted the main steps. Approximately eighty words—taken from the standard passage—were used in the captioned illustrations. In three separate experiments, students who read the summary performed better on tests of retention and transfer than students who received the whole passage—in some cases, producing twice as many steps in the causal chain on the retention test and twice as many solutions on the transfer test. Mayer, Bove, Bryman, Mars, and Tapangco, (1996, p. 64) conclude that this research helps show "when less is more."

DESIGN DILEMMA: RESOLUTION

We began with a multimedia presentation intended to give an overview of a quality management process. Then we sought ways to make it more interesting. First, we considered adding background music and environmental sounds. Second, we considered inserting short video clips depicting dramatic consequences of faulty products in other industries. Third, we considered inserting short verbal segments containing interesting details about recalls against faulty products. However research and theory on the coherence effect convinced us to reject all of these attempts to spice up the lesson. In summary, the coherence principle suggests that you should *avoid adding extraneous sounds, pictures, or words to a multimedia presentation.*

When you report back to the quality director that you do not want to spice up the presentation, you might be accused of wanting to take all the enjoyment out of learning. How should you respond? We recommend that you make a distinction between *emotional interest* and *cognitive interest*. Emotional interest occurs when a multimedia experience evokes an emotional response in a learner, such as reading a story about a life-threatening event or seeing a graphic video. There is little evidence that emotion-grabbing adjuncts—which have been called *seductive details*—promote deep learning (Garner, Gillingham, and White, 1989; Renninger, Hidi, and Krapp, 1992). In short, attempts to force excitement do not guarantee that students will work hard to understand the presentation. In contrast, cognitive interest occurs when a learner is able to mentally construct a model that makes sense. As a result of attaining understanding, the learner feels a sense of enjoyment. In summary, understanding leads to enjoyment. The achievement of cognitive interest depends on active reflection by the learner rather than exposure to entertaining but irrelevant sights and sounds. Thus, your response to the director can be that your aim is to promote cognitive interest rather than emotional interest.

Overall, the research and theory summarized in this chapter show that designers should always consider the cognitive consequences of adding interesting sounds, pictures, or words. In particular, designers should consider whether the proposed additions could distract, disrupt, or seduce the learner's process of knowledge construction.

WHAT TO LOOK FOR IN e-LEARNING

☐ Lessons that DO NOT include extraneous sounds in the form of background music or unrelated environmental sounds.

☐ Lessons that DO NOT use graphics and video clips that are related but not essential to the knowledge and skills to be learned.

☐ Lessons that present content in lean text or narration that presents the main points.

COMING NEXT

We have seen in this chapter that sounds, graphics, and textual details added for interest can depress learning compared to more concise lessons. In the next chapter on the *personalization principle,* we ask about the learning effect of formal versus informal language in e-lessons and preview an area of emerging research on the use of virtual coaches.

Suggested Readings

Avoid Adding Extraneous Sounds

Moreno, R., and Mayer, R.E. (2000). A Coherence Effect in Multimedia Learning: The Case for Minimizing Irrelevant Sounds in the Design of Multimedia Instructional Messages. *Journal of Educational Psychology, 92,* 117–125.

Avoid Adding Extraneous Pictures

Mayer, R.E., Heiser, J., and Lonn, S. (2001). Cognitive Constraints on Multimedia Learning: When Presenting More Material Results in Less Understanding. *Journal of Educational Psychology, 93,* 187–198.

Avoid Adding Extraneous Words

Harp, S.F., and Mayer, R.E. (1998). How Seductive Details Do Their Damage: A Theory of Cognitive Interest in Science Learning. *Journal of Educational Psychology, 90,* 414–434.

Mayer, R.E., Heiser, J., and Lonn, S. (2001). Cognitive Constraints on Multimedia Learning: When Presenting More Material Results in Less Understanding. *Journal of Educational Psychology, 93,* 187–198.

Renninger, K.A., Hidi, S., and Krapp. A. (1992). *The Role of Interest in Learning and Development.* Hillsdale, NJ: Lawrence Erlbaum Associates.

CHAPTER OUTLINE

Personalization Principle One: Use Conversational Rather Than Formal Style

Psychological Reasons for the Personalization Principle

Evidence for Using Conversational Style

Personalization Principle Two: Use Onscreen Coaches to Promote Learning

What Are Pedagogical Agents?

Do Agents Improve Student Learning?

Do Agents Need to Look Real?

Do Agents Need to Sound Real?

8

Applying the Personalization Principle

USE CONVERSATIONAL STYLE AND VIRTUAL COACHES

CHAPTER PREVIEW

SOME e-LEARNING lessons rely on a formal style of writing to present information. In this chapter we summarize the empirical evidence that supports a conversational style of writing that uses first- and second-person language. A learning agent is an onscreen character who helps guide the learning processes during an instructional episode. While research on agents is quite new, we present evidence for the learning gains achieved in the presence of an agent as well as for the most effective ways to design and use agents. The psychological advantage of conversational style and learning agents is to induce the learner to engage with the computer as a social conversational partner.

DESIGN DILEMMA

Suppose your team has just developed a prototype e-learning lesson on quality management processes for your company. As team leader you review the storyboards before sending them for programming. As you read them you feel a little uncomfortable with the tone borrowed from the reference materials used to research some of the content. You fear that the formal writing style may cause some employees to feel alienated from the computer as a training environment and therefore not try as hard as they could to understand the material. For example, as seen in Figure 8.1, the textual explanation that goes along with the graphics is written in an impersonal style. In a bid to make your e-learning course more personal, and hence more engaging for the employees, you decide to reword the script slightly. For example, you use more first- and second-person constructions. You also decide to add a coach in the form of Joe Quality to provide helpful tips (see Figure 8.2).

Figure 8.1. Use of Impersonal Language to Present a Procedure.

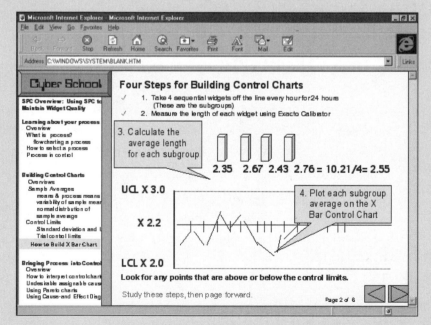

Happy with your revisions, you show your training director what you have done. She becomes quite upset. Stunned with the informal style you've created, your

Figure 8.2. Use of Personal Language and an Onscreen Coach to Explain a Procedure.

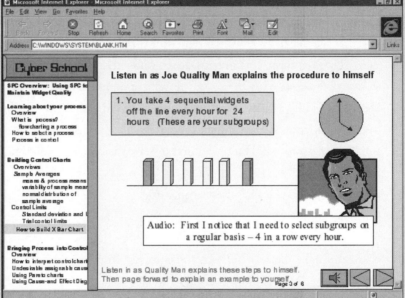

director thinks its better to keep things formal. "After all, the new quality initiative is serious business. Using such informal language and a cartoon makes it all seem a bit too Mickey Mouse for my taste," she says. "These are adults; they will be insulted by having a cartoon character talk to them!" How can you resolve this conflict between your intuition that conversational style and a friendly coach will stimulate learning and your director's intuition that it will stifle learning?

Personalization Principle One: Use Conversational Rather Than Formal Style

Does it help or hurt to change printed or spoken text from formal style to conversational style? Would the addition of a friendly onscreen coach distract from or promote learning? In this chapter, we explore research and theory that directly addresses these issues.

Consider the procedural demonstration shown in Figure 8.1. As you can see, the explanatory text uses a formal style. The overall feeling is quite impersonal. Now, compare this with the demonstration in Figure 8.2. In this case, the text presents exactly the same information but uses a more personal writing style by adding second-person pronouns and an onscreen coach. Together the resulting instruction more closely resembles human-to-human conversation. Of course, learners know that the character is not really in a conversation with them, but they may be more likely to act as if the character is like a conversational partner. Based on cognitive theory and research evidence, we recommend that you create or select e-learning courses that include some spoken or printed text that is conversational rather than formal.

Let's look at a couple of e-learning examples. The screen in Figure 8.3 is giving safety rules for handling of pyrotechnics. Note that both the onscreen text and the audio are very formal. A simple rewrite uses second-person pronouns to make the text more conversational: "You should be very careful if

Figure 8.3. Formal Language Used in Text and Narration.

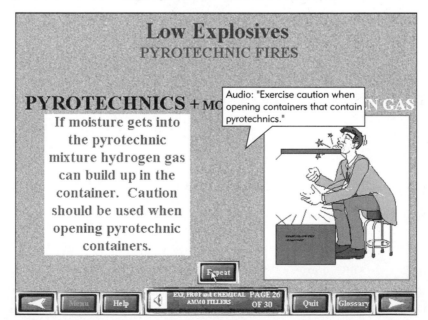

Figure 8.4. Conversational Language Used in Text.

With permission from DigitalThink.

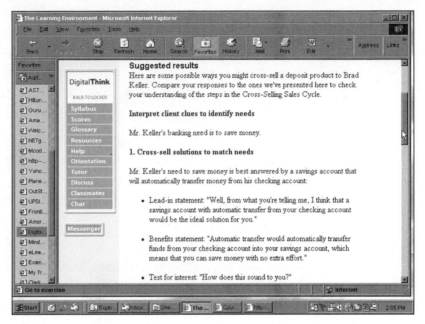

you open any containers with pyrotechnics." In contrast to the pyrotechnics lesson, the text under "Suggested Results" shown in Figure 8.4 uses second- and first-person language to give feedback to an exercise.

Psychological Reasons for the Personalization Principle

Let's begin with a common sense view that we do not agree with. The rationale for putting words in formal style is that conversational style can detract from the seriousness of the message. After all, learners know that the computer cannot speak to them. The goal of a training program is not to build a relationship but rather to convey important information. By emphasizing the personal aspects of the training—by using words like "you" and "I"—you convey a message that training is not serious. Accordingly, the guiding principle is to keep things simple by presenting the basic information.

This argument is based on an information delivery view of learning in which the instructor's job is to present information and the learner's job is to acquire the information. According to the information delivery view, the training program should deliver information as efficiently as possible. Formal style meets this criterion better than conversational style.

Why do we disagree with the call to keep things formal and the information delivery view of learning on which it is based? Although the information delivery view seems like common sense, it is inconsistent with how the human mind works. According to cognitive theories of learning, humans strive to make sense of presented material by applying appropriate cognitive processes. Thus, instruction should not only present information but also prime the appropriate cognitive processing in the learner. Research on discourse processing shows that people work harder to understand material when they feel they are in a conversation with a partner rather than simply receiving information (Beck, McKeown, Sandora, Kucan, and Worthy, 1996). Therefore, using conversational style in a multimedia presentation conveys to the learners the idea that they should work hard to understand what their conversational partner (in this case, the course narrator) is saying to them. In short, expressing information in conversational style can be a way to prime appropriate cognitive processing in the learner.

Evidence for Using Conversational Style

Although this technique as it applies to e-learning is just beginning to be studied, there is already preliminary evidence concerning the use of conversational style in e-learning lessons. In a set of five experimental studies involving a computer-based educational game on botany and a multimedia lesson on lightning formation, researchers (Moreno and Mayer, 2000b) compared versions in which the words were in formal style with versions in which the words were in conversational style. For example, Figure 8.5 gives the introductory script spoken in the computer-based botany game; the top portion shows the formal version and the bottom shows the personalized version. As you can see, both versions present the same basic information, but in the personalized version the computer is talking directly to the learner. In five out of five studies, students who learned with per-

Figure 8.5. Formal Versus Informal Lesson Introductions Compared in Research Study.

From Moreno and Mayer, 2000b.

Introductory Portion of Text Spoken in a Botany Computer Game

Formal Version

"This program is about what type of plants survive on different planets. For each planet, a plant will be designed. The goal is to learn what type of roots, stem, and leaves allow the plant to survive in each environment. Some hints are provided throughout the program."

Personalized Version

"You are about to start a journey where you will be visiting different planets. For each planet, you will need to design a plant. Your mission is to learn what type of roots, stem, and leaves will allow your plant to survive in each environment. I will be guiding you through by giving out some hints."

sonalized text performed better on subsequent transfer tests than students who learned with formal text. Overall, participants in the personalized group produced between 20 to 46 percent more solutions to transfer problems than the formal group. Figure 8.6 shows results from one study where improvement was 46 percent and the effect size was 1.55, which is considered to be large.

Figure 8.6. Better Learning from Personalized Narration.

From Moreno and Mayer, 2000a.

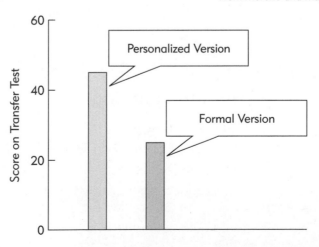

These results should not be taken to mean that personalization is always a useful idea. There are cases in which personalization can be overdone. For example, consider what happens when you add too much personal material, such as, "Wow, hi dude, I'm here to teach you all about _____, so hang on to your hat and here we go!" The result can be that the advantages of personalization are offset by the disadvantages of distracting the learner and setting an inappropriate tone for learning. Thus, in applying the personalization principle it is always useful to consider the audience and the cognitive consequences of your script—you want to write with sufficient informality so that the learners feel they are interacting with a conversational partner but not so informally that the learner is distracted or the material is undermined. In fact, implementing the personalization principle should create only a subtle change in the lesson; a lot can be accomplished by using a few first- and second-person pronouns.

Complementary results come from related studies. For example, people read a story differently and remember different elements when the author writes in the first person (from the "I/we" point of view) than when the author writes in the third person (he, she, it, or they) (Graesser, Bowers, Olde, and Pomeroy, 1999). Recent research summarized by Reeves and Nass (1996) shows that, under the right circumstances, people "treat computers like real people." Part of treating computers like real people is to try harder to understand their communications. Consistent with this view, Mayer, Sobko, and Maatone (in press) found that people learned better from a narrated animation on lightning formation when the speaker's voice was human rather than machine-simulated.

Personalization Principle Two: Use Onscreen Coaches to Promote Learning

In the previous section, we provided evidence for writing with first- and second-person language to establish a conversational tone in your training. A related new area of research focuses on the beneficial effects of onscreen coaches, called *pedagogical agents*, on learning.

What Are Pedagogical Agents?

Personalized speech is also an important component in animated pedagogical agents developed as onscreen tutors in educational programs (Cassell, Sullivan, Prevost, and Churchill, 2000; Moreno, Mayer, Spires, and Lester, 2001). Pedagogical agents are onscreen characters who help guide the learning process during an e-learning episode. Agents can be represented visually as cartoon-like characters, as talking-head video, or as virtual reality avatars; they can be represented verbally through machine-simulated voice, human recorded voice, or printed text. Agents can be representations of real people using video and human voice or artificial characters using animation and computer-generated voice. Our major interest in agents concerns their ability to employ sound instructional techniques that foster learning.

Onscreen agents are appearing frequently in e-learning. For example, Figure 8.7 introduces Jim in a lesson on reading comprehension. Thoughout

---

Figure 8.7. Onscreen Coach Used to Give Reading Comprehension Demonstrations.

With permission from Plato Learning Systems.

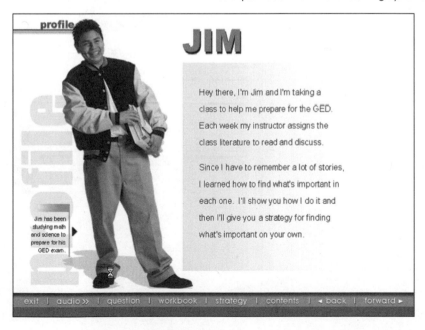

the lesson, Jim demonstrates techniques he uses to understand stories and then learners apply Jim's guidelines to comprehension exercises. Figure 8.8 from a course on commercial bank lending uses a coach to provide guidance about evaluating a loan application.

Figure 8.9 shows a screen from a guided discovery e-learning game called Design-A-Plant in which the learner travels to a planet with certain environmental features (such as low rainfall and heavy winds) and must choose the roots, stem, and leaves of a plant that could survive there. An animated pedagogical agent named Herman-the-Bug (in lower left corner of Figure 8.9) poses the problems, offers feedback, and generally guides the learner through the game. As you can see in the figure, Herman is a friendly little guy and research shows that most learners report liking him (Moreno and Mayer, 2000b; Moreno, Mayer, Spires, and Lester, 2001).

Figure 8.8. The Coach Provides Guidelines for Researching a New Bank Loan Application.

With permission from Moody's Financial Services.

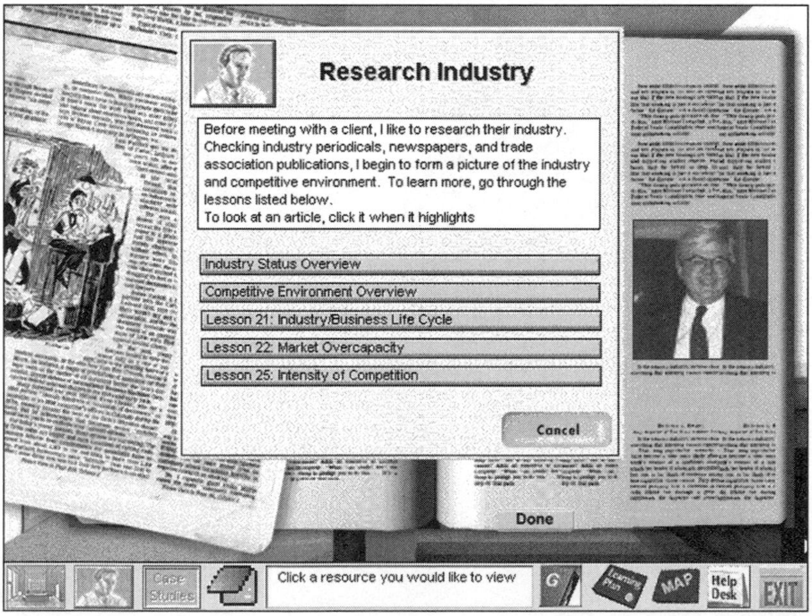

Figure 8.9. Herman-the-Bug Used in Design-A-Plant Instructional Game.
Moreno, Mayer, Spires, and Lester, 2001.

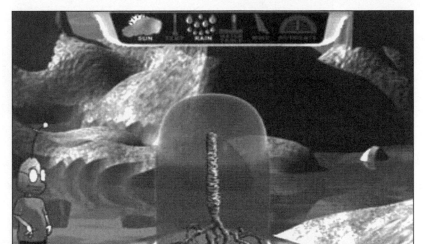

In another program an animated pedagogical agent is used to teach students how to solve proportionality word problems (Atkinson, 2002). In this program, an animated pedagogical agent named Peedy provides a step-by-step explanation of how to solve each problem. Although Peedy doesn't move much he can point to relevant parts of the solution and make some simple gestures, as he guides the students. Peedy and Herman are among a small collection of agents who have been examined in controlled research studies.

Computer scientists are doing a fine job of producing life-like agents who interact well with humans (Cassell, Sullivan, Prevost, and Churchill, 2000). For example, an onscreen agent named Steve shows students how to operate and maintain the gas turbine engines aboard naval ships (Rickel and Johnson, 2000); an onscreen agent named Cosmo guides students through the archi-tecture and operation of the internet (Lester, Towns, Callaway, Voerman, and Fitzgerald, 2000); and an onscreen agent named Rea interacts with potential home buyers, takes them on virtual tours of listed properties, and tries to sell them a house (Cassell, Sullivan, Prevost, and Churchill, 2000).

In spite of the continuing advances in the development of onscreen agents, research on their effectiveness is just beginning (Atkinson, 2002; Moreno and Mayer, 2000b; Moreno, Mayer, Spires, and Lester, 2001). Let's look at some important questions about agents in e-learning courses and see how the preliminary research answers them.

Do Agents Improve Student Learning?

An important primary question is whether adding onscreen agents can have any positive effects on learning. Even if computer scientists can develop extremely lifelike agents that are entertaining, is it worth the time and expense to incorporate them into e-learning courses? In order to answer this question, researchers began with an agent-based educational game, called Design-A-Plant, described previously (Moreno, Mayer, Spires, and Lester, 2001). Some students learned by interacting with an onscreen agent named Herman-the-Bug (agent group), whereas other students learned by reading the identical words and viewing the identical graphics presented on the computer screen without the Herman agent (no-agent group). Across two separate experiments, the agent group generated 24 to 48 percent more solutions in transfer tests than did the no-agent group.

In a related study (Atkinson, 2002), students learned to solve proportionality word problems by seeing worked-out examples presented via a computer screen. For some students, an onscreen agent spoke to students, giving a step-by-step explanation for the solution (agent group). For other students, the same explanation was printed as onscreen text without any image or voice of an agent (no-agent group). On a subsequent transfer test involving different word problems, the agent group generated 30 percent more correct solutions than the no-agent group. Although these results are preliminary, they suggest that it might be worthwhile to consider the role of animated pedagogical agents as aids to learning.

Do Agents Need to Look Real?

As you may have noticed in the previously described research, there were many differences between the agent and no-agent groups so it is reasonable to ask which of those differences has an effect on student learning. In short, we want to know what makes an effective agent. Let's begin by asking about the looks of the agent, such as whether people learn better from human-looking agents or cartoon-like agents. To help answer this question, students learned about botany principles by playing the Design-A-Plant game with one of two agents—a cartoon-like animated character named Herman-the-Bug or a talking-head video of a young male who said exactly the same words as Herman-the-Bug (Moreno, Mayer, Spires, and Lester, 2001). Overall, the groups did not differ much in their test performance, suggesting that a real character did not work any better than a cartoon character. In addition, students learned just as well when the image of the character was present or absent as long as the students could hear the agent's voice. These preliminary results suggest that a lifelike image is not always an essential component in an effective agent.

Do Agents Need to Sound Real?

Even if the agent may not look real, there is compelling evidence that the agent has to sound conversational. First, across four comparisons (Moreno, Mayer, Spires, and Lester, 2001; Moreno and Mayer, in press), students learned better in the Design-A-Plant game if Herman's words were spoken rather than presented as onscreen text. This finding is simply an indication that the *modality effect* (as described in Chapter Five) applies to onscreen agents. Second, across three comparisons (Moreno and Mayer, 2000b), students learned better in the Design-A-Plant game if Herman's words were spoken in a conversational style rather than a formal style. This finding is simply an indication that the *personalization effect* (as described in this chapter) applies to onscreen agents. Finally, Atkinson (2002) found some preliminary evidence that students learn to solve word problems better from an onscreen agent when the words are spoken in a human voice rather than a machine-simulated voice. Overall, these preliminary results show that the agent's voice is an important determinant of instructional effectiveness.

Although it is premature to make firm recommendations concerning onscreen pedagogical agents, we are able to offer some suggestions based on the current state of the field. We suggest that you consider using onscreen agents, and that the agent's words be presented as speech rather than text, in conversational style rather than formal style, and with human-like rather than machine-like articulation. Although intense work is underway to create entertaining agents who display human-like gestures and facial expressions, their educational value is yet to be demonstrated.

We further suggest that you use agents to provide instruction rather than for entertainment purposes. For example, in Chapters Nine and Ten we illustrate ways to use an agent to help learners ask questions of themselves when studying expository text and to self-explain worked examples. The cartoon general in Figure 8.10, for example is *not* an agent since he is

---

Figure 8.10. General Character Plays No Instructional Role So Is Not an Agent.

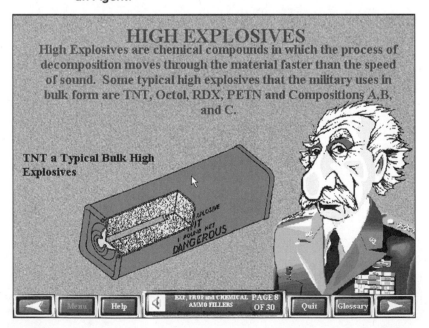

never used for any instructional purpose. Likewise there is a common unproductive tendency to insert theme characters from popular games and movies who are added only for entertainment value and serve no instructional role. These embellishments are likely to depress learning, as discussed in Chapter Seven.

Based on the cognitive theory and research we have highlighted in this chapter, we can propose the *personalization principle:* First, present words in conversational style rather than formal style. In creating the script for a narration or the text for an on-screen passage, you should use some first- and second-person constructions (that is, involving "I," "we," "me," "my," "you," and/or "your") to create the feeling of conversation between the course and the learner. However, you should be careful not to overdo the personalization style because it is important not to distract the learner. Second, use onscreen agents to provide coaching in the form of hints, worked examples, demonstrations, and explanations.

DESIGN DILEMMA: RESOLUTION

Now that you have some justification for personalization, we can return to the dilemma you encountered at the start of this chapter concerning the design of your e-learning course on quality processes. When your training director balks at including some personalized words and a friendly coach in your e-learning course, you can explain that your goal is to create a sense of conversational communication in learners. According to cognitive theory, you explain, when learners see the computer as a conversational partner, they will try harder to understand what the computer is saying. If the director is not convinced by your explanation of cognitive theory, you can point out that there is a growing body of research evidence that people learn more deeply when important instructional methods such as demonstrations or worked examples are presented by a pedagogical agent speaking in a personal manner. You also suggest that since the physical appearance of the agent is not that important to the learning outcome, you plan to test several different representations to see which appeals most to the learners.

WHAT TO LOOK FOR IN e-LEARNING

☐ Instructional content presented in conversational language using "you," "your," "I," "our," and "we."

☐ Coaching provided via conversational narration from onscreen characters (agents).

  ☐ Agents may be visually realistic or line art.

  ☐ Agent dialog presented via audio narration.

  ☐ Voice quality and script should be natural and conversational.

  ☐ Agents serve a valid instructional purpose.

COMING NEXT

This chapter completes the basic set of principles dealing with best use of media elements in e-learning. These principles apply to training produced to inform as well as to increase performance; in other words they apply to all forms of e-learning. If your training goal is to build job-specific skills, your e-learning should provide practice opportunities. In the next chapter we will look at how practice should be designed to best promote learning and will show you how to apply the principles described in Chapters Three through Eight when you design practice exercises.

Suggested Readings

Mayer, R.E., Sobko, K., and Mautone, P.D. (in press). Social Cues in Multimedia Learning: Role of Speaker's Voice. *Journal of Educational Psychology.*

Moreno, R., Mayer, R.E., Spires, H., and Lester, J. (2001). The Case for Social Agency in Computer-Based Teaching: Do Students Learn More Deeply When They Interact with Animated Pedagogical Agents? *Cognition and Instruction, 19,* 177–214.

Moreno, R., and Mayer, R.E. (2000). Engaging Students in Active Learning: The Case for Personalized Multimedia Messages. *Journal of Educational Psychology, 93,* 724–733.

Reeves, B., and Nass, C. (1996). *The Media Equation: How People Treat Computers, Television, and New Media Like Real People and Places.* New York: Cambridge University Press.

CHAPTER OUTLINE

Design of Practice in e-Learning

Practice Principle One: Interactions Should Mirror the Job

Psychological Reasons for Job-Relevant Practice

   Practice to Support Selecting and Integrating

   Practice to Support Retrieval: The Encoding Specificity Principle

Evidence for the Benefits of Practice

   Asking Why Improves Learning

   Assigning a Pro and Con Analysis Improves Learning

Practice Principle Two: Critical Tasks Require More Practice

Psychological Reasons for Multiple Distributed Practice Exercises

The Evidence for Multiple Distributed Practice Exercises

   More Practice Yields Improved Performance

   The Relationship Between Practice and Expertise

   Effects of Amount of Practice in e-Learning

   Distribution of Practice

Practice Principle Three: Apply the Media Elements Principles to Practice Exercises

   Contiguity Principle

   Modality and Redundancy Principles

   Personalization Principle

Practice Principle Four: Train Learners to Self-Question During Receptive e-Lessons

Psychological Reasons for Training Self-Questioning Skills

Evidence for Training Self-Questioning

9

Does Practice Make Perfect?

CHAPTER PREVIEW

TO SAVE time and cost, some e-learning courseware may skip or minimize practice exercises, which are labor intensive to build. At the other extreme, some may include games to make the learning more fun. Both options ignore important psychological processes and evidence showing that learners benefit from periodic opportunities to practice in job-relevant ways. In this chapter we summarize the empirical evidence regarding the design, frequency, and layout of effective practice in e-learning. The psychological advantage of including frequent job-relevant practice is that it provides multiple overt rehearsal opportunities for working memory that result in encoding in long-term memory.

In some situations, learners must study expository materials lacking practice opportunities. We present research evidence that shows that learners can be trained to self-question what they are reading or hearing and thus promote rehearsal themselves.

DESIGN DILEMMA

Your two main clients, the director of quality and the vice president of operations are discussing the preliminary design plan for your latest Web-based training assignment with you and your boss.

Director of quality: "The chief operating officer wants this quality program to roll out fast. She has been following the latest lawsuits in the industry over the past year and has got the president's attention. She wants training. She wants it fast. And she wants it on our intranet. We'll need to cut out some of the fat—like all these practice exercises. Cutting most of them will save you at least two months of development time!"

Vice president of operations: "Hold on—my operators aren't going to sit there reading hundreds of screens. A training program has got to be fun to hold their interest. Instead of all those boring questions, how about a Jeopardy™-type game? Or better yet—let's make it a Tomb Raiders™ game!"

As the discussion drags on, you rough out a storyboard based on a Jeopardy™ format (Figure 9.1). You wonder what would be best, a page-turner with no practice or a program with games? Is there another, better alternative?

Figure 9.1. A Sketch for a Jeopardy™-Theme Practice Exercise.

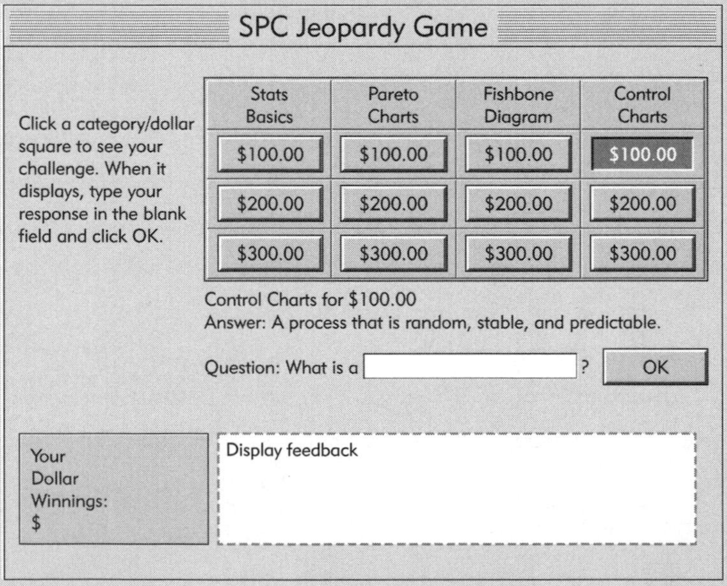

SPC Jeopardy Game

Click a category/dollar square to see your challenge. When it displays, type your response in the blank field and click OK.

Stats Basics	Pareto Charts	Fishbone Diagram	Control Charts
$100.00	$100.00	$100.00	$100.00
$200.00	$200.00	$200.00	$200.00
$300.00	$300.00	$300.00	$300.00

Control Charts for $100.00
Answer: A process that is random, stable, and predictable.

Question: What is a [   ] ?   [OK]

Your Dollar Winnings: $

Display feedback

Design of Practice in e-Learning

e-Learning should promote psychological engagement between the learner and the lesson content in ways that help learners to select, integrate, and retrieve new knowledge. First, they must select the important information in the training. Then they must integrate the new information into existing knowledge in long-term memory. Finally, they must be able to retrieve new knowledge and skills out of long-term memory when they are on the job. Effective e-learning will support all three of these processes by providing practice exercises with features that mirror the physical and psychological environment of the job.

One path to engagement is through overt learner responses to lesson practice exercises. Practice exercises, often referred to as interactions in computer learning environments, appear in a variety of formats. Some are questions similar to those used in the classroom, such as selecting the right answer in a list or saying whether a statement is true or false. Others use formats that are unique to computers, such as *drag and drop* and *simulations* (such as the bank loan analysis case study shown in Figure 9.2). But, more

---

Figure 9.2. A Simulation Interaction in Which a Learner Recommends a Bank Loan.

With permission from Moody's Financial Services.

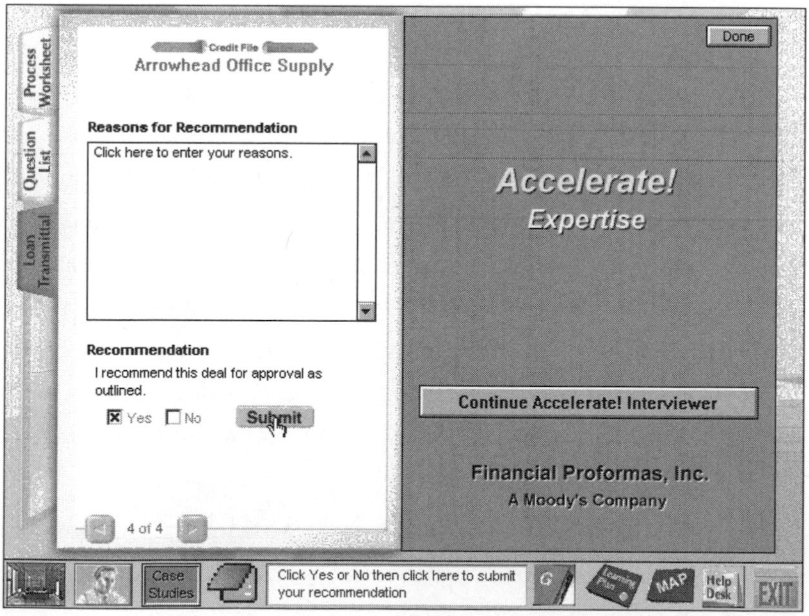

Figure 9.3. A Question That Requires Only Recognition of Lesson Information.

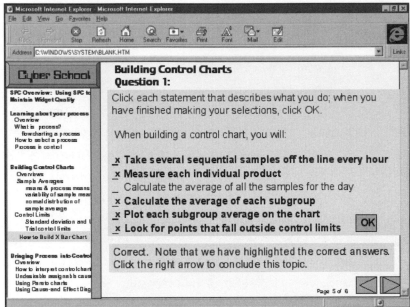

significant to learning than the practice exercise format are the psychological processes the questions require of the learner. Consider the questions shown in Figures 9.3 and 9.4. They both ask the learner to select the correct answers from multiple options, but the exercise in Figure 9.3 requires only that the learner recognize information that was presented previously, while the question in Figure 9.4 requires the learner to apply the new knowledge to a job-like situation. Adding interactions to computer lessons—especially application or simulation questions like those shown in Figures 9.2 and 9.4—requires time to develop and time for the learner to complete during the training. In that sense interactions are expensive. How can practice exercises be most effectively designed to realize a return on that investment? Based on empirical evidence, we recommend four guidelines for effective practice in e-learning:

- Interactions should mirror the thinking processes and environment of the job.

Figure 9.4. A Question That Requires the Learner to Apply New Knowledge.

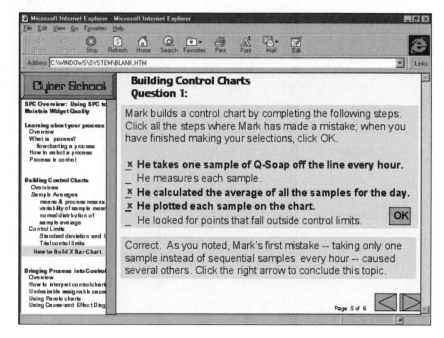

- Better learning results from more practice questions interspersed throughout the lesson.

- Practice questions should be formatted to be consistent with the media elements principles summarized in Chapters Three through Eight.

- Learners should be trained to provide their own questions when they are studying from receptive (expository) materials.

Practice Principle One: Interactions Should Mirror the Job

Practice exercises in e-learning should require learners to process information in a job-realistic context. Questions that ask the learner to merely recognize or recall information previously provided in the training will not promote learning that transfers to the job.

Designing effective exercises requires performing a job and task analysis to define the specific cognitive and physical processing required by the job. From this analysis the e-learning designer should create *transfer appropriate interactions*—activities that require learners to respond in similar ways during the training as they will on the job. The more the features of the job environment are integrated into the interaction, the more likely the right cues will be encoded into long-term memory for later transfer. The storyboard designed for the Jeopardy™ game (Figure 9.1) requires only recall of information. Neither the psychological nor the physical context of the work environment is reflected. In contrast, the simulation and application questions in Figures 9.2 and 9.4 require the learners to make the kind of decisions they would make on the job and therefore are more likely to support transfer of learning.

A good rule of thumb is to *avoid e-learning with many questions that require simple regurgitation of information provided in the training program.* These questions do not support the psychological processes needed to integrate new information with existing knowledge. They can be answered without any real understanding of the content, and they don't implant the cues needed for retrieval on the job. Instead, as you review e-learning alternatives, keep in mind the ways that your workers will need to apply new knowledge to their jobs. Also keep in mind the important physical features and psychological requirements of your work environment. Then look for interactions that mirror those job applications.

Table 9.1 summarizes our recommendations for the best types of interactions for training of procedural tasks, principle-based tasks, processes, concepts, and facts (Clark, 1999). We include two screen examples to illustrate effective interactions for procedure and principle tasks. Figure 9.5 is a simulation from the Dreamweaver course designed to help learners practice the application of procedure steps to create a Web page. Figure 9.6 is a case-study practice designed to help bank employees apply sales guidelines to identify and present banking products relevant to the client's needs. This kind of interaction will build effective knowledge structures in long-term memory for job performance improvement because it gives learners an opportunity to apply what they are learning to realistic, job-related situations.

Table 9.1. Interactions for Five Types of Content in e-Learning.

Based on Clark, 1999.

Content Type	Interaction Description	Example: Web Page Creation
Fact	Use the fact to complete a task. Provide a job aid for memory support.	Use the codes on your reference aid to access the application.
Concept	Identify a new instance of the concept.	Select the Web page that applies effective design features.
Process	Solve a problem or make a prediction.	Predict the impact of a miscoded page property specification on the final Web page output.
Procedure	Perform a task by following steps.	Select the text font from the pull-down menu.
Principle	Perform a task by applying guidelines.	Design an effective Web page.

Figure 9.5. A Simulation Question to Teach a Software Procedure.

With permission from Element K.

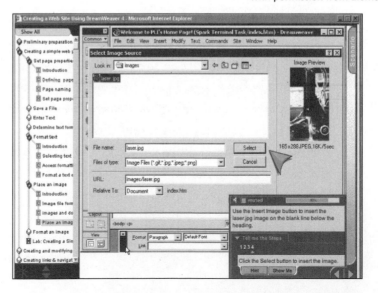

Figure 9.6. An Interaction That Requires Learners to Apply Guidelines to Respond to a Customer.

With permission from DigitalThink.

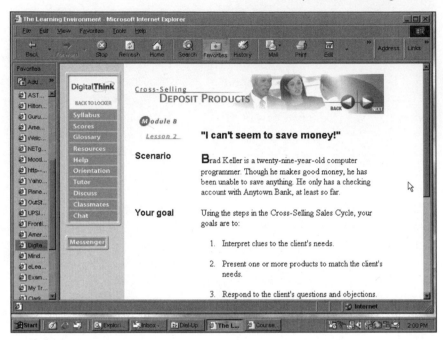

Psychological Reasons for Job-Relevant Practice

In Chapter Two we summarized five processes that must take place for lesson content to be transformed into new learner knowledge and skills. Here we focus specifically on the processes of selecting, integrating, and retrieving new knowledge. The *selecting process* means that the learner must focus attention on the important elements of the instruction. The *integrating process* means the learner must link the new lesson information in working memory into existing knowledge structures in long-term memory. The *retrieving process* means that new knowledge and skills stored in long-term memory must be retrieved and transferred back into working memory when needed on the job. These three processes can be initiated by the learners themselves and/or they can be stimulated by the instructional materials.

Practice to Support Selecting and Integrating

Almost any kind of practice question will direct learners' attention to the content being practiced. However, simply asking learners to repeat information they were given in the training does not stimulate integration of new information with preexisting knowledge. We call these types of questions rote or memorization practice. In contrast, questions that require applying new information to job-related situations stimulate learners to link the new information in working memory with existing knowledge in long-term memory.

Practice to Support Retrieval: The Encoding Specificity Principle

However, it is not enough to encode new knowledge into long-term memory. The knowledge also must be retrievable when needed on the job. For retrieval to happen, practice exercises need to be based on the *encoding specificity principle*. The *encoding specificity principle* states that transfer is maximized when the conditions at retrieval (on the job) match those present at encoding (during learning). Transfer of learning back to the job requires that new memories formed during training include the retrieval cues from the job environment. Retrieval cues are the hooks that stimulate the activation of newly learned knowledge on the job. In other words, the work environment itself triggers the use of the new skills. Although knowledge and skills presented without any job context may be encoded into long-term memory, the learner might not be able to retrieve them when needed after training.

For an everyday example of this, think about listing the months of the year. You could recall them without difficulty. But suppose you were asked to list the months of the year in alphabetic order. Since this is not the way you learned this information originally, you would not have the retrieval cues to do this easily. A colleague tells about a time when she received an "A" in a sailing class because she scored high on all the written tests even though she never learned to sail with any degree of proficiency. Her practice responding to questions about sailing did not translate into sailing skills. Activity alone *is not sufficient* for transfer. The activity must incorporate features and processes that match the features and processes of the work environment.

Evidence for the Benefits of Practice

Since practice exercises will add to the expense of e-learning, what evidence do we have for their effectiveness? In this section we review several research studies that demonstrate that practice does improve learning.

Asking Why Improves Learning

In the 1980s researchers reported that learning from text was improved by adding a *why* question to the end of the text. In a recent version of this research, McDaniel and Donnelly (1996) compared the effect of text alone, text modified with additional details, and modified text with why questions added. A sample why question is: "Why does an object speed up as its radius gets smaller?" They found that the question technique resulted in greater factual and inference learning. Specifically, the inserted question resulted in 70 percent accuracy on application of new knowledge compared to 59 percent from the two versions without a question.

Assigning a Pro and Con Analysis Improves Learning

Researchers have also found that requiring learners to consider both sides of an issue in the form of an argument, as well as to integrate multiple sources, resulted in deeper and more original mental processing and, in turn, better learning. Wiley and Voss (1999) compared the learning impact of four different activities assigned in conjunction with reading historical text presented either as a book chapter or as source documents on the Internet. The assignments were to read the sources and write an essay in the form of either a narrative, a summary, an explanation, or an argument. Students were tested for both memory and application learning. The researchers evaluated the quality of the essays as well as the final test results. They found that the essays written in the form of an argument included more original student analysis and less copied information than did the narratives or summaries. The essays were even more original when learners had to obtain information from multiple sources on the Internet rather than simply read a textbook chapter.

This study indicates that the assignment to write an argument from multiple sources requires greater organization and integration of the materials. In other words, having to formulate different points of view and express them in an argument essay as well as to integrate the various sources of information requires deeper processing of content. The different assignments resulted in no differences on answers to questions requiring the *recognition* of information on the test. However, the argument assignment resulted in higher scores of test questions based on the principles inherent in the passages. In Chapter Eleven we describe how this type of assignment can be adapted to Web-based training.

Practice Principle Two: Critical Tasks Require More Practice

An important question for developers who are trying to balance development costs and program length with effective learning is: If a few good questions promote learning, would more good questions result in even better learning? In general the answer is yes, although there will be diminishing returns on the investment. To determine the value added by additional practice opportunities, consider the level of proficiency required by the job. For critical tasks, such as those with safety consequences, we recommend lots of practice. In situations where greater job proficiency can be gained during actual work assignments with the use of job aids, fewer practice exercises will suffice.

Also, the distribution of the questions within the lessons makes a difference to effective learning. Research has consistently shown that practice distributed throughout the training period results in better long-term retention than the same practice completed in a shorter time frame (National Research Council, 1991). This suggests that the practice exercises should be interspersed throughout a lesson rather than all placed at the end. For example, the lesson outline in Figure 9.7 shows several practice exercises placed after each new topic in the lesson.

Psychological Reasons for Multiple Distributed Practice Exercises

Encoding refers to the integration of new knowledge and skills with existing knowledge in long-term memory. Well-designed practice exercises provide encoding opportunities. In general, the more encoding opportunities an

Figure 9.7. Frequent Practice Exercises Are Distributed Throughout the Lesson.

Lesson Outline: Sampling for Control Chart Lesson

Introduction
Topic 1: Samples and Subgroups
-Populations, samples, and subgroups
   -Practice: given work samples, distinguish among subgroups, samples, and
     populations
   -Practice: determine the subgroup average for widget height
   -Practice: select subgroup for Part Z and determine its average diameter
Topic 2: Characteristics of Sample Averages
-Means approaching process means as number of subgroups increases
   -Practice: which subgroup mean is closest to process mean: widgets?
   -Practice: select subgroup that will yield closest process mean: Part Z
   -Practice: which example approximates X-doublebar?
-Relationship between variability of sample averages and individual units
   -Practice: which subgroup variation is closest to individual unit variation?
   -Practice: which sample would be best for the control chart?
   -Practice: which subgroup variability is half that of individual units?

individual has, the better the long-term retention. This is because each encoding can promote more connections with existing knowledge in long-term memory. More connections mean a higher probability of finding the new knowledge or skill when you need it.

The Evidence for Multiple Distributed Practice Exercises

We offer four lines of evidence about the amount and placement of practice in instruction:

- Research on the relationship between practice and task proficiency

- Studies on the relationship between practice and expert performance

- Comparisons of outcomes from e-lessons containing greater and lesser numbers of practice exercises

- Research on the distribution of practice during learning

More Practice Yields Improved Performance

While practice may not make perfect, it will improve performance indefinitely although at diminishing levels. Timed measurements of workers using a machine to roll cigars found that after thousands of practice trials conducted over a four-year period, proficiency continued to improve (Crossman, 1959). Proficiency leveled off only after the speed of the operator exceeded the physical limitations of the equipment. In plotting time versus practice for a variety of motor and intellectual tasks a logarithmic relationship has been observed between amount of practice and time to complete tasks (Rosenbaum, Carlson, and Gilmore, 2001). Thus the logarithm of the time to complete a task decreases with the logarithm of the amount of practice. This relationship is called the *power law* of practice. Figure 9.8 diagrams this relationship from one study. As you can see, while the greatest amount of proficiency gains occur on early trials, even after thousands of practice sessions, incremental improvements

Figure 9.8. The Power Law of Practice: Speed Increases with Practice.

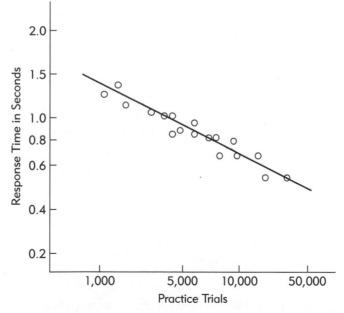

continue to accrue. Practice likely leads to improved performance in early sessions by learners finding better ways to complete the tasks and in later practice sessions by increased chunking of subskills and by achieving automaticity.

The Relationship Between Practice and Expertise

What do world-class performers have in common? A number of studies have examined what it takes to achieve high levels of expertise in such various domains as sports, music, and chess playing (Ericsson, 1990). One of the most important findings was that skill development and expertise are *strongly related to the time and efficiency of deliberate practice*. In other words, the more a person practices, the better he or she gets *regardless of initial talent and ability*. In fact, in the absence of practice, the more talented individuals will lose their edge compared to less talented individuals who continue a regimen of deliberate practice. These studies provide persuasive evidence of the relationship between sustained practice and high levels of proficient performance.

Effects of Amount of Practice in e-Learning

More directly related to e-learning, Schnackenberg and others compared learning from two versions of computer-based training, one offering more practice than the other (Schnackenberg, Sullivan, Leader, and Jones, 1998; Schnackenberg and Sullivan, 2000). They found that the version with more practice increased learning for both higher- and lower-ability learners. The authors conclude: "When instructional designers are faced with uncertainty about the amount of practice to include in an instructional program, they should favor a greater amount of practice over a relatively small amount if higher student achievement is an important goal" (Schnackenberg, Sullivan, Leader, and Jones, 1998, p. 14). See the following box for details about this research.

More practice means a longer lesson, however. In this study, high-ability learners taking the full lesson achieved about a 15 percent improvement in learning and took 25 percent longer compared to those taking the lesson with less practice. For low-ability learners, a similar improvement of about 15 percent took 75 percent longer than the lesson with less practice. Does the additional time spent warrant the learning improvement? To decide how much practice your e-learning courses should include, evaluate the criticality of job proficiency to determine whether the extra training time is justified by the improvements in learning.

MORE PRACTICE IN e-LEARNING RESULTED IN MORE LEARNING

Two identical lessons on educational psychology were created as part of a required course for third-year university students: a full version with 174 information screens and sixty-six practice exercises and a lean version with the same 174 information screens with twenty-two practice exercises. Learners, who were divided into high- and low-ability groups based on their GPAs, completed a fifty-two-question test along with an attitude questionnaire after training. Table 9.2 shows the results, including test scores and time to complete the training for the lower- and higher-ability learners. As expected, higher-ability learners scored higher and the full version took longer to complete. In comparing the two versions, note that the full version resulted in higher average scores with an effect size of .45, which is considered to be moderate. The only difference in learner course ratings was that those taking the full program agreed more strongly than those in the lean program that they had enough opportunities to practice answering questions (Schnackenberg, Sullivan, Leader, and Jones, 1998).

Table 9.2. Outcome Scores and Learning Time in Higher- and Lower-Ability Learners from e-Learning with Less and More Practice.
From Schnackenberg, Sullivan, Leader, and Jones, 1998.

	66 Practices		22 Practices	
Ability Level	Low	High	Low	High
Test Scores	32.25	41.82	28.26	36.30
Time to Complete (minutes)	146	107	83	85

Distribution of Practice

As we said earlier in this chapter, practice is more effective when it is distributed throughout the lesson rather than placed in one location. The earliest research on human learning conducted by Ebbinghaus in 1913 showed that distributed practice yields better long-term retention. According to the National Research Council, "The so-called spacing effect—that practice sessions spaced in time are superior to massed practices in terms of long-term retention—is one of the most reliable phenomena in human experimental psychology. The effect is robust and appears to hold for verbal materials of all types as well as for motor skills" (1991, p. 30). As long as eight years after an original training, learners whose practice was spaced showed better retention than those who practiced in a more concentrated time period (Bahrick, 1987).

The spacing effect, however, does not result in better *immediate* learning. It is only after a period of time that the benefits of spaced practice are realized. Since most training programs do not measure delayed learning, this effect would typically not be noticed. Only in long-term evaluation would this advantage be seen. Naturally, practical constraints will dictate the amount of spacing that is feasible.

Practice Principle Three: Apply the Media Elements Principles to Practice Exercises

In Chapters Three through Eight, we presented six principles for design of multimedia pertaining specifically to the use of graphics, text, and audio in e-learning. Here are some suggestions for ways to apply those principles to the design of practice interactions.

Contiguity Principle

According to the *contiguity principle,* text should be presented close to the graphics it is explaining to assist learners with integration. Applying this principle to the design of practice exercises, we recommend that directions for practice exercises be clearly distinguished by placement, color, or font and be placed adjacent to the question. In addition, when laying out practice that will include feedback to a response, leave an open screen area for feedback near the question and as close to the response area as possible so learners can easily link the feedback to their response and to the question. The correct options should be highlighted in multiple choice or multiple select items. After reading the feedback and reviewing the correct options, learners can easily see whether their response was or was not appropriate for the question asked. Thus when the learner answers a question, he or she should see four components on the screen: directions, question, response, and feedback, as illustrated in Figure 9.4.

Modality and Redundancy Principles

According to the *modality principle* described in Chapter Five, audio should be used to explain graphics in the lesson. However, audio is too transient for practice exercises. Learners need to refer to the directions while responding to questions. Any instructions or information learners need in order to answer a question should remain in text on the screen while the learner decides on a response. Feedback should also be presented in text format so that learners can review their responses in relationship to the question. Based on the *redundancy principle* described in Chapter Six, use text alone for most situations. Do not narrate onscreen text directions or practice questions.

WHEN AUDIO OR VIDEO IS NEEDED FOR PRACTICE

In courses where audio or video is needed for practice, there should be a replay option. For example, in a telephone customer service course, a practice exercise might require learners to respond to customer comments. A replay option gives them a chance to study the customer's words, tone of voice, and inflection before selecting the best response. If a case exercise is presented in a video clip, the learner should have access to a text review of the essential elements of the case.

Personalization Principle

According to the personalization principle described in Chapter Eight, e-lessons should use conversational language and virtual coaches called agents to provide help in the form of hints, worked examples, and demonstrations. In the case of practice exercises, directions and hints should use the first and second person, as illustrated in most of the examples in this chapter. In the next section, we will explain the use of a coach to teach learners how to self-question.

Practice Principle Four: Train Learners to Self-Question During Receptive e-Lessons

We have discussed the benefits of multiple practice exercises that mirror the environment of the job and that are dispersed throughout the training materials. But in some situations learners will be required to learn from lessons that lack practice interaction—lessons we refer to as *receptive*. To learn from receptive training, learners will need to ask questions of themselves regarding the content presented. For example, a learner reading about a new software program might ask: "How can I apply the program features to my job?" Or, "How does the new program differ from the one I'm using now?"

E-learning can be used to train learners to ask and answer their own questions while reading or listening to lessons. Constructing this type of training will be time-consuming. Once completed, however, it should increase the reading comprehension of all participants on any instructional materials that lack explicit practice. Train learners to self-question by showing examples of self-questioning followed by practice that requires learners to self-question instructional materials. As an example, Figure 9.9 illustrates a tutor agent used to demonstrate the use of question stems to improve comprehension of text in part of the Quality Management lesson.

Psychological Reasons for Training Self-Questioning Skills

A fundamental assumption of our book is that learning requires an active engagement of the mind with new information. We have recommended and shown evidence that multiple practice exercises matched

Figure 9.9. A Storyboard Using an Agent to Coach on Self-Explanation.

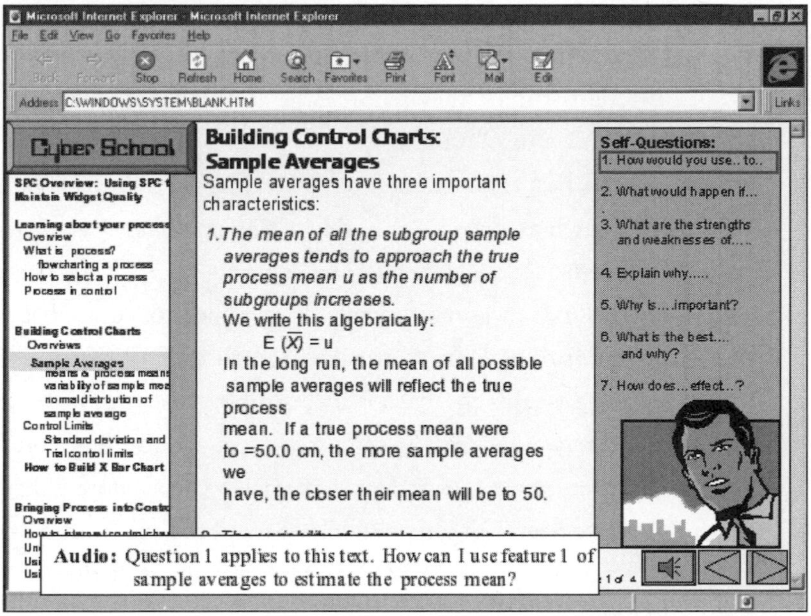
Microsoft Internet Explorer - Microsoft Internet Explorer
File Edit View Go Favorites Help
Back Forward Stop Refresh Home Search Favorites Print Font Mail Edit
Address C:\WINDOWS\SYSTEM\BLANK.HTM
Links
Cyber School
Building Control Charts:
Sample Averages
Sample averages have three important characteristics:
1. The mean of all the subgroup sample averages tends to approach the true process mean u as the number of subgroups increases.
We write this algebraically:
E (X̄) = u
In the long run, the mean of all possible sample averages will reflect the true process mean. If a true process mean were to =50.0 cm, the more sample averages we have, the closer their mean will be to 50.
Self-Questions:
1. How would you use.. to..
2. What would happen if...
3. What are the strengths and weaknesses of....
4. Explain why.....
5. Why is....important?
6. What is the best.... and why?
7. How does....effect..?
Audio: Question 1 applies to this text. How can I use feature 1 of sample averages to estimate the process mean?
1 of 4

to the processing requirements of the job result in better learning than fewer exercises or activities that require only rote processing. However, learners with high metacognitive skills (see Chapters Two and Twelve) as well as high prior knowledge of the course topics may be able to effectively and spontaneously provide their own processing of new content. Thus, our recommendations apply mainly to less knowledgeable or less skilled learners.

However, be careful in the assumptions you make about your learners. Most people process information mindlessly, resulting in poor understanding, learning, and memory. Without explicit practice exercises, processing of content is not as complete as it might be. Learners who are successful spontaneous processors of information are more the exception than the rule because doing this processing requires time and effort, interrupts the flow of text, and is likely to be seen as an obstacle to learning (Pressley, Wood, Woloshyn, Martin, King, and Menke, 1992).

Evidence for Training Self-Questioning

A recent review summarizes a number of studies that trained learners to generate questions to improve their comprehension of textual materials (Rosenshine, Meister, and Chapman, 1996). In an evaluation of twenty-six different studies, they report large and significant learning improvements from this type of training.

The best results came from providing learners with generic questions or stems such as: *"How are . . . and . . . alike?" "How would you use . . . to. . . ." "What are the strengths and weaknesses of . . . ?" "How does . . . affect . . . ?"* Studies that measured learning from expository materials with the generic questions resulted in an overall effect size of 1.12 (King, 1992). The reviews suggest that this approach is successful because it provides explicit direction, is concrete, and is easy to teach and apply. The authors conclude that generic questions and question stems may have "been more effective because they promote deeper processing, initiate recall of background knowledge, require integration of prior knowledge, and provide more direction for processing" (p. 200).

In summarizing all the questioning training programs in the twenty-six studies, they recommend the following guidelines:

- Provide learners with prompts such as the generic question stems listed previously.

- Provide models of appropriate responses—in other words, give worked examples of how to adapt the question stems to formulate specific questions relevant to the material being read and answer them. Models can be given before, during, and after practice as feedback.

- Anticipate potential difficulties. During training, help learners discriminate among questions that are not likely to work effectively, such as questions that are too narrow or that cannot be answered by the materials being read.

- Start with simple materials and build to more complex. Training started with small text segments—ranging from a sentence to a short paragraph—and over time built up to long passages.

- Provide job aids to remind learners of the question stems. A cue card or pop-up screen with a list of the generic question stems should be available.

- Provide practice and feedback in generating and responding to questions.

- Assess learner mastery of the technique.

DESIGN DILEMMA: RESOLUTION

At the design meeting, your clients expressed different ideas about the practice in the quality management course. One manager suggested skipping the practice entirely in order to get the training done faster. Another manager suggested inserting games to make the lesson entertaining. However, your research has shown that practice that includes the context and mental processes of the job is needed to support learning. Here's what you might say to the managers:

"Although a few individuals can learn from materials that have little interaction, our target audience doesn't match that profile. We need to include interactivity in the program to hold attention and to maintain interest. We also need to build that interactivity so it helps the operators apply the skills to their quality monitoring tasks. While a game like Jeopardy™ might be fun, it will not build the right mental connections to help operators on the job. Here is an example of the type of interaction that research demonstrates will lead to building skills that will transfer to the job (Figure 9.10). Note that the exercise mirrors real work decisions and actions. See how the question context is realistic to the job. It may even be fun, and it will certainly give you the job results you are paying for in this training."

Figure 9.10. A Storyboard of a Practice Exercise that Simulates a Job Task.

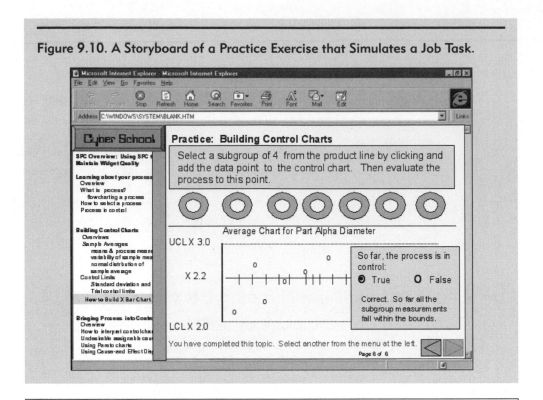

WHAT TO LOOK FOR IN e-LEARNING

☐ Several practice exercises per topic.

☐ Exercises that require learners to apply knowledge and skills to job-realistic situations and environments.

☐ Few or no questions that require only rote recall of information (unless the job requires recall of information without a job aid).

☐ Distribution of exercises throughout the lessons rather than placement in one location.

☐ More practice opportunities for highly critical tasks than for less critical tasks.

☐ Directions to practice exercises presented in text clearly visible near the question.

☐ Feedback appearing in text close to the question.

☐ Memory support visible near the application question.

☐ Training in self-questioning when e-lessons lack practice exercises.

COMING NEXT

In this chapter, we have looked at the psychology and research recommending design of effective practice interactions for skill-building. But we know that designing and completing practice exercises takes time—time for the course designer and time for the learner. In the next chapter, we will look at empirically proven ways you can save time and get good learning results by substituting worked examples for some practice questions.

Suggested Readings

Clark, R.C., (1999). *Developing Technical Training: A Structured Approach for Developing Classroom and Computer Based Instructional Materials.* Silver Spring, MD: International Society for Performance Improvement.

Ericsson, K.A. (1990). Theoretical Issues in the Study of Exceptional Performance. In K.J. Gilhooly, M.T.G. Keane, R.H. Logie, and G. Erdos (Eds.). *Lines of Thinking: Reflections on the Psychology of Thought.* New York: John Wiley & Sons.

Mayer, R.E. (1996). Learning Strategies for Making Sense Out of Expository Text: The SOI Model for Building Three Cognitive Processes in Knowledge Construction. *Educational Psychology Review, 8*(4) 357–371.

Rosenshine, B., Meister, C., and Chapman, S. (1996). Teaching Students to Generate Questions: A Review of the Intervention Studies. *Review of Educational Research, 66*(2), 181–221.

CHAPTER OUTLINE

Worked Examples: Fuel for Learning

    What Are Worked Examples?

Worked Example Principle One: Replace Some Practice Problems with Worked Examples

Psychological Reasons for Using Worked Examples

Evidence for Benefits of Worked Examples

    How Should Worked Examples Be Sequenced?

Worked Example Principle Two: Apply the Media Elements Principles to Examples

    Contiguity Principle

    Modality Principle

    Personalization Principle

Psychological Reasons for Applying the Media Elements Principles

Evidence for the Media Elements Principles

Worked Example Principle Three: Use Job-Realistic *or* Varied Worked Examples

Psychological Reasons to Adapt Examples to Task Types

    Transfer of New Procedural Skills

    Transfer of Principle-Based or Problem-Solving Skills

The Evidence for Worked Examples That Support Transfer

    When Using Varied Examples, Make Them Worked Examples

    Break Complex Worked Examples into Clearly Labeled Sub-Problems

Worked Example Principle Four: Teach Learners to Self-Explain Examples

Psychological Reasons for Training Self-Explanations

The Evidence for Self-Explanations

10

Leveraging Examples in e-Learning

CHAPTER PREVIEW

WHILE EXAMPLES have been a popular instructional method for years, recent research gives us new ways to save learning time and to effectively teach tasks by substituting worked examples for some practice exercises. A worked example is a step-by-step demonstration of how to solve a problem or perform a task. The psychological advantage of worked examples is that they reduce mental work. In this chapter we describe and illustrate the best types of worked examples for teaching procedural and principle-based tasks. We also show how best to use text, audio, and graphics to apply the media elements principles described in Chapters Three through Eight to worked examples. However, even the best worked examples do no good if they are ignored. We end the chapter with empirical research that shows that teaching learners how to study a worked example improves learning.

DESIGN DILEMMA

The e-learning design team has just finished reviewing the first-draft storyboards for the lesson on building control charts with the main client, the manager of quality. The storyboards include a worked example of how to build a control chart like the one shown in Figure 10.1 followed by four practice exercises requiring learners to build control charts from simulated product data. The quality manager jumps right in: "We can't take operators off the line for more than an hour without seriously impacting production. All these practice exercises are going to take them a lot of time to complete. You have to keep each lesson to no more than five to seven minutes!" You know from research (summarized in Chapter Nine) that without practice exercises, e-learning becomes a page-turner and learning may be compromised. You wonder if there are some ways to accelerate learning—ways that don't sacrifice the outcomes.

Figure 10.1. A Worked Example to Demonstrate a Step-by-Step Solution: Version 1.

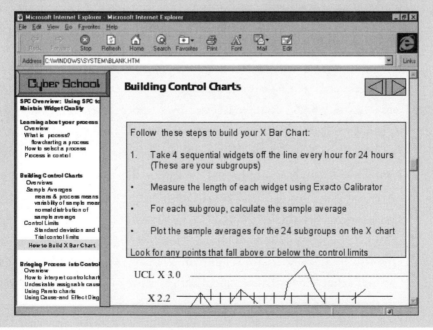

Worked Examples: Fuel for Learning

Worked examples are one of the most powerful methods you can use to build new and rich knowledge in long-term memory, and they are popular with learners. Learners often choose worked examples over verbal descriptions. For example, learners in a LISP programming tutorial ignored verbal descriptions of LISP procedures in favor of worked examples (Anderson, Farrell, and Sauers, 1984). In another study, learners were free to study either textual descriptions or worked examples to help them complete problem assignments. The information in the text was deliberately written to contradict the examples. By evaluating the learners' solutions, it was clear that the learners used the examples, not the text, as their preferred instructional resource (LeFevre and Dixon, 1986).

What Are Worked Examples?

In this chapter we write about a specific type of example called a worked example. A worked example is a step-by-step demonstration of how to perform a task or solve a problem, as shown in Figure 10.1. Worked examples can assume many forms including illustrations showing step-by-step problem solutions, animated demonstrations, textual descriptions, videotaped expert demonstrations, and representations of the thoughts of expert performers like the one shown in Figure 10.2. While using worked examples in lessons is not new, today we have research providing guidelines on the most effective type, distribution, and layout of examples to teach job tasks.

Worked examples for highly structured topics like math typically illustrate a step-by-step solution similar to the one shown in Figure 10.3. Most of the research has used mathematics and science problems as the instructional content because the high structure of these kinds of problems makes step-by-step demonstrations of learning straightforward. However, it's not necessary to be a mathematician or scientist to understand or apply the principles learned from these studies. In fact, in this chapter, we apply the findings from this research to tasks commonly found in large organizations

Figure 10.2. A Worked Example of Effective Selling Techniques.
With permission from DigitalThink.

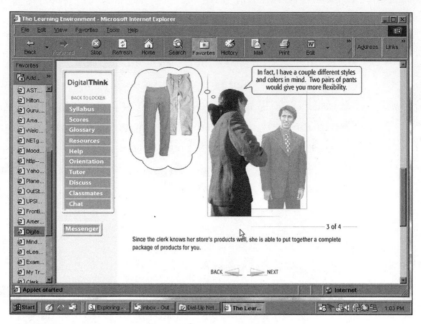

Figure 10.3. Partial Worked Math Problem Example.
Adapted from Renkl and others, 1998.

You are planning to invest part of the money you inherited from your aunt in a savings certificate. The remaining amount, however, should be invested at the highest interest rates possible, bearing therefore a higher risk, too. After you have read over various literature on this subject, you decide to buy Russian junk-bonds with a life-span of 5 years (n = 5 years) and an interest rate of 30% (p = 30%). The interest is booked as compound interest.

Which amount do you have to invest in the Russian junk-bonds as start capital, if you want to receive $8,000 (K5 = $8,000) at the end of 5 years?

Solution:

Step one: select the givens

K5 = $8,000   K5: end capital after 5 years
P = 30%   P: interest rate
N = 5 years   N: life-span in years
To be searched: K0   K0: start capital

Step two: select the correct formula
K0 = Kn : qn
K0 = K5 : q5

such as learning to use a new automated software system, making a sale, or researching a bank loan application.

Based on empirical evidence, we recommend four guidelines regarding best use of examples in e-learning:

- Worked examples should replace some practice exercises for novice learners.

- Principles regarding best use of text, audio, and graphics are applied to present worked examples.

- Worked examples are job realistic and diverse to build useful mental models for procedural and principle-based job tasks.

- Training in self-explanation of examples is available. These guidelines address the what, when, and how of effective examples to save learning time and improve learning outcomes.

Worked Example Principle One: Replace Some Practice Problems with Worked Examples

Traditional wisdom dictates that the best way to learn to solve problems is to practice solving lots of problems. A typical math text shows a couple of sample problems worked out followed by a number of problems for the learners to work themselves. Most of us can recall the hours of labor spent completing those school math problem assignments. Could we learn as effectively in less time by replacing some of the assigned problems with worked examples?

In Chapter Nine, we recommended that e-courses include a number of practice exercises that are job relevant. However, based on the research evidence and psychological processes summarized below, we offer a slightly modified version of that guideline: *In courses that are teaching new tasks, learning time can be saved by replacing some practice assignments with worked examples designed following the guidelines in this chapter.*

There are a couple of caveats to this guideline. One is that worked examples are only effective if the learner studies them. If they are ignored or bypassed, they are of little value. One way to circumvent this problem is to design worked examples as "completion" problems. These are worked examples with parts missing that the learner must fill in. Another solution is to make the worked example interactive by inserting a question that requires the learner to study the worked example, as illustrated in Figure 10.4. A second limitation is that novices will benefit most from worked examples. Learners with experience in the course topics may learn as effectively or better from working out problems themselves as from studying worked examples.

Figure 10.4. A Worked Example with an Inserted Question.

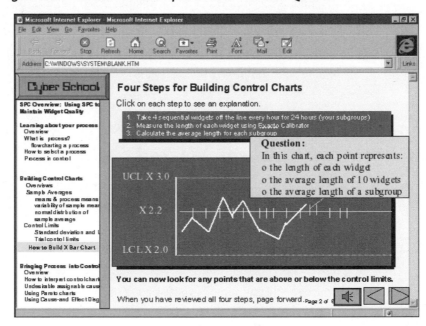

Psychological Reasons for Using Worked Examples

Working memory has a limited capacity that becomes inefficient when having to retain even a few items. If the only way to build job-relevant skills is to perform many practice exercises, working memory can become overloaded by the mental work required to complete these exercises. However, if limited working memory resources could be used to study worked examples and build new knowledge from them, some of this labor-intensive effort could be bypassed. Worked examples are more efficient for learning new tasks because they reduce the load in working memory, thereby allowing the learner to learn the steps in problem solving.

Sweller and his colleagues distinguish between the *intrinsic load* of instructional materials that results from the inherent complexity of the content itself and the *extraneous load* imposed by the instructional design (Sweller, 1999; Sweller, Van Merrienboer, and Pass, 1998). Learners who are studying complex topics will have to deal with high intrinsic mental load, especially if it's new information. However, good e-learning can help learners manage that load by using effective instructional methods. Replacing some assigned problems with worked examples reduces the extraneous load, freeing working memory to allocate resources to the learning process. This recommendation applies primarily to courses for novice learners who are most susceptible to cognitive overload.

Evidence for Benefits of Worked Examples

There is a lot of evidence for the effectiveness of learning from worked examples. As an example, in one study twelve geometry problems were used. In the conventional group the learners solved all twelve problems as practice. In the worked examples group, the learners received eight problems already worked out to study and then four problems to solve as practice. Students in the worked examples group spent significantly less time studying and scored higher on a test than did those in the conventional group. Furthermore, the worked examples group scored higher not only on test problems similar to those used during practice but also on different types of problems requiring application of the principles taught (Paas, 1992). The investigators conclude that "training with partly or completely worked-out problems leads to less effort-demanding and better transfer performance and is more time efficient" (p. 433). In fact, in one study, the use of worked examples allowed learners to complete a three-year mathematics course in two years (Zhu and Simon, 1987). Positive effects of worked examples have been reported in a variety of courses teaching well-defined problems, including algebra, geometry, statistics, and programming.

An exception may be with learners familiar with the skills. A group of twenty-four trade apprentices was trained on writing various types of programs for circuits. Half used worked examples and the other half solved all the problems themselves. Learning was measured after each of several training sessions lasting about one hour each. While learners benefited from worked examples in the first sessions, in later sessions solving problems was more effective than studying worked examples. The researchers propose that for learners with some experience in an area, "interpreting a worked example may be redundant and impose a greater cognitive load than simply providing a solution to the problem" (Kalyuga, Chandler, Tuovinen, and Sweller, 2001, p. 580).

How Should Worked Examples Be Sequenced?

What is the best way to sequence worked examples with problems assigned for practice? For example, would it be better to follow four worked examples with four assigned problems or to alternate a single worked example with a practice problem four times? Using LISP programming lessons, a study compared alternating one example and one practice with using groups of examples followed by groups of practice. The alternating example-practice instruction resulted in faster and more accurate solutions. The authors conclude that "the most efficient way to present material to acquire a skill is to present an example, then a similar problem to solve immediately following" (Trafton and Reiser, 1993, p. 1022). The psychological reason is that while learning to solve new problems, having an analogous problem immediately available in memory supports its application to the new problems.

Worked Example Principle Two: Apply the Media Elements Principles to Examples

In Chapters Three through Eight we presented six principles for design of multimedia pertaining to the use of graphics, text, and audio in e-learning. Here are some suggestions for ways to apply those principles to the design of worked examples.

Contiguity Principle

According to the contiguity principle, text should be placed close to the
graphics it is explaining to assist learners with integration. To solve the problem of limited screen real estate in Web-based training, designers frequently
use a scrolling page to present a complete worked example, as illustrated in
Figure 10.1. This technique can result in a physical separation of the text
from the illustration so that, after scrolling through the steps to look at the
illustration, the steps are no longer visible or vice versa. This separation
requires the learner to expend scarce working memory resources on mentally
searching through the visual elements. Figure 10.5 improves the layout of
the worked example in Figure 10.1 by replacing the scrolling screen with a
fixed screen display. The four steps in text remain fixed in the upper frame
and the visual illustration changes as the learner selects each step. Another
solution is the use of baby graphics, as illustrated in Figure 10.6. On this

Figure 10.5. Integration of Text with Graphic Elements on a Fixed Screen.

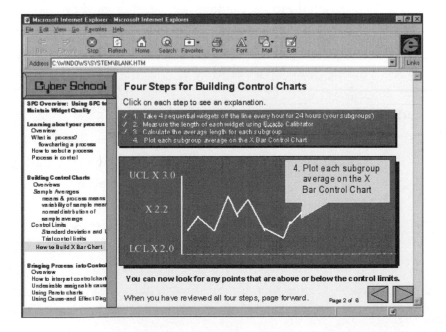

Figure 10.6. Use of Baby Screens to Integrate Graphics and Text.

With permission from Element K.

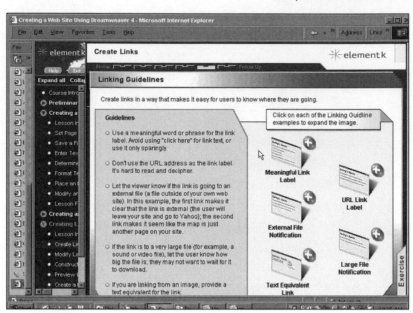

screen several guidelines for creating meaningful links on Web pages stated in text on the left side of the screen are illustrated by miniature screens on the right side of the screen. The learner can click on each miniature to view an enlarged version. When using this technique, be sure the enlarged baby does not cover up the related text.

Modality Principle

According to the modality principle described in Chapter Five, audio should be used to explain graphics in the lesson. Figure 10.7 illustrates a worked example in which audio has replaced text to explain the steps. An advantage to using audio is greater use of limited screen real estate which otherwise is consumed by text explanations. If the graphic is quite complex, such as in an animated worked example, help the learner by providing visual cues with arrows or colored boxes. For example, the worked example in the Web-based course (Figure 10.8) uses an arrow to direct the eye to the software application button being described.

Figure 10.7. Audio Is Used to Explain Visual Elements of a Worked Example.

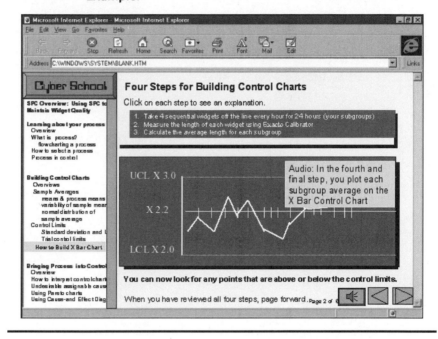

Figure 10.8. An Arrow Directs Attention in a Worked Example.

With permission from Element K.

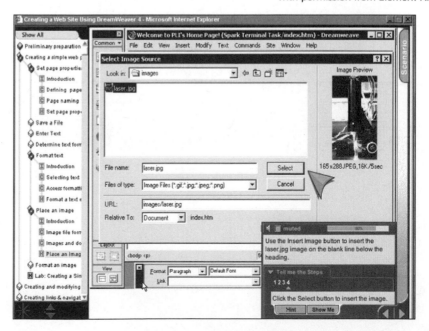

Personalization Principle

According to the personalization principles described in Chapter Eight, learning is improved by the use of conversational text and virtual coaches, called agents. Note the use of the second person "you" in the examples in this chapter. Later in this chapter we show the use of a learning agent to demonstrate how to best learn from a worked example.

Psychological Reasons for Applying the Media Element Principles

The psychological basis for these guidelines was described in detail in Chapters Three through Eight. Therefore we only briefly recap the main ideas. Most of the guidelines are effective because they reduce extraneous mental load, thereby freeing working memory capacity for learning. If audio cannot be used, placing text in close proximity to the graphic illustration on the screen integrates the information for the learner. However, when technically feasible, it is more effective to use audio narration to explain a graphic in order to use the visual and auditory channels of working memory most effectively. Similarly, it is better to avoid adding duplicate text to audio narration that is describing a graphic to avoid overloading the visual channel of working memory. Finally, the informal language suggested by the personalization principle tends to engage learners more actively into a social dialog with the computer.

Evidence for the Media Elements Principles

In Chapters Three through Eight we summarized the research basis for the *media elements principles* so we will only briefly revisit that research as it specifically relates to worked examples.

1. *Integrate Visual Elements.* If the example is to be presented in a visual mode only, a physical integration of text with a diagram is more effective than presenting the explanatory text away from the diagram. Figure 10.9 shows two versions of a geometry worked example

Figure 10.9. A Comparison of Textual Elements Separate from and Integrated into Graphic.

From Sweller, Chandler, Tierney, and Cooper, 1990.

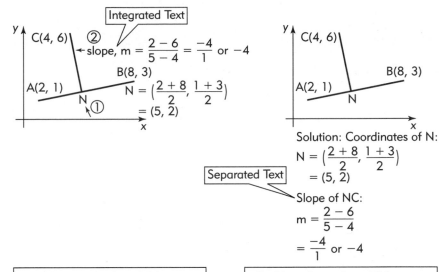

Problem: Points A and B have coordinates (2, 1) and (8, 3), respectively. N is the Midpoint of AB. What is the slope of the Straight line that joins N to the point C (4, 6)?	**Problem:** Points A and B have coordinates (2, 1) and (8, 3), respectively. N is the Midpoint of AB. What is the slope of the Straight line that joins N to the point C (4, 6)?
Integrated Version	**Traditional Version**

from a research study. In one version the equations are placed within the diagram, whereas in the other version the equations are placed below the diagram. The integrated versions consistently resulted in better learning (Sweller, Chandler, Tierney, and Cooper, 1990).

2. *Use Audio to Expand on Graphics—Do Not Narrate Onscreen Text.* Better learning has been reported in lessons in which a graphic element was explained by narration alone, compared to narration and identical text (Mayer, Heiser, and Lonn, 2001).

3. *Use Visual Cues in Complex Visual Displays.* If the worked example involves a complex visual display and audio explanation, a visual cue such as an arrow or highlighting to draw learner attention to the

aspect of the worked example being described improves learning (Jeung, Chandler, and Sweller, 1997). This does not apply to less complex worked examples.

Worked Example Principle Three: Use Job-Realistic *or* Varied Worked Examples

So far we have seen that we can save instructional time by replacing problem assignments with worked examples and by formatting those worked examples in ways that integrate the audio and visual elements. Other important points relating to worked examples are what type to use and how many are needed. For example, should all the examples be similar or should they be diverse? This question has direct impact on the issue of transfer— how effectively will your learners be able to apply the skills you train back to their jobs?

The number and type of examples that work best will depend on the type of task that is being taught. For procedural tasks—also called *near transfer* skills—a single job-realistic worked example that clearly illustrates the steps is usually sufficient. The goal is to provide an easy-to-follow model for the learner. These types of worked examples are commonly called demonstrations. In e-learning, a good demonstration can be replayed many times by the learner as needed, and should be readily accessible as reference during practice. Figures 10.4, 10.5, 10.7, and 10.8 illustrate demonstrations of procedures.

In contrast, when teaching tasks that require judgment and problem-solving—tasks known as *far transfer*—more than one example will be needed. Some examples of far transfer tasks include making a sale, designing a visual, or writing a report. There is no one right method for performing these tasks, since each job situation will be different. Solving these far transfer tasks, whether in highly structured domains such as programming or mathematics or in more ill-defined arenas such as sales or negotiations, requires more flexible knowledge in long-term memory. The knowledge must be adaptable so the worker can apply it to the diverse job problems that will arise.

In e-lessons that teach far transfer tasks, look for several examples in which the storyline varies but the underlying principles remain the same. For example, in a sales course, you should see several dialogs in which the sales associate is talking with various clients and adapts the basic sales guidelines to each client's unique needs. Because studying examples that are different on the surface can add cognitive load, this is a situation in which worked examples really pay off.

Psychological Reasons to Adapt Examples to Task Types

Transfer of New Procedural Skills

The psychological processes involved in the transfer of procedural versus principle-based tasks are different. In Chapter Nine we described the *encoding specificity principle* as the basis for transfer from the training to the job. *Encoding specificity* states that transfer is maximized when the conditions at retrieval match those present at the time of training. In other words, the environment of the job needs to be simulated in the instructional environment. It is easy to apply *encoding specificity* to procedural tasks since the steps on the job are always performed in the same way and in the same environment. Therefore, the worked example needs to provide a realistic model of how to do the task on the job. For example, if you want workers to use a new computer system, they need to see a demonstration and have practice opportunities on that system or a faithful simulation of it like the example in Figure 10.8. The purpose of these worked examples is to provide a model for the learner to imitate in a faithful way.

Transfer of Principle-Based or Problem-Solving Skills

As we mentioned previously, to solve far transfer tasks based on principles, a flexible knowledge base is needed that can be adapted to the many different incarnations of a problem. One characteristic of experts is that they size up a problem by identifying the underlying principles that are not apparent to a novice. For example, an expert physicist is able to look at a problem that involves pulleys and realize the problem is really about the conservation of linear momentum. For a novice, it would appear to be simply a "pulley problem." Experts gain this ability through experience with hundreds of different real problems encountered in their specialty field. Over time, experts abstract robust mental models in long-term memory to apply to daily problems. The first thing someone needs to figure out when faced with a problem is, "what kind of problem is it?" Just as with real-world experience, learners can derive principles by studying a number of diverse examples in training. In this way providing learners with a number of worked examples that use varied contexts or scenarios can accelerate the development of expertise.

The Evidence for Worked Examples That Support Transfer

Transfer of learning has been the subject of a lot of research. In one study individuals solved the tumor problem shown in the following box. Prior to tackling that problem, different groups had different prework assignments. One group read a story about a general who captured a mined fortress by splitting up his troops and attacking from different directions. Another group read the fortress story, plus a story about putting out a fire on an oil rig. A single hose was not large enough to disperse sufficient foam, so the fire was put out by directing many small hoses toward the middle of the fire. As you have probably surmised, although the context of each story was quite different, the underlying principle—a convergence principle—was the same. The research showed that most individuals who tried to solve the tumor problem without any other stories did not arrive at the convergence solution. Even those who read the fortress problem prior to the tumor problem did not have much better luck. But the group that read both stories had much greater success (Gick and Holyoak, 1980). From this research we learn to appreciate the power of multiple examples that have a different context but share a similar set of guidelines or principles.

THE TUMOR PROBLEM

Suppose you are a doctor faced with a patient who has a malignant tumor in his stomach. It is impossible to operate on the patient, but unless the tumor is destroyed, the patient will die. There is a kind of ray that at a sufficiently high intensity can destroy the tumor. Unfortunately, at this intensity, the healthy tissue that the rays pass through on the way to the tumor will also be destroyed. At lower intensities, the rays are harmless to healthy tissue but will not affect the tumor either. How can the rays be used to destroy the tumor without injuring the healthy tissue? (Duncker, 1945)

The challenge with using examples of various contexts is they add cognitive load to the learning process. In the following section, we summarize research that suggests that varied examples can be made easier for learners by presenting them in a worked format and also by breaking a complex worked example into chunks and highlighting each chunk.

When Using Varied Examples, Make Them Worked Examples

Paas and Van Merrienboer (1994b) gave learners math problems that were either all quite similar or all quite different from each other. However, for each set of similar or diverse problems, the learners either studied worked examples or were asked to solve the problems as exercises. Table 10.1 summarizes the research plan and results. Consistent with prior research, they

Table 10.1. A Comparison of Learning from Different and Similar Practice Problems and Worked Examples.

Low-Variability Examples		High-Variability Examples	
Traditional	Worked	Traditional	Worked
			Best Learning

found that worked examples were more effective than practice problems due to management of cognitive load. Further, studying examples that were different was more effective than studying examples that were similar because they supported transfer better. But study of different examples was effective only when they were worked out so that cognitive resources could be invested in study of each example. Based on this research, we recommend that multiple varied worked examples be used in training designed to build complex far transfer skills.

Break Complex Worked Examples into Clearly Labeled Sub-Problems

When a worked example involves multiple steps, format the worked example's steps in ways that draw attention to the problem's sub-goals. Catrambone (1996, 1998) added annotations or labels to highlight the sub-goals and also physically spaced the sub-goals from each other, as illustrated in Figure 10.3. E-learning designers can use this research to their benefit since tasks are usually chunked into segments for demonstration purposes. Simply basing lesson segments on problem sub-goals and drawing attention to them via labels can improve learning.

Worked Example Principle Four: Teach Learners to Self-Explain Examples

Some learners make better use of worked examples than others, and the techniques of these successful learners can be taught to others. In a nutshell, the successful learners can explain worked examples to themselves and their explanations focus on the principles behind the example. In e-courseware, look for lessons that help students learn from worked examples by teaching them how to self-explain. Specifically look for demonstrations of a worked example being explained. In other words, the lesson should have a worked example of how to process a worked example. Here is a great opportunity to use a learning agent as a virtual coach. In Figure 10.10 we illustrate how we might use an agent to demonstrate self-explaining of a worked example.

Figure 10.10. A Worked Example Using an Agent to Demonstrate Self-Explaining.

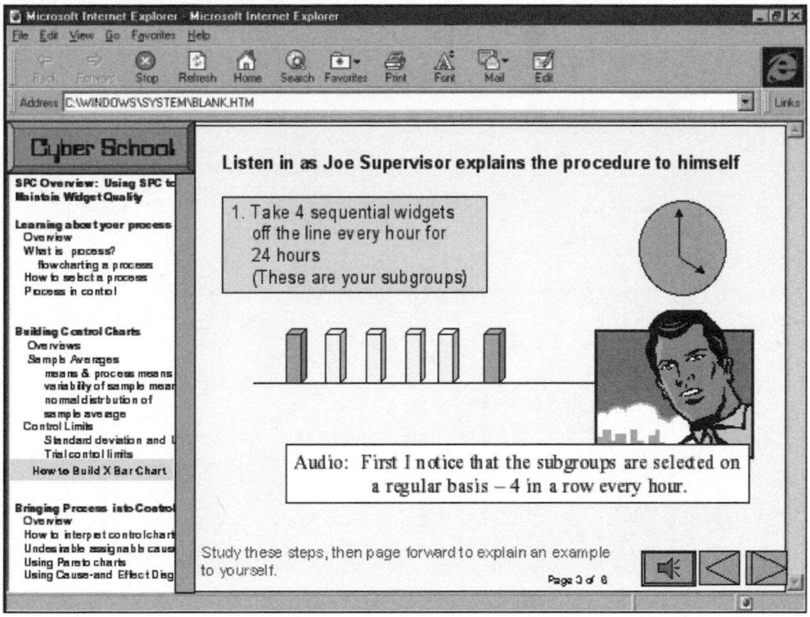

Microsoft Internet Explorer - Microsoft Internet Explorer

File Edit View Go Favorites Help

Back Forward Stop Refresh Home Search Favorites Print Font Mail Edit

Address C:\WINDOWS\SYSTEM\BLANK.HTM   Links

Cyber School

SPC Overview: Using SPC to Maintain Widget Quality

Learning about your process
 Overview
 What is process?
 flowcharting a process
 How to select a process
 Process in control

Building Control Charts
 Overviews
 Sample Averages
  means & process means
  variability of sample means
  normal distribution of
  sample average
 Control Limits
  Standard deviation and
  Trial control limits
 How to Build X Bar Chart

Bringing Process into Control
 Overview
 How to interpret control chart
 Undesirable assignable cause
 Using Pareto charts
 Using Cause-and Effect Diag

Listen in as Joe Supervisor explains the procedure to himself

1. Take 4 sequential widgets off the line every hour for 24 hours (These are your subgroups)

Audio: First I notice that the subgroups are selected on a regular basis — 4 in a row every hour.

Study these steps, then page forward to explain an example to yourself.

Page 3 of 8

Practice in self-explanations such as the one illustrated in Figure 10.11 should follow the demonstration. In these practices, learners should focus their explanations on why the example uses a particular technique to solve a problem, as well as on how the worked example illustrates the application of a specific principle. After one or two practices, periodically reminding the learner to self-explain should be sufficient.

Psychological Reasons for Training Self-Explanations

If the role of an example is to build the right knowledge in long-term memory, the more effectively the learner processes the example, the better the learning. At one extreme, if learners ignore the examples they will not have any of the benefits summarized in this chapter. Likewise if learners give examples only cursory processing, the benefits will be limited. We know that to build new knowledge, learners need to make sense of the new information

Figure 10.11. A Practice Exercise on Self-Explaining a Worked Example.

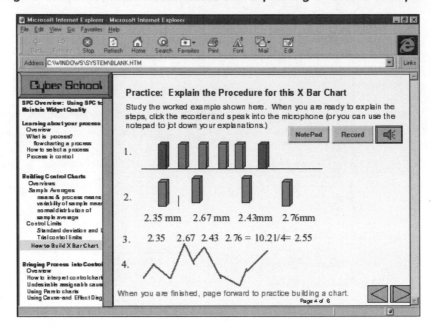

being presented; and they need to connect new information with existing knowledge in long-term memory. This knowledge-building process requires active engagement by the learner with the worked example. Self-explanations promote this active processing.

The Evidence for Self-Explanations

College students talked aloud as they studied worked physics problems. Later the students were tested with new problems, and successful and unsuccessful learners were compared regarding the number and quality of their self-explanations. The average number of explanations per worked example ranged from a low of fewer than two to a high of more than twenty-five. Learning correlated with the number of self-explanations generated. Students who generated many self-explanations solved 86 percent of the problems correctly, whereas students who generated only a few solved 42 percent of problems correctly. The quality of self-explanation also made a difference. The more productive explanations:

- Focused on when and why solution equations were used

- Related solution steps to the physics principles

- Incorporated more self-monitoring of comprehension

There were no differences in the successful and unsuccessful groups as to their prior knowledge or ability. Thus, this technique can be applied to a wide range of learners who will benefit regardless of their background (Chi, 2000; Chi, Bassok, Lewis, Reimann, and Glaser, 1989; Chi, De Leeuw, Chiu, and La Vancher, 1994).

DESIGN DILEMMA: RESOLUTION

In response to a request from your client to save instructional time, you found a number of ways to speed learning by reducing cognitive load. First you converted several of the assigned problems into worked examples—interspersing them with practice problems. Next, you found you could improve your worked examples by making the text and the graphic simultaneously visible on the screen. Then, even better, you removed much of the text by presenting the descriptions in audio narration. To make the content more friendly you added a tutor agent to explain examples.

Because your target audience will need to apply the new skills to diverse product lines and metrics, you further revised your worked examples to include situations that used a variety of products and product metrics. Last, to help learners process the worked examples effectively, you used your virtual tutor to explain a worked example to himself, followed by a practice exercise that focused on self-explaining.

When you schedule a follow-up storyboard review, you are pleased to report that, in fact, the team has been able to apply a number of research-based principles to the training that will decrease the amount of time and effort the learners will need to apply to acquire the skill. You demonstrate your changes with your new storyboards and end by offering to share some of the research that helped the team implement the changes.

WHAT TO LOOK FOR IN e-LEARNING

☐ Worked examples that illustrate task performance and replace some practice problems for novice learners.

☐ Worked examples are interspersed among practice problems.

☐ Textual explanations are integrated into the graphic elements of an example.

☐ Audio is used to elaborate on a graphic illustration or animated demonstration.

☐ Conversational script and agents are used to present worked examples.

☐ For near transfer skills (procedures), worked examples in the form of demonstrations incorporate job context.

☐ For far transfer skills (principles), several diverse worked examples show application of guidelines to diverse job scenarios.

☐ Complex worked examples are formatted to draw attention to the sub-goals of the problem.

☐ Demonstrations and practice in self-explanations of worked examples are included.

COMING NEXT

One of the unique features of computer training delivered via intranet or Internet is the opportunity for collaboration during self-study. Collaborative tools, including e-mail, message boards, conferencing, and chats, can be used to convert solo learning into a social experience. In the next chapter we will look at what research tells us about the benefits of collaborative learning and how to structure group assignments for maximum benefit.

Suggested Readings

Atkinson, R.K., Derry, S.J., Renkl, A., and Wortham, D. (2000). Learning from Examples: Instructional Principles from the Worked Examples Research. *Review of Educational Research, 70*(2), 181–214.

Chi, M.T.H. (2000). Self-Explaining Expository Tests: The Dual Processes of Generating Inferences and Repairing Mental Models. In R. Glaser (Ed.), *Advances in Instructional Psychology: Educational Design & Cognitive Science.* Hillsdale, NH: Lawrence Erlbaum Associates.

CHAPTER OUTLINE

What Is Collaborative Learning?

Collaborative Learning Versus Knowledge Management

Options for Collaboration in Internet e-Learning

Which Collaborative Tools to Use

What Is Concurrency?

What Are Your Anticipated Learning Goals?

What We Know About Collaboration During Learning

Learning Together Can Be Better Than Learning Alone

Models for Productive Group Collaborations

Jigsaw

Adapting Jigsaw to e-Learning

Structured Controversy

Adapting Structured Controversy to e-Learning

Seven-Jump Method

Adapting Seven-Jump to e-Learning

Scripted Cooperation

Adapting Scripted Cooperation to e-Learning

Psychological Reasons for Collaborative Assignments

The Evidence for Online Collaborative Learning

11

Learning Together on the Web

CHAPTER PREVIEW

e-LEARNING DELIVERED on the Internet or intranets can make use of collaborative facilities such as chat, message boards, online conferencing, and e-mail. Because these computer collaborative opportunities are relatively new, we do not have a strong research base for their value in e-learning. However, we do have many studies showing the learning gains realized from collaborative work in classrooms. In this chapter we summarize the empirical evidence regarding features of collaborative assignments that contribute to classroom learning and suggest how proven classroom collaborative activities could be adapted to e-learning environments.

DESIGN DILEMMA

Three Web-based training vendors have made presentations to the Quality Management Program training selection committee. Quik Learn uses collaborative tools built into their interface that allow learners to participate in chats or discussions about course topics. Figure 11.1 shows a screen from their presentation. The second vendor, Cyber Smart, also includes collaborative opportunities in the form of project assignments and exercises that require learners to work as teams using message boards, chats, and e-mail. Figure 11.2 illustrates a storyboard from their design. The third vendor, Digital School, did not include any collaborative activities in their proposed design.

Figure 11.1. Collaborative Exercise Using a Discussion Board.

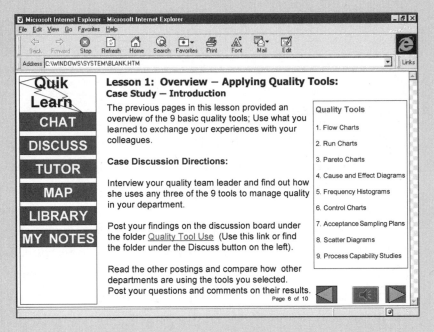

Mark: "I don't think those group activities are a good idea. The whole point of this is to be able to learn only what you need when you need it. If we are going to do a lot of group work, let's just put together a classroom course. I vote for Digital School!"

Marcie: "That's true, Mark, but remember our projections show that it would be costly to pull learners together in a classroom, so maybe we could still get some social interaction through the intranet. I like the interface and discussions we see in Quik Learn."

Mark: "Any kind of group interaction is going to add time to the course. And what benefit do we get from it?"

Marcie: "You're right, but I think there are some advantages to working together. Let me do some research and let's postpone our decision until our next meeting."

Figure 11.2. A Collaborative Team Assignment Using a Discussion Board.

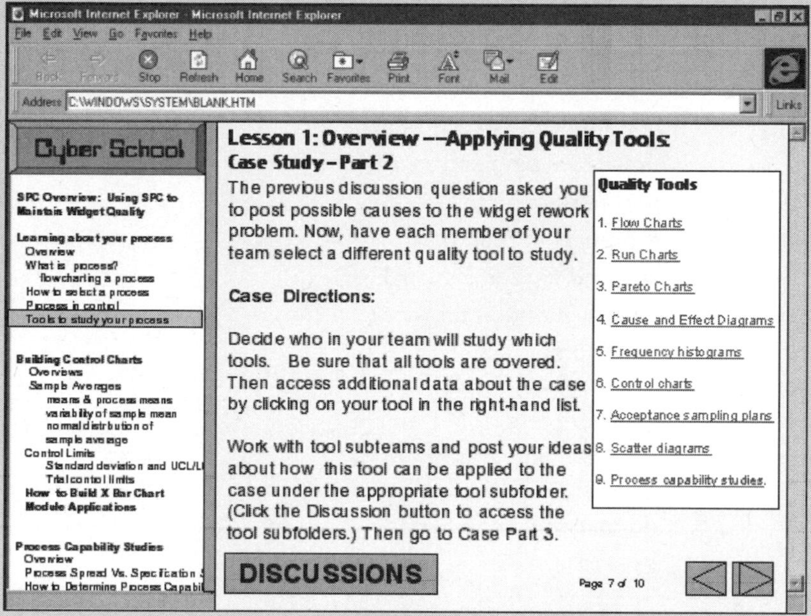

What Is Collaborative Learning?

The first generations of computer-delivered training were designed for solo learning. There were no practical ways to integrate other learners or an instructor into the experience. However, the technology underlying the Internet has changed all of that. Chats, message boards, online conferences, and e-mail provide an array of channels for collaboration. We define collaboration as a structured exchange between two or more participants designed to enhance achievement of the learning objectives. Table 11.1 summarizes these collaborative tools and some of their common applications in e-learning. In spite of the availability of collaborative tools, few organizations other than

Table 11.1. Common Applications of Collaborative Facilities in e-Learning.

Facility	Description	Use in e-Learning
Chats	Two or more participants communicate at the same time, usually by text but sometimes by audio. Usually moderated by a facilitator. (See Figure 11.11.)	• Role-play practice • Group project work • Pair collaborative study
Message Boards	A number of participants communicate at different times by typing comments that remain on the board for others to read and respond to (See Figure 11.3). Usually monitored by a moderator.	• Topic-specific exchanges • Post-class exchanges
Threaded Discussion Boards	A message board in which related comments appear in threads. A running discussion is maintained over time.	• Comments on specific sub-topics
Online Conferencing	A number of participants online at once with a moderator. Offers features to hear comments, send messages (audio or text), display visuals, collaboratively work on a product, and vote. (See Figure 11.12.)	• Guest speakers • Group project work
E-Mail	Two or more participants communicating at different times. Comments received and managed at the individual's mail site.	• Group project work • Instructor-student exchanges • Pair collaborative study

Table 11.1 (Continued).

Facility	Description	Use in e-Learning
List-Servs	Group e-mail where individuals comment on a specific topic and comments are sent to everyone on the list. Recipients can choose digests of list-servs receiving periodic consolidated emails.	• Class announcements

educational institutions are making use of them in e-learning (Galvin, 2001). Is this a missed learning opportunity? In this chapter we address that question by summarizing collaborative assignments for which there is empirical evidence of improved learning outcomes.

Collaborative Learning Versus Knowledge Management

In addition to supporting learning of course content, collaborative tools can also serve a knowledge management function by encouraging learners to exchange their own experiences related to the course topic. For example, Figure 11.3 illustrates some of the discussion topics set up for a quality management course. One of them is a discussion among new users of automated quality tools. That discussion is not designed to promote processing of the course content per se, but rather to add value to the course through participant sharing of work experiences. Learning through knowledge exchange is a valuable feature of online learning.

Options for Collaboration in Internet e-Learning

Some Internet collaboration tools are *synchronous*, that is, occurring simultaneously in real time. You may already be familiar with chat rooms and online conferences—these are synchronous. Others are *asynchronous*, that is, occurring at different times. Message boards and e-mails are asynchronous tools. Some e-learning providers have integrated a variety of collaborative options at the course and lesson interface. For example, the lesson shown in

Figure 11.3. Sample Online Discussion Topics for Information Exchange.

Figure 11.4 offers learners access to chats, discussions, and tutor e-mail at all times via the buttons in the left frame.

Based on empirical evidence from classroom collaborative work, we recommend the following guidelines for use of collaboration tools in e-learning:

- Assign projects to e-learning groups using proven collaborative methodologies such as jigsaw and structured controversy.

- Assign structured discussions to e-learning groups using proven collaborative methodologies such as problem-based learning and peer tutoring.

Which Collaborative Tools to Use

Several factors determine which, if any, collaborative tools will facilitate learning in your instructional situation. Two major factors are the degree of learner concurrency and the learning goal.

Figure 11.4. Courseware That Builds Collaborative Features into the Interface.

With permission from DigitalThink.

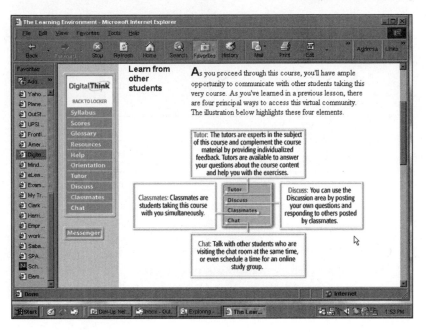

What Is Concurrency?

Concurrency refers to the number of learners active in an e-course in the same time period. To organize our discussion, we look at communication options along a continuum illustrated in Figure 11.5. Highly concurrent learning environments such as distance-learning university courses have set start and end dates. Assignments are completed independently but in a coordinated time frame. For example, consider a class of forty-five learners that starts in October and will be working on Units One and Two during that month. This is a highly concurrent environment. It is thus feasible to make group assignments and plan synchronous and asynchronous exchanges using a range of tools including chats, conferences, e-mail, and message boards.

Some corporate and government training scenarios may have training situations of *moderate concurrency,* in which learners are likely to engage in the same training at roughly the same time. For example, a new e-course on

Figure 11.5. Degrees of Student Concurrency in Online Learning.

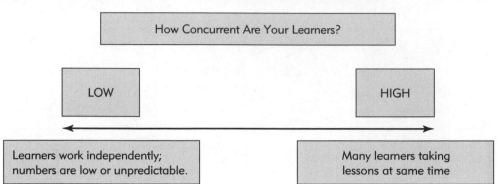

product updates is released for a large group of account representatives who have fourth-quarter goals based on the sale of the new product. Although learners work independently, it is likely that at any given time period, a number of account representatives will be engaged in the training. Another example is a mandatory online course for new hires. If staffing rates are sufficiently high, a number of learners will likely participate simultaneously. In these two situations, tools such as discussion boards, chats, and e-mails or a scheduled expert presentation via conferencing are practical.

In contrast, low concurrent learning environments are characterized by individuals who may start and finish training at any time. They don't start together, they don't use the same amount of elapsed time to complete the course, and they don't finish together. There are no predictable waves of learners going through the training. They may study different course segments, depending on their prerequisites and job needs. Some may complete a learning event quickly and others may not. In other words, everyone enjoys a unique schedule, and the number of learners who are simultaneously engaged in a given instructional unit is unpredictable. In this situation, synchronous events like chats or conferences linked to the instruction are less practical, while message boards and instructor e-mail can play a greater role.

In summary, the degree of learner concurrency in your training environment is a major pragmatic factor that dictates which collaborative techniques and tools you can use to achieve your learning goals.

What Are Your Anticipated Learning Goals?

The training goals are another variable that influence the type of collaborative techniques and tools to use. Procedural courses, such as those that teach new software applications, benefit from different types of collaborative interactions more than conceptual courses focusing on far transfer skills. For example, procedural courses should provide access to instructor e-mail for resolving difficulties. Also, message boards can offer opportunities for participants to share experiences of a new procedure. In contrast, more conceptual courses that focus on far transfer tasks or conceptual knowledge (how to close a sale or design a new product) lend themselves more effectively to collaborative team projects.

What We Know About Collaboration During Learning

If you are designing or evaluating e-learning options, how important are the collaboration features? Does collaboration have a positive impact on learning? How should collaboration be structured? What impact does collaboration have on completion of e-learning? As mentioned earlier, the majority of Web-delivered training, other than that designed by educational institutions, does not use collaborative facilities. About 77 percent of all e-learning is designed for solo use (Galvin, 2001). What evidence is there for the learning value of collaboration during instruction?

Since computer-supported collaborative interactions are relatively new, there is little controlled research from which to draw guidelines. However, we do have many years of research on the benefits of face-to-face collaborative learning. In this chapter we will summarize that research and make suggestions for adapting the findings from classroom collaboration to online environments. As the technology matures, we anticipate more research will shape the guidelines we provide here. In the meantime, we summarize what we know about collaborative learning today.

Learning Together Can Be Better Than Learning Alone

Many studies conducted with all age groups over the past forty years provide evidence that participants who study together often learn more than those who study alone. This has proven true for diverse subject areas and a wide range of tasks and for learners working in small groups as well as in pairs (Johnson and Johnson, 1990). For example, one hundred college students taking a course in abnormal psychology were assigned to four study groups that varied both in degree of collaboration and structure. The *collaborative structured* group required students to study in pairs. Each member of the pair constructed twenty-five multiple choice questions along with answers and explanations. Before each major test, pair members administered their questions to their partners, followed by coaching. The *collaborative unstructured* students also worked in pairs and were given a broad assignment to "discuss course topics" in preparation for the test. The *individual structured* students worked alone generating multiple choice questions, while the *individual unstructured* students worked alone to prepare discussion topics. The final examination test scores are shown in Table 11.2. The results showed best outcomes for learners working together and for learners who followed the structured study format. The highest average was from the pairs that used a structured assignment. From this study we learn that both collaboration and structure contribute to better learning (Fantuzzo, Riggio, Connelly, and Dimeff, 1989).

Not all forms of collaborative learning are equally effective. In a large-scale review, Johnson and Johnson (1990, p. 34) concluded: "Simply placing students in groups and telling them to work together does not in itself promote higher achievement." Similarly, in another review, most studies reported no positive effect for collaborative learning when students studied

Table 11.2. Average Test Scores for Students Working Together and Alone with Structured and Unstructured Study Assignments.
From Fantuzzo, Riggio, Connelly, and Dimeff, 1989.

	High Structure	Low Structure
Together	84.8	70.1
Alone	69.0	66.3

together but were tested individually or when they studied together and created a group product (Slavin, 1983). However, most studies reported a positive learning effect when students studied together and were given a group reward based on the individual progress of all learners in the group (Slavin, 1983). A recent analysis of many research studies found that when learning from computer-delivered training in classroom settings, small groups learned significantly more than individuals learned under optimal conditions that included previous group work experience and use of cooperative group learning strategies (Lou, Abrami, and d'Apollonia, 2001). The use of collaborative methods in e-learning is a potentially powerful technique but one that warrants a great deal of additional research to define the circumstances under which collaboration is best used.

The educational community has acknowledged the potential benefits of collaborative learning and is now working to define the specific factors that make collaborative learning most powerful (Cohen, 1994; National Research Council, 1994a). The following guidelines summarize the best practices for implementation of collaborative learning in classroom environments that are likely to apply to e-learning collaboration as well.

Guideline One: Make Assignments That Require Collaboration Among Learners. Unless there is some reason to interact, learners assigned to groups may still tackle tasks individually. For example, we often ask learners to get acquainted in small groups at the start of a class. We ask one person to be a spokesperson and summarize the experience and learning goals of their group to the whole class. Our intention is to stimulate introductory group dialog. However, some groups avoid interaction by assigning each person to write a personal summary on a piece of paper and turn it in to the spokesperson. If verbal interaction is our goal, we need to develop a better assignment that requires group interaction. To get learning benefit, collaborative tasks must be designed in a way that requires learners to interact and contribute to a group outcome. The lesson must make structured assignments of sufficient scope and complexity that cannot be achieved by a single participant working alone. In this chapter we summarize some face-to-face techniques you can adapt to e-learning that reflect this guideline.

Guideline Two: Assign Learners to Groups in Ways That Optimize Interaction.
Collaborative learning assignments yield best outcomes for learners working
in pairs or in small groups. Group sizes above five or six are discouraged since
the larger size may not offer sufficient opportunity for everyone to interact
fully. In addition, research has shown that heterogeneous groups get better
learning outcomes than homogeneous groups. Therefore, assign teams based
on an assessment of learner background knowledge. When possible, mix
students with different backgrounds rather than allowing learners to self-select
their own learning teams.

Guideline Three: Structure Group Assignments Around Products or Processes. We
know that collaborative learning benefits from structured assignments.
Effective collaborative assignments can require the development of a project
or can simply specify a process for a structured discussion. We will look at
these two alternatives in the following paragraphs.

Product-Oriented Collaboration. In product-oriented collaboration, a tangible output such as a report or design is a vehicle for stimulating group collaboration with subsequent learning. For conceptual learning that involves
product design or problem-solving and no one correct solution, assign collaborative projects to foster maximum interaction, mutual exchange, and in-
depth discussions. Research has shown that when working on these types of
projects, the amount of interaction in the group is predictive of learning
(Cohen, 1994). We recommend that you develop project assignments that
adapt a proven classroom structured collaborative methodology. These
methodologies provide a process for groups to follow as they work together
on a final product. This product may be a report, software designed to
achieve specified outcomes, a marketing plan for a new product, or engi-
neering specifications for a manufacturing process. The lesson must provide
sufficient guidance and resources to ensure productive collaboration but leave
enough openness and ambiguity to stimulate creativity and challenge.

Process-Oriented Collaboration. Process-oriented collaboration does not
involve production of a tangible product per se, but rather focuses on the
learning that can be gained from structured group exchange. As an example,

some medical schools in the 1980s moved from traditional science lecture and lab formats to a form of collaborative learning called problem-based learning (PBL). At some universities the PBL format has expanded beyond medical education. For example, at the University of Maastricht, the Netherlands, PBL is used in the law, economics, medical, and psychology curricula and has been extensively evaluated (Schmidt and Moust, 2000). In these classes, groups start a lesson with a problem-discussion meeting. They follow a structured process to discuss the problem, define learning issues, conduct independent study, and reconvene to discuss problem solutions. There is no tangible product generated in PBL; the learning is stimulated by the group interaction around a problem and the follow-up research activities. Other process-oriented techniques involve various forms of peer tutoring in which pairs work together following study guidelines to prepare for course tests such as the mutual question-asking technique used by the college students in the abnormal psychology class described previously.

Whether you select product or process models, effective structuring of the collaborative assignment to maximize interactions is a critical factor for success. In addition, the degree of concurrency in your learning environment and the types of collaborative facilities your technology support will shape the collaborative learning assignments that you can implement. In the next section we provide specific principles for adapting structured collaborative classroom techniques to your e-learning environment.

Models for Productive Group Collaborations

A number of structured methodologies for productive face-to-face collaborative learning interactions have evolved over the past forty years. Since these have been shown to improve learning in the classroom, they make a good starting place for planning productive e-learning collaborative assignments. We will have to look to future research to validate their effectiveness in the online environment. The specific techniques we will discuss are summarized in Table 11.3 and include: jigsaw, structured controversy, seven-jump method of problem-based learning, and scripted cooperation for peer tutoring.

Table 11.3. Features of Structured Collaborative Techniques.

Technique	Task	Size	Outcome
Jigsaw	Far Transfer Conceptual	Small Group (4–5)	Tangible Product
Structured Controversy	Far Transfer Conceptual	Two Pairs	Tangible Product
Problem-Based Learning	Far Transfer Conceptual	Small Group (5–8)	Group Process
Peer Tutoring	Near or Far Transfer	Pairs	Process

Jigsaw

The jigsaw method uses two team structures—home teams and specialty sub-teams. Several home teams made up of five to seven members work independently on an assignment such as to design a product, to prepare a report, or to complete some project related to the instructional goal. The assignment must be of sufficient scope and challenge to invite multiple sources of knowledge and skills. After an initial period of work, home teams divide and meet with members from different home teams to form sub-teams, which focus on a specific aspect related to the core assignment. Each home team member participates in a separate sub-team. Sub-teams work together to master their topic and then the members return to their home team. Each member then teaches a piece of the conceptual puzzle to fellow home team members and applies that piece to the final product. For example, if the class has three home teams of six members each, six sub-teams of three members each would work together to gain expertise on a sub-topic related to the home team assignment. When the home teams reconvene, each member would have different expertise to share with the home team, which would then assimilate all lessons learned into the final assignment.

Adapting Jigsaw to e-Learning

Applying jigsaw to e-learning is straightforward in environments of high or moderate concurrency and can also be adapted to situations of low concurrency. In high or moderate concurrency, learners will form home teams similar to standard classroom procedures. A project is assigned in the e-course, such as the widget rework case shown in Figure 11.6 from the quality management course. Learners link with other online participants to begin the home team assignment. After working on an initial project, each home team member is then assigned to a sub-team. For example, in the quality course, learners individually select a quality tool to study with their sub-team, as shown in Figure 11.7. Members of each sub-team can go to a message board with an assignment linked to one of the sub-topics. Ideally they can work with others active on that sub-topic to review previous discussions and, after researching available resources, make their own additions and synthesis of the discussion to take back to the home team. In the final phase, the home team uses e-mail, chat, or conference session to integrate the findings of each member into a final project, as shown in Figure 11.8.

Figure 11.6. Jigsaw Home Team Case Assignment.

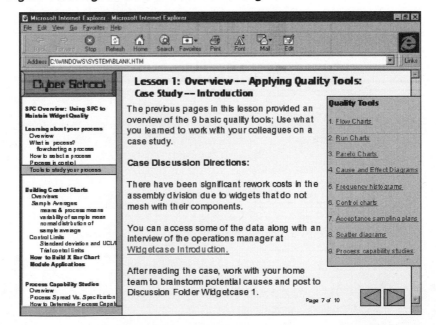

Figure 11.7. Jigsaw Sub-Team Case Assignment.

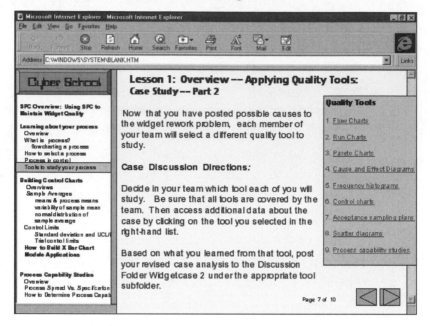

Figure 11.8. Jigsaw Final Home Team Case Assignment.

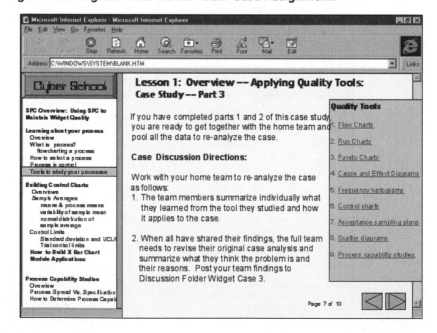

Environments with low learner concurrency can use a form of jigsaw in which an individual learner contributes to an ongoing learning project. After reviewing the status of the project to date on a project Web page, the learner selects a topic to research from specified subtopics and can use both sub-topic message boards and individual research to build expertise on his or her chosen topic. The individual learner then makes a change or contribution to the ongoing learning project based on his or her specialty topic. Figure 11.9 illustrates how the widget rework collaborative case assignment has been revised for low learner concurrency environments. While this adaptation lacks the benefits of synchronous collaboration, it does allow course members to access the work of others and to contribute to an ongoing effort.

Structured Controversy

In Chapter Nine we summarized a study that showed that learners who were given an assignment to write a pro and con argument learned more than learners asked to write a narration or summary (Wiley and Voss,

Figure 11.9. Jigsaw Assignment Adapted for Low Concurrency Environment.

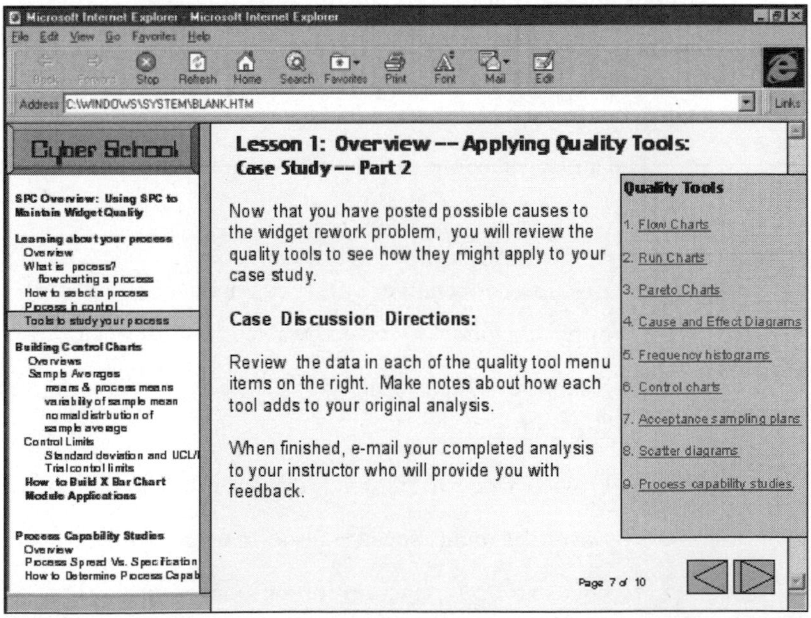

1999). The deeper processing stimulated by synthesizing opposing aspects of an issue led to more learning than merely writing a summary. You can take advantage of a natural tendency for conflict to arise in a group assignment by channeling it in a productive direction. Johnson and Johnson (1992) developed a structured methodology for group argumentation they call *structured controversy*. In the classroom, learners are assigned to heterogeneous teams of four. The teams are presented with an issue or problem that lends itself to a pro and con position. The teams divide into pairs, each of which takes one side and researches it, developing a strong position for their perspective. After a period of time, the team of four reconvenes and one pair presents their argument to the other. After the presentation, the receiving pair must state back the argument adequately to the presenting pair to demonstrate their understanding of the presentation team's argument. Then the pairs reverse roles. All team members develop an understanding of both perspectives. After the argumentation stage, the full team moves into a synthesis stage where the opposing perspectives are merged into a reasoned position that culminates in a group report or presentation.

Comparing the structured controversy method of collaborative learning with several alternative assignments, including debates, individual learning, or groups that stressed concurrence, the structured controversy method proved more effective, with effect sizes ranging from .42 to .77 (Johnson and Johnson, 1992).

The authors recommend the following factors for successful constructive controversy:

- Ensure a cooperative context where the goal is first understanding the opposing views, followed by a synthesis of perspectives.
- Structure groups to include learners of mixed background knowledge and ability.
- Provide access to rich and relevant information about the issues.
- Ensure adequate social skills to manage conflict.
- Focus group interactions on rational arguments.

Adapting Structured Controversy to e-Learning

Since this collaborative technique involves small groups of four, it could readily be adapted to e-learning environments of high- or medium-learner concurrency. At an appropriate Web site, accessible within the course or from the online classroom environment, design an application problem or case that lends itself to two or more alternative perspectives. Also provide links to relevant resources. Instruct participants to take one of the positions and find an online classmate interested in that same position. The pair will then work through e-mail or chat to research their position and develop their case. Next they post their argument to the message board, and either together or individually review opposing arguments. They can post their summary of those arguments to verify understanding. To complete the exercise, either the pair or an individual can produce and post a final product to an online gallery that represents a synthesis of all perspectives. Figures 11.10 and 11.11 illustrate

Figure 11.10. Application of Structured Controversy Method to an Online Assignment.

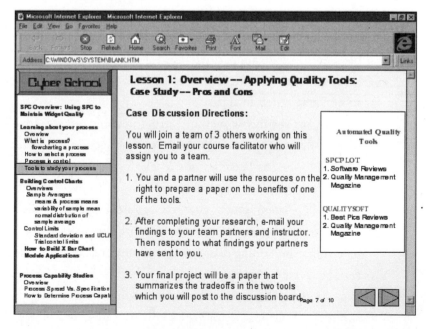

Figure 11.11. Use of Chat for Discussion of Structured Controversy Topics.

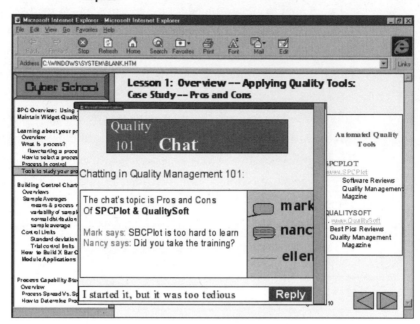

how this might be adapted to the quality management course. In these screens, learning pairs are assigned to research one of two quality tools, making a case for its benefits. After responding to the benefits of the other tool posted by other team partners, the four learners synthesize what they have learned about the benefits and tradeoffs of the two tools in an online chat session and write a final paper.

As with the jigsaw method, structured controversy involves development of several products. As the degree of concurrency decreases, the management of teams becomes overwhelming and the benefits derived from ongoing interactions with others diminishes. However, the opportunity to research a position, post a report or argument, and synthesize one's position with opposing positions posted by others still remains. For example, a graduate course in training design assigns a project that requires learners to contrast behavioral with cognitive instructional methods. A learner selects one of the two approaches and conducts research on it. After submitting her research summary to the instructor via e-mail, she can view a Web page that offers opposing viewpoints and prepare a summary that captures the opposite view.

Alternatively, she can participate in a message board discussion in which other learners have posted their viewpoints for either approach. Finally, she would prepare a synthesis of both viewpoints and e-mail it to the instructor.

Seven-Jump Method

The University of Maastricht in the Netherlands has adopted problem-based learning (PBL) in various curriculum areas and has evaluated it extensively (Schmidt and Moust, 2000). Groups of eight to ten students without any prior preparation meet with a tutor to discuss a problem like the one shown in the following box. In working with PBL, the faculty found that maximum benefit was gained with a structured group process they call seven-jump. After reading the problem, the group process follows this sequence:

1. Clarify unknown terms and concepts.

2. Define the problem in the case.

3. Analyze the problem by brainstorming different plausible explanations.

4. Critique the different explanations produced and try to draft a coherent description of the process.

5. Define the learning issues.

6. Engage in self-directed study to fill the gaps specified by the learning issues.

7. Meet with the group, share learnings, and develop a final description of the process.

A SAMPLE CASE PROBLEM USED IN PBL

THE MISERABLE LIFE OF A STOMACH

The protagonist of our story is the stomach of a truck driver who used to work shifts and who smokes a lot. The stomach developed a gastric ulcer and so the smoking stopped. Stomach tablets are now a regular part of the intake.

While on the highway in Southern Germany, our stomach had to digest a heavy German lunch. Half an hour later, a severe abdominal pain developed. The stomach had to expel the meal. Two tablets of acetylsalicylic acid were inserted to relieve the pain.

A second extrusion some hours later contained a bit of blood. In a hospital in Munich an endoscope was inserted. The stomach needed to be operated upon in the near future. Explain. (Schmidt and Moust, 2000)

Adapting Seven-Jump to e-Learning

While developed for face-to-face meetings, the structure of the seven-jump method may lend itself to online collaboration through computer conferencing, chats, or e-mail. In this collaborative technique, there is little emphasis on a tangible product, so it is the process that is most critical. Thus, it may be that collaborative tools with minimal communication time lag, such as chat or conference, will provide the best vehicles for online implementation. Ideally, a small group of learners could jointly read a case and follow the seven-jump process. Step three (involving brainstorming) is best facilitated through some type of synchronous interaction. Steps one, two, four, five, and seven could be handled asynchronously via e-mail and/or postings to a group discussion board. Figure 11.12 shows an online conference from the quality

Figure 11.12. Use of Conferencing Software to Collaborate on a Project.

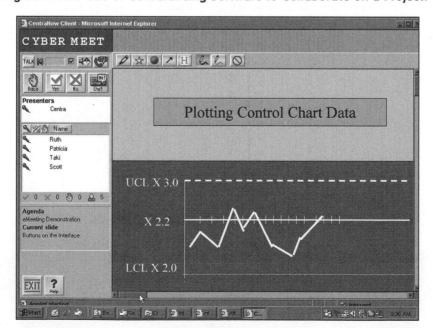

management course about a case involving control charts. Depending on the specific Web ware used for the conference session, the control chart can be updated by participants in the conference, or at least manipulated by the moderator in response to specific participant comments.

In situations of low learner concurrency, the advantages of dynamic discussions may be lost. These issues are topics of current research that will provide us guidelines in the future.

Scripted Cooperation

Scripted cooperation has been successfully used with college students working in pairs to study textual instructional materials. Pairs who used the methodology learned more than individuals studying alone (O'Donnell and Dansereau, 1992). Scripted cooperation requires pairs of learners to follow a structured assignment as they study together. A sample process for the pair to follow is:

Each member of the pair reads the same text assignment.

One member then summarizes the key points to the listener.

The listener points out any inaccuracies or omissions by the summarizer.

They both work to find effective study strategies for the material, such as forming analogies, creating images, and so on.

After completing the study strategies, they read a second selection of text, reversing roles on summarization and critique.

The following guidelines have been derived from more than ten years of research on learning with scripted cooperation:

Use pairs, since interaction is maximized between two individuals. Research showed that participants who remain relatively passive consistently perform worse than those who are actively engaged.

Provide pairs with specific interactive process guidelines (scripts) rather than allowing participants to develop their own process.

Assign heterogeneous pairs with respect to ability or cognitive style. The performance of high-ability individuals does not suffer and that of lower-ability learners is improved.

Adapt the interactive script to the characteristics and task-relevant skills of
   participants.

In a recent study, groups of information technology students were assigned
a case problem to design a technology solution that would increase customer
satisfaction in a retail setting. Learners worked on the problem alone and in
pairs and with and without questions such as, "How would you define the
problem?" and "What are the arguments for your proposed solution?" Overall, pairs engaged in better problem-solving than individuals, learners with
questions engaged in better problem-solving than learners without questions,
and the combination of pairs with questions did the best (Ge and Land, 2002).

Adapting Scripted Cooperation to e-Learning

The use of synchronous exchanges via chats or conferences would provide an
online communication environment closest to the face-to face experience of
the classroom scripted-cooperation method. Would similar benefits be realized by pairs that follow a script in an asynchronous fashion? How would
their outcomes compare with learners working alone and with learners working synchronously through chats? Would asynchronous scripts need to differ
from synchronous scripts? These questions will require further research on
collaborative virtual learning.

Psychological Reasons for Collaborative Assignments

In Chapter Two we summarized the need for learners to attend to important
information in the lesson and to integrate new knowledge with existing
knowledge in long-term memory. Well-structured collaborative assignments
that maximize interactions among all participants support both of these
processes.

For PBL small-group discussions, it is the cognitive process of integration that mediates learning (Schmidt and Moust, 2000). Effective integration
requires the activation of prior knowledge in long-term memory. College students who had studied osmosis in high school discussed one of two problems: the behavior of red blood cells in distilled and salty water or the factors

affecting airplane takeoff. After the group discussions, all students read a text on osmosis and diffusion. On a follow-up test, students who participated in the blood cell discussion groups recalled almost twice as much information about osmosis as the airplane discussion group, even though both groups studied the same text on osmosis. The discussion of the red cell problem activated the osmosis knowledge students had learned in high school. This activation of relevant prior knowledge promoted better integration of new information, resulting in improved learning.

Of course, other techniques can be used to activate prior knowledge in learners. For example, learners might be asked to answer questions or write down everything they know about a topic. However, the same study compared the relative effect of discussion groups versus individual analysis. Small group discussions had a larger positive effect than individual assignments. Confronting a problem and discussing the problem in a small group have independent positive effects on prior knowledge and subsequent learning (Schmidt and Moust, 2000).

The Evidence for Online Collaborative Learning

At the start of the chapter we summarized research findings on collaborative learning in the classroom environment. As of this time, we do not have sufficient replicated evidence on learning outcomes from online collaboration to make definitive statements about them. Two recent reports compared the quality of communication in face-to-face with online collaborative discussions for learners in programs on leadership (Jonassen and Kwon, 2001), and medicine (Kamin, O'Sullivan, and Deterdin, 2002). Both report patterns of deeper communication in the online discussions, possibly due to greater accountability, visibility, and opportunities for reflection afforded by the written asynchronous online discussions.

Online collaborations that were supported by guiding statements such as "We have not yet reached consensus concerning these aspects" or "My proposals for an adjustment of the analysis are" resulted in deeper communications and better learning outcomes than collaborations that had no supporting questions or had specific content-oriented questions (Mandl, Weinberger, and

Fischer, 2002). Since online communication is an active area of current research, we anticipate more guidelines will emerge in the next few years.

DESIGN DILEMMA: RESOLUTION

When Mark and Marcie reconvene their meeting the following week, Marcie takes charge of the discussion. She says, "I found out that collaboration can improve learning outcomes and that most learners like it. But to really get value out of collaboration, it needs to be structured in a way to ensure participation of everyone involved in meaningful ways. Since we have over one hundred operators and supervisors worldwide who will be taking the course in a three-month timeframe during the quality management rollout, we can maximize their learning by selecting a vendor who offers online collaboration. I'm going to recommend Cyber Smart. The reason is that their team exercises are designed in a way that will require the operators to work with each other and with their supervisors to complete well-designed projects. There is some solid research behind the type of collaborative exercises that Cyber Smart has used."

WHAT TO LOOK FOR IN e-LEARNING

☐ Structured group assignments requiring project outcomes that are based on well-designed cases, along with resources to work those cases

☐ Assignments that use e-mail, chat, conferencing, and message boards appropriate to the degree of concurrency in the learning environment

☐ Structured group discussions on well-designed case problems that make use of chats or conferencing, accompanied by resources to research follow-up issues

☐ Structured study assignments for pairs of learners that make use of e-mail or chats

☐ Knowledge management facilities to extend learning through discussion boards

☐ Student-instructor e-mail used for questions and for evaluating projects

Suggested Readings

Cohen, E.G. (1994). Restructuring the Classroom: Conditions for Productive Small Groups. *Review of Educational Research, 64*(1), 1–35.

Lou, Y., Abrami, P.C., and d'Apollonia, S. (2001). Small Group and Individual Learning with Technology: A Meta-Analysis. *Review of Educational Research, 71*(3), 449–521.

National Research Council. (1994). Cooperative Learning. In D. Druckman and R. Bjork (Eds.), *Learning Remembering Believing.* Washington D.C.: National Academy Press.

Schmidt, H.E., and Moust, J.H.C. (2000). Factors Affecting Small-Group Tutorial Learning: A Review of Research. In D.H. Evensen and C.E. Hmelo (Eds.) *Problem Based Learning.* Mahwah, New Jersey: Earlbaum.

CHAPTER OUTLINE

Learner Control Versus Program Control
>   Popularity of Learner Control
>
>   Navigational Features to Implement Learner Control

Do Learners Make Good Instructional Decisions?
>   Do You Know What You Think You Know? Calibration Accuracy
>
>   Do Learners Like Lesson Features That Lead to Learning?

Psychological Reasons for Poor Learner Choices

Learner Control Principle One: Use Learner Control for Learners with High Prior Knowledge or High Metacognitive Skills
>   Who Learns Best Under Learner Control?
>
>   Evidence That Program Control Is Best
>
>   Evidence That Learner Control Works Better Later in Learning

Learner Control Principle Two: Make Important Instructional Events the Default Navigation Option

Learner Control Principle Three: Add Advisement to Learner Control

Navigational Guidelines for Learner Control
>   Use Links Sparingly to Augment the Lesson
>
>   Allow Learners to Control Pacing
>
>   Use Course Maps to Provide an Overview and Orient Learners
>
>   Provide Basic Navigation Options on All Screens

12

Do Surfing and Learning Mix?

THE EFFECTIVENESS OF LEARNER CONTROL IN e-LEARNING

CHAPTER PREVIEW

LEARNER CONTROL, in which navigational features allow learners to select the topics and instructional elements they prefer, has always been popular with learners. High user control defines the Internet, so learners taking courses on the Internet will expect similar choices. Unfortunately, high learner control often is not the best design when high levels of skill attainment are important. Many learners do not make good instructional decisions. Psychologically this is due to variation in learning management (metacognitive) skills among learners. In this chapter we present the evidence to recommend that you design navigational options based on the tradeoffs among the following: learner preferences, production costs and time, criticality of skill attainment, and the profile of your learning audience.

DESIGN DILEMMA

You and your e-learning design team are discussing the navigation controls for the quality management training currently under development:

Sam: "Here's my first cut at the navigation controls. (See Figure 12.1.) We'll set it up so the learner can jump to any topic she wants and can skip lesson topics she doesn't find relevant. And I'm adding a lot of links so the learner can jump to the practice exercises if she wants them or skip them if she feels she understands the concepts. I'll also make new terms hot links so learners can bring up definitions. That's what people expect on the Web. They are used to going where they want and doing what they want."

Figure 12.1. Navigational Elements Designed for High Learner Control.

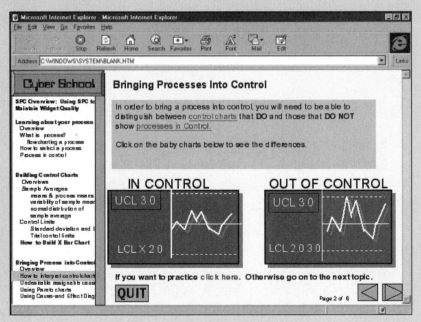

Sue: "But Sam, learning a new skill is not the same as surfing for information. We are building the lessons and topics in a logical sequence and including worked examples and practice exercises that should not be bypassed. I think all those control options you've designed put the instruction at risk. Many learners don't really know what they should select."

Sam: "You instructional folks have to quit holding learners by the hand. They are grown-ups and can make these decisions themselves! And they will like it much better if they can make their own choices. The whole point of e-learning is choices—take those away and you lose the power of the Internet!"

Sam and Sue are disagreeing about learner control. Control over learning has been a common feature of computer-delivered instruction. Certainly the underlying scheme of the Internet is freedom of movement. But what about Sue's concerns for learning? How effective is learner control in training? Fortunately we have evidence from research and from cognitive theory to resolve this dilemma.

Learner Control Versus Program Control

In contrast to classroom instruction, e-learning can allow learners to select the topics they want, control the pace at which they progress, and decide whether to bypass some lesson elements such as examples or practice exercises. When learners have the option to make these kinds of choices, we say the instruction offers *learner control*. In contrast, when the course and lesson offer few learner choices, the instruction is under *program control*. Most classroom instruction operates in program control mode. Classroom training typically progresses at the same pace for everyone, follows a linear sequence, and uses the same teaching techniques for all. The instructor and textbook provide a single learning path. On the other hand, computer-delivered instruction can offer many or few options and thus can be designed to be learner controlled or program-controlled.

Although the term learner control is often used generically, the actual type of control varies. Thus, two courses that are depicted as "high in learner-control" may in fact offer quite different learner options. In general, control options fall into three arenas:

1. *Content Sequencing.* Learners can control the order of the lessons, topics, and screens within a lesson. Many e-courses allow content control through a course menu from which learners select lessons in any sequence they wish.

2. *Pacing.* Learners can control the time spent on each lesson. With the exception of short video or audio sequences, a standard adopted in virtually all e-learning allows learners to progress through the training at their own rate, spending as much or as little time as they wish on any given screen. Likewise, the option to exit is made available on every screen.

3. *Access to Learning Support.* Learners can control instructional components of lessons such as examples or practice exercises. Within a given lesson, learners may find navigation buttons, links, or tabs that, if selected, lead to course objectives, definitions, additional references, coaches, examples, or practice exercises. In contrast, a program-controlled lesson would provide all instructional components as the learners click the "forward" button.

Figure 12.2 shows a screen for a course that allows control over all three of these arenas. At the bottom right of the screen the directional arrows

Figure 12.2. A Lesson with Multiple Navigational Control Elements.
With permission from Element K.

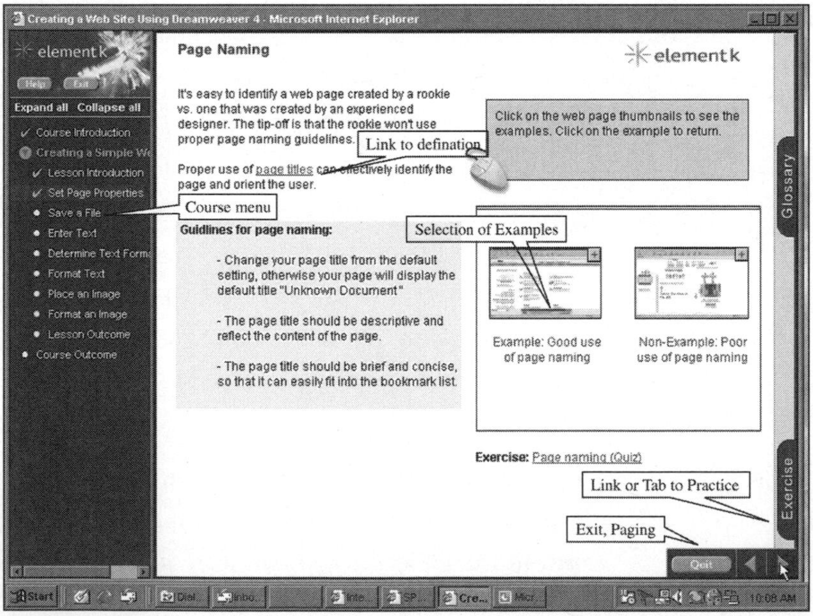

provide for movement forward or backwards at the learner's own pace. The course uses Microsoft standard control buttons in the upper right-hand corner of the screen as well as the orange button in the lower right to exit. In the left-hand frame, the course map allows learners to select lessons in any sequence. Within the central lesson frame, the learner can decide to study the examples by clicking on the baby screens to enlarge them. Learners can also select a practice exercise by either clicking on the link below the examples or on the navigational tab on the right-hand side.

Popularity of Learner Control

Learning outcomes from learner and program control are mixed. However, there is one consistent finding—learners like learner control! To the extent that appeal to the learner is a major goal of your instructional projects, learner control is a definite satisfier. Given the high control features inherent on the Internet, it is likely that learners will expect the same kind of freedom in e-learning courses.

Navigational Features to Implement Learner Control

In e-learning there are several common navigational techniques for implementing learner control, including:

- Course menus, often placed in the left-hand frame, allow learners to select specific lessons and topics within a lesson, as illustrated in Figures 12.1 and 12.2. Alternative formats include menu screens at the introduction and section "tabs" analogous to workbook lesson tabs. In other situations, separate windows accessed from a navigation button on the screen contain the course map. To help learners track progress within a course, it is common to highlight modules, lessons, or topics that have been completed.

- Links placed within the primary teaching frame allow learners to access content from other sites on the Internet or from other sections within the course. Links may lead to separate sites, to different pages in the course, or to windows that overlay the page. The links shown in Figure 12.2 lead to practice exercise pages in the course or definitions from the course glossary that appear in windows over the page.

- Pop-ups or mouse-overs provide additional information, without the learner having to leave the page. For example in Figure 12.3, placing the mouse-over parts of the software screen brings up a short explanation that "pops" up near the relevant part.

- Buttons that activate forward, backward, and quit options permit movement within the lesson and are standard features in e-learning.

- Guided tours are overviews accessible from the main menu screen that demonstrate the resources available in a course. These are most typically used in courses that offer high learner control and include multiple resources for the learner.

Figure 12.3. Explanatory Text Boxes Appear When Parts of the Application Screen Are Touched by the Mouse.

With permission from Element K.

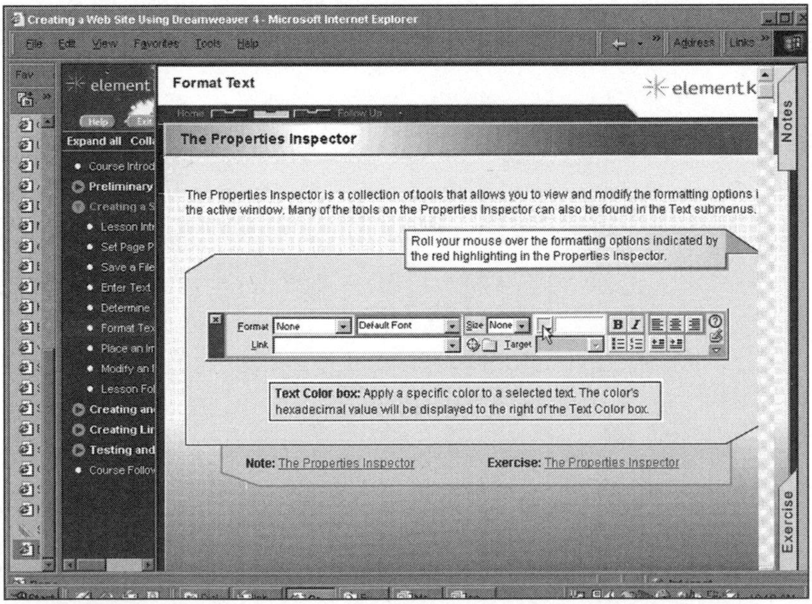

Rather than advise for or against learner control, we provide guidelines and illustrations for *when and how* learner control can most effectively be provided. Additionally, we summarize both the evidence and the psychological reasons for these guidelines to help you adapt them to your own unique situations. Learner control can be effective if learners are able to make accurate decisions about their learning needs. But how accurate are learner self-assessments?

Do Learners Make Good Instructional Decisions?

The extent to which learners can make accurate determinations of their existing knowledge will have a major impact on what kinds of decisions they make in a highly learner-controlled environment. For example, if learners can accurately assess which topics they do and do not comprehend, they can make good selections about topics to study and how much time and effort to put into studying those topics. In short, they are capable of good achievement under conditions of learner control. We have two lines of evidence addressing this question: calibration accuracy and student lesson ratings.

Do You Know What You Think You Know? Calibration Accuracy

Suppose you have to take a test on basic statistics. Prior to taking the test, you are asked to estimate your level of confidence in your knowledge. You know that even though you took statistics in college, you are a little rusty on some of the formulas. But you figure that you can score around 70 percent. After taking the test, you find your actual score is 55 percent. The correlation between your confidence estimate and your actual performance is called calibration. Had you guessed 55 percent, your calibration would have been perfect. Test your own calibration now by answering this question: What is the capital of Australia? As you state your answer, also estimate your confidence in your answer as high, medium, or low. We will return to this example later.

HOW CALIBRATION IS MEASURED

In a typical calibration experiment, learners read a text and then are asked to make a confidence rating about their accuracy in responding to test questions about the text. The correlation between their confidence ratings, typically on a one to six scale, and their actual score is *calibration*. If there is no relationship between confidence and accuracy, the correlation is close to zero. Calibration is an important skill. If learners are well-calibrated, they can make accurate estimates of their knowledge and should be able to make appropriate instructional decisions in courses high in learner control. The focus of calibration measurement is not so much on what we actually know, but on the accuracy of what we think we know. If you don't think you know much and in fact your test score is low, you have good calibration.

Research on calibration has shown that, while most of us do in fact have a good general sense of what we do and do not know, our specific calibration accuracy tends to be poor (Stone, 2000). Glenberg and his associates (1987) found that calibration correlations were close to zero, leading them to conclude that "contrary to intuition, poor calibration of comprehension is the rule, rather than the exception" (p. 119).

In comparing calibration of individuals before and after taking the test, accuracy is generally better after responding to test questions than before. Therefore, providing questions in training should lead to more accurate calibrations. Walczyk and Hall (1989) found this to be true in a study in which they compared the calibration of learners who studied using four resources: text alone, text plus examples, text plus questions, and text plus examples and questions. Calibration was best among those who studied from the version with examples and questions. Along similar lines, a pretest that matches the knowledge and skills of post-tests has been reported to improve calibration (Glenberg, Sanocki, Epstein, and Morris, 1987). Glenberg and his colleagues (1992) refer to the subjective assessment of knowledge as "illusions of knowing." By the way, the capital of Australia is not Sydney, as many people guess with high confidence. It is Canberra.

Do Learners Like Lesson Features That Lead to Learning?

Similar findings have been found in studies that compared *actual learning* with *learner ratings* of how much they learned and liked the instruction after the course. Dixon (1990) compared course ratings with actual learning for more than 1,400 employees who participated in classroom training on implementation of a new manufacturing process. At the end of the class, learners completed an end-of-course rating form in which they assessed the amount of new information they learned, rated their enjoyment of the session, and rated the skill of the instructor. These ratings were then correlated with the amount of actual learning determined by a valid post-test. The result? There was no correlation between ratings and actual learning.

Do students learn more when matched to their preferences in lesson features? In one recent study, participants were surveyed before taking a course regarding their preferences for amount of practice—high or low. They were then assigned to two e-learning courses—one with many practice exercises and a second identical course with half the amount of practice. Half the learners were matched to their preference and half mismatched. The results showed that *regardless of their preference,* those assigned to the full practice version achieved significantly higher scores on the post-test than those in the shorter version (Schnackenberg, Sullivan, Leader, and Jones, 1998). The authors conclude that "the results are more consistent with past evidence that students' preferences and judgments often may not be good indicators of the way they learn best" (p. 14).

Psychological Reasons for Poor Learner Choices

Metacognition is the mind's operating system. In short, metacognition is awareness of how one's mind works. Individuals with high metacognitive skills set realistic learning goals and use effective study strategies. They have high levels of learning management skills. For example, if faced with a certification test, they would plan a study schedule. Based on accurate assessments of their current strengths and weaknesses, they would focus their time and efforts on the topics most needed for achievement. They would use appropriate study techniques based on an accurate assessment of the requirements of the certification. However, learners with poor metacognitive skills are prone to poor understanding of how they learn, which will lead to flawed decisions under conditions of high learner control.

How can you best apply the evidence and the psychology behind learner control to your selection and design of effective e-courses? Based on empirical evidence, we recommend three guidelines for the best use of learner control to optimize learning:

- Use learner control for learners with high prior knowledge or metacognitive skills and/or in lessons or courses that are advanced rather than introductory.

- When learner control is used, design the default navigation options to lead to important instructional course elements.

- Include advice based on valid test questions to help learners make effective instructional decisions.

Learner Control Principle One: Use Learner Control for Learners with High Prior Knowledge or High Metacognitive Skills

As we have seen, learners prefer to have full control over their instructional options but often don't make good judgments about their instructional needs—especially those who are novice to the content and/or who lack good metacognitive skills. Hence the e-learning designer and consumer must consider the multiple tradeoffs of learner control, including learner satisfaction, the profile of the target learners, the cost of designing learner-controlled instruction, and the criticality of skills being taught. Fortunately there are design options that can provide both learner control and instructional effectiveness.

Who Learns Best Under Learner Control?

A review of research on learner versus program control concludes that two types of learners do not excel in a learner-controlled environment: learners with little prior knowledge of the subject, and learners with poor metacognitive skills when they take moderate to complex courses (Steinberg, 1989). Learner control is more likely to be successful:

- When learners have prior knowledge of the content and skills involved in the training

- When the subject is a more advanced lesson in a course or a more advanced course in a curriculum

- When learners have good metacognitive skills

- When the course is of low complexity

Evidence That Program Control Is Best

Young (1996) compared outcomes of learners with high and low self-regulatory (metacognitive) skills who took four computer lessons in either a learner control or program control mode. Under learner control, participants could select or bypass definitions, examples, and practice exercises, whereas those in the program-controlled version were presented with all the above options. Those in the learner-controlled version looked at less than 50 percent of the total number of screens available. As summarized in Table 12.1,

Table 12.1. Test Scores of High and Low Metacognitive Learners Studying Under Learner or Program Control.

From Young, 1996.

	Learner Controlled	Program Controlled
Low Metacognitive Skill	20%	79%
High Metacognitive Skill	60%	82%

Young found that learners with low metacognitive skills learned less in the learner-controlled mode than any of the other three groups.

Evidence That Learner Control Works Better Later in Learning

A computer-based lesson in chemistry compared the outcomes from program control and learner control over the sequence of tasks and number of practice exercises completed (Lee and Lee, 1991). The outcomes were further compared for early stages of learning versus later stages of learning, when learners would have acquired a knowledge base. Program control gave better results during initial learning, while learner control was more effective at later stages. This supports the hypothesis that learners with greater prior knowledge are able to make more appropriate decisions under conditions of learner control. Based on evidence to date, we recommend that when selecting or designing courseware for novice learners who lack good learning regulation skills, look for courses with greater program control—at least in the beginning lessons in a course.

Learner Control Principle Two: Make Important Instructional Events the Default Navigation Option

Practice during learning is an important instructional method that leads to expertise. We also know that learners prefer learner control, and in many e-learning environments, they can easily drop out if not satisfied. Therefore, if you are using high learner control, set up the default option to lead to important instructional elements such as practice exercises. In other words, require the learner to make a deliberate choice to bypass practice.

Research by Schnackenberg and Sullivan (2000) supports this guideline. Two navigational versions of the same lesson were designed. As illustrated in Figure 12.4, in one version, pressing "continue" *bypassed practice* while in the other version pressing "continue" *led to practice*. In the "more practice" default (version 2), participants viewed nearly twice as many of the screens as those in version 1 and scored higher on the final test. Details about this study are summarized in the following box.

Figure 12.4. Default Navigation Options That Bypass Practice
Compared to Those That Lead to Practice.

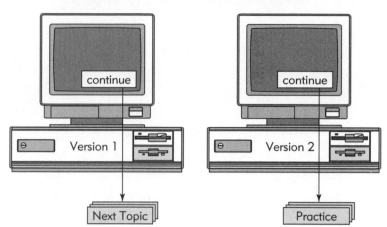

RESEARCH ON LEARNING FROM DIFFERENT NAVIGATIONAL OPTIONS

Two versions of the same course—one with twenty-two practice exercises and a second with sixty-six practice exercises—compared outcomes of high- and low-ability learners in the following conditions:

- Program control in the short- and full-practice versions

- Learner control in the full version, where the default navigation option led to more practice

- Learner control in the full version, where the default navigation option bypassed practice and led to the next topic

Participants completing the full-practice versions scored higher than those completing the short-practice version. In the "more practice" default version (condition 2), participants viewed nearly twice as many of the optional screens (68 percent) as participants in the "skip practice" (condition 3) default version (35 percent). Learners were more likely to select the "continue" button and take the default versions in both learner-control conditions (2 and 3). Typical of most learner-control studies, participants assigned to the learner control mode had more positive attitudes than those in program control (Schnackenberg and Sullivan, 2000).

The authors conclude that programs that make a high amount of practice available as the default route are more likely to result in higher achievement than those that make less practice available as the default route. They suggest that since learner-controlled programs have no instructional advantages, have been shown in other studies to be disadvantageous for low-ability learners, and cost more than program control, program control should be a preferred mode.

However, their subjects consisted of students taking a required university course. In environments where learners have greater choices about whether to take or complete e-learning, a designer cannot downplay user preferences to the extent recommended in this study. When designing programs with high learner control, set navigation controls so that critical aspects of the program (such as examples or practice exercises) are the default options.

Learner Control Principle Three: Add Advisement to Learner Control

Adaptive control is a process in which the content of the training is adjusted by the instructional program based on an evaluation of how learners are responding. If the learner is not responding correctly to questions, the program automatically provides more information and/or practice. Likewise, if learning is demonstrated, fewer instructional elements are provided. Adaptive control has proven to yield higher achievement than learner control for the reasons we have discussed (Tennyson, Tennyson, and Rothen, 1980). A disadvantage of adaptive control is the expense of building and validating the test items and decision rules.

Advisement is a variation of adaptive control that leaves learner control in place. In advisement the computer program assesses learner needs based on their responses. Rather than automatically branching to appropriate sections of the instruction as in adaptive control, the advisement version of adaptive control provides recommendations to the learner regarding what to select in the training. In the end, the learner maintains control and is free to ignore or take the advice. A study by Tennyson (1980) found that advisement and adaptive control versions gave equivalent results—both better than full learner control.

There are three main advantages to adaptive instruction with advisement. First, as shown previously, it leads to better learning outcomes than straight learner control. Second, if you have a learning audience that is quite mixed regarding their background knowledge and skills, you can save time by advising learners with more background to bypass lessons or topics already familiar to them. Third, you still keep the more popular learner-control options. The disadvantage is the time required to construct and validate diagnostic questions that make the advisement effective.

We recommend that designers take into consideration the cost benefit of building advisement programs in terms of the criticality of the learning and the potential savings in learning time. Consumers of e-learning need to look for adaptive features in prospective programs in situations of high task criticality and high audience heterogeneity. However, in situations when most of the audience is likely to be novice, high levels of skill attainment are critical, and development budgets/time are limited, we recommend program control.

Navigational Guidelines for Learner Control

Tours, course maps, links, forward, back, and exit buttons are the most common navigational tools supporting learner control. Below are some recommendations on use of these navigational devices.

Use Links Sparingly to Augment the Lesson

Links that take the learner off the teaching screen as well as links leading to important instructional events should be used sparingly. By definition, links signal to the user that the information is adjunct or peripheral to the main content of the site. Learners will bypass many links. Based on the research described previously, we discourage using links for access to essential skill building elements such as worked examples or practice, especially with novice audiences.

One study (Neiderhauser, Reynolds, Salmen, and Skolmoski, 2000) correlated use of navigation options including links to learning outcomes. They found that high use of links in a lesson was negatively correlated to learning, probably due to cognitive overload.

LINK USE LED TO POORER LEARNING: RESEARCH DETAILS

Two related concepts were presented in two separate lessons. In each lesson, links led learners to correlated information about the concept in the other lesson. For example, if reading about the benefits of concept A in Lesson 1, a link would bring up benefits of concept B in Lesson 2 for purposes of contrast. They found that nearly half the learners frequently made use of these links. The other half either never used the links or used them briefly before abandoning them in favor of a more linear progression where they moved through one lesson from start to finish before moving to the other. Contrary to the authors' expectations, they found that extensive use of the links was negatively related to learning. They attribute their findings to adverse impact of hypertext navigation on cognitive load (Neiderhauser, Reynolds, Salmen, and Skolmoski, 2000).

These findings may reflect another example of the *contiguity principle* discussed in Chapter Four, where learning suffers from separated information that requires the learners to perform the integration themselves. The action of selecting a link and relating contrasting information to the primary instructional material may increase cognitive load in similar ways, as when learners integrate explanatory text with pictures that are physically separated.

Allow Learners to Control Pacing

Most e-learning programs allow learners to proceed at their own pace through lessons by pressing the "forward" button. Video or animated demonstrations typically have slider bar controls indicating progress as well as "quit" options. Recent research by Mayer and Chandler (2001) affirms this practice. They tested learning outcomes from short animated scientific descriptions comparing learners who could control the display by pressing the "continue" button to learners who received a continuous presentation.

They found that performance on a subsequent transfer test was significantly better when learners could control the rate of presentation. They attribute these results to cognitive overload that results from continuous flow of information.

Use Course Maps to Provide an Overview and Orient Learners

Research has been mixed on the contribution of course maps to learning. In the experimental hypertext program described previously, a topic map was also included containing a graphic representation of the hierarchical structure of the hypertext. Learners could access any screen in the hypertext from the topic map. A trace of user paths found that many learners did access the topic map frequently but rarely used it to navigate. Most would access the map, review the levels, and return to where they were reading. A few participants never accessed the topic map. In correlating map use with learning, the study found only a slight benefit. It may be that course maps are less important for navigational control than for providing learners, with an advance orientation to the content structure. This may be especially useful for novice learners, who are most sensitive to cognitive overload and who benefit most from a linear structure of logically sequenced units of instruction.

Provide Basic Navigation Options on All Screens

At the very least, navigation elements for forward and backward movement, course exit, and menu reference should be easily accessible from every display. In courses that use scrolling pages, navigation should be accessible from both the top and bottom of the page to avoid overloading learners with unnecessary mouse work (having to scroll back to the top of the page to click "next"). Additionally, some sort of a "fuel indicator," to borrow a term from the gaming industry, is useful to learners so that they know where they are in a topic and how far they have to go to complete it. The simplest manifestation of the fuel indicator is the "Page 1 of 10" type footer.

DESIGN DILEMMA: RESOLUTION

After reviewing the research on learner and program control, Sue decides to collect some data from the target audience so she can be better prepared to meet Sam's challenges at the next design meeting. She schedules a dozen thirty-minute interviews with team leads and shift supervisors and designs a structured interview to assess their prior knowledge regarding quality tools, their experience with the Internet, and what level of learning management skills they have. She also reviews the interviews done earlier with senior managers regarding priorities and constraints. From her interviews, she builds the following profile of her audience:

- The majority of the operators don't know the details about specific job applications of quality tools and techniques.

- Most of the operators have not had recent opportunities to build good learning management skills.

Additionally, based on prior management discussions, Sue is aware that:

- A positive reaction to the training by learners and managers alike is a high priority since this is one of their first major company-wide ventures into e-learning.

- High skill attainment and job transfer are important since there are safety, legal, and economic consequences to inadequate task performance.

- Management is anxious to roll out the training quickly at a relatively low cost.

Although Sue personally likes advisement strategies, due to lack of resources and the fact that most of the audience is relatively novice, she decides there is insufficient justification for the extra time and cost involved. And while program control would be her second choice, she knows that Sam is right—the satisfaction ratings would fall with the use of program control. She decides that the best approach for her situation will be learner control with default options leading to important instructional elements. Figure 12.5 shows Sue's rework of Sam's original design. She has eliminated links to practice, thereby making it the default option. She also has placed the examples on the screen and directed learners to view all of them. For ease of use she puts paging arrows at both the top and the bottom of the scrolling page. Control over course topics, pacing, and exit are left the same as Sam had planned.

Figure 12.5. Learner Control with Default Navigation Leading to Important Instructional Elements.

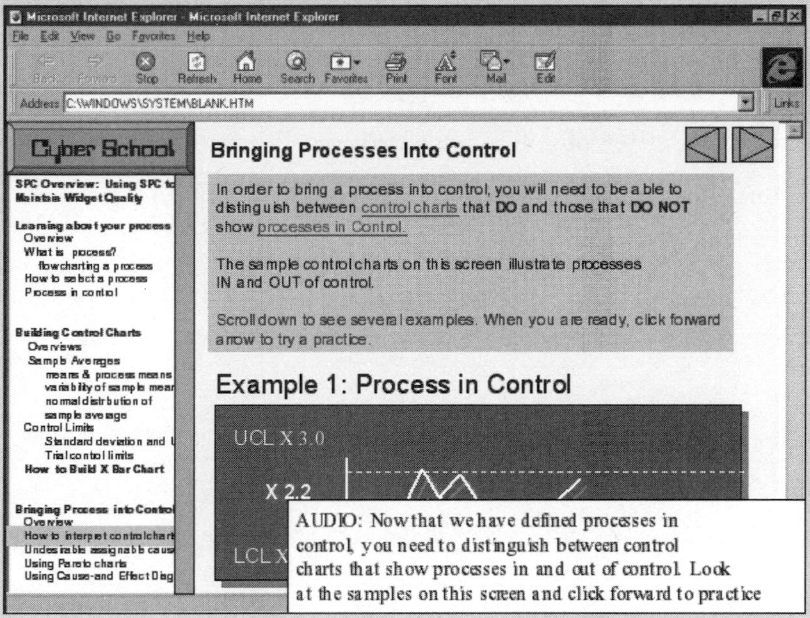

WHAT TO LOOK FOR IN e-LEARNING

CONSIDER A COURSE HIGH IN LEARNER CONTROL WHEN:

☐ Your goal is primarily to provide information rather than to build skills.

☐ Your content is relatively low in complexity and topics are not logically interdependent.

☐ Your audience is likely to have high metacognitive or learning self-regulation skills.

☐ Your audience is likely to have prior knowledge of the content.

☐ The lessons or courses are later in a series so that learners have built a knowledge base.

(*Continued*)

CONSIDER e-LEARNING THAT USES ADVISEMENT WHEN:

☐ Your audience has a mix of background knowledge and skills related to the content.

☐ Saving learning time is a high priority.

☐ Reaching high levels of skill and knowledge proficiency is a high priority.

☐ Resources are available to create the questions and decision logic necessary for advisement.

☐ Training is a regularly scheduled event, or is primarily for compliance purposes, or demonstrated competence would save considerable learner time.

CONSIDER e-LEARNING THAT USES PROGRAM CONTROL WHEN:

☐ Your audience is primarily novice and a high level of proficiency is a priority.

COMING NEXT

In Chapter One we distinguished between instructional goals that are procedural and those that require far transfer (or problem-solving). The majority of e-learning courses currently in use are designed to teach computer skill procedures. What is the potential of e-learning to teach more complex problem-solving skills? In the next chapter we look at this question.

Suggested Readings:

National Research Council (1994). Illusions of Comprehension, Competence, and Remembering. In D. Druckman and R.A. Bjork (Eds.), *Learning, Remembering, Believing*. Washington, D.C.: National Academy Press.

Nelson, T.O. (1996). Consciousness and Metacognition. *American Psychologist, 51*(2), 102–116.

Steinberg, E.R. (1989). Cognition and Learner Control: A Literature Review, 1977–1988. *Journal of Computer-Based Instruction, 16*(4), 117–121.

Stone, N.J. (2000). Exploring the Relationship Between Calibration and Self-Regulated Learning. *Educational Psychology Review, 12*(4), 437–475.

CHAPTER OUTLINE

What Are Problem-Solving Skills?

What Are Metacognitive Skills?

Problem-Solving Principle One: Use Job Contexts to Teach Problem Solving *Processes*

SICUN

Accelerate Expertise

Psychological Reasons for Job-Specific Training

Evidence for Job-Specific Problem-Solving Training

Sherlock and the Acceleration of Expertise

Problem-Solving Principle Two: Focus Training on Thinking Processes Versus Job Knowledge

Adapting Problem-Solving Process Training to e-Learning

Psychological Reasons to Provide Metacognitive Worked Examples

Problem-Solving Principle Three: Make Learners Aware of Their Problem-Solving Processes

Assign Activities to Worked Examples of Problem-Solving Processes

Ask Learners to Document Problem Solving Plans

Make Problem-Solving Processes Visible

Psychological Reasons for Assigning Practice in Problem-Solving

Evidence for Guided Discovery Designs

Problem-Solving Principle Four: Incorporate Job-Specific Problem-Solving Processes

Cost-Benefit Analysis

13

e-Learning to Build Problem-Solving Skills

CHAPTER PREVIEW

IN AN economy dependent on knowledge work, there is an increasing need to build problem-solving skills in workers. Some e-lessons may attempt to use puzzle problems for this purpose. However, cognitive theory on learning transfer and empirical evaluations of thinking skills training do not support this approach. Instead, we recommend a focus on the processes that expert workers use when solving real job problems.

E-learning offers unique opportunities to help workers learn how to solve problems by making the mental *processes* as well as the products of problem-solving explicit. In this chapter we describe the use of e-learning courseware to demonstrate problem-solving actions and thoughts, to provide practice for solving realistic job cases, and to grow awareness of the problem-solving processes. Because the use of multimedia to build job-specific problem-solving skills is quite recent, there is not yet a strong empirical basis to support these approaches. However, since worked examples, practice, and feedback have proven effective for other skills, we have reason to believe these recommendations will be validated in future research.

DESIGN DILEMMA

"I wish our employees were better thinkers! I know most are committed to doing good work. But when they are faced with a new problem, it's like they can't see beyond their noses. They just keep trying the same old things and don't ask themselves what else they might consider. This is the information age! Our company's success relies on the problem-solving skills of our workforce. I want creative thinking skills training!"

That was the message from upper management to the training department. Your team leader kicked off the follow-up meeting: "Upper management wants training on problem-solving skills and they want it for all workers in the organization, including operators, technicians, engineers, and supervisors! One vice president specifically mentioned a book on creative thinking skills that he saw featured at a recent conference. We've got one week to respond with a plan to include what will be in the training and how it will be designed. Well, maybe not all the details, but at least a high-level design to show management. Otherwise, they are going to look outside for a consultant to develop this training."

That evening while browsing in the psychology section of your favorite bookstore you find the book mentioned by the vice president. It's called *Brain Busters: How to Think Creatively*, and it's filled with puzzles and tips on how to solve them. The next morning you come in early and rough out some storyboards using some of the puzzles. Figure 13.1 is one of the storyboards you have created. You see a lot of potential for animation and simulation. "Hmmm—this could be a lot of fun to produce—but I wonder if it will help people on their jobs?"

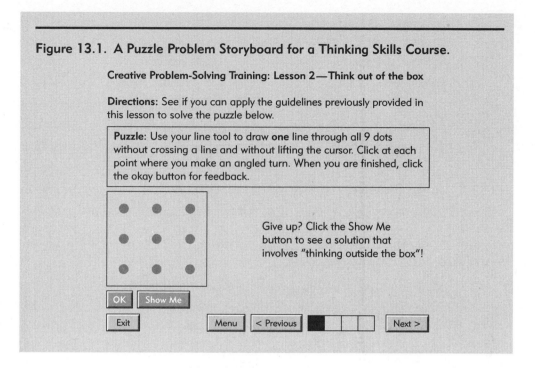

Figure 13.1. A Puzzle Problem Storyboard for a Thinking Skills Course.

Creative Problem-Solving Training: Lesson 2—Think out of the box

Directions: See if you can apply the guidelines previously provided in this lesson to solve the puzzle below.

Puzzle: Use your line tool to draw **one** line through all 9 dots without crossing a line and without lifting the cursor. Click at each point where you make an angled turn. When you are finished, click the okay button for feedback.

Give up? Click the Show Me button to see a solution that involves "thinking outside the box"!

OK   Show Me

Exit   Menu   < Previous   Next >

What Are Problem-Solving Skills?

As the economy increasingly relies on knowledge work—work that depends as much on heads as on hands—the need for effective problem-solvers in the workplace grows. By this we mean someone who can apply knowledge and skills to solve routine as well as unique problems in a given career field. Success in problem-solving relies on:

- *Cognitive Skills*—the facts, concepts, and procedures unique to a skill field

- *Metaskills*—the ability to plan, monitor, and assess actions associated with problem-solving

- *Motivation*—an investment of effort to persist and solve the problem (Mayer, 1998).

This chapter focuses on the use of e-learning to support the cognitive and metacognitive skills that underpin successful problem solving.

We know that neither job-specific knowledge nor metacognitive skills alone are enough for successful problem-solving. For example, consider the following math problem. *An army bus holds thirty-six soldiers. If 1,128 soldiers are being bused to their training site, how many buses are needed?* Seventy percent of respondents did the math correctly. But 29 percent selected the answer: 31 remainder 12. Eighteen percent said 31 buses needed, while 23 percent gave the correct answer of 32 (Schoenfeld, 1987). Here we see a good example of problem-solvers who knew the mathematical operations—that is, they had the cognitive skills. It was their metacognitive skills that were lacking. They failed to ask themselves: "What is the problem asking—does my answer make sense?" And so they chose too few buses or "fractions" of buses. Success in problem-solving requires both cognitive and metacognitive skills.

What Are Metacognitive Skills?

Metacognition is the skill that sets goals, monitors progress, and makes adjustments as needed. People with good metacognitive skills focus not only on the outcome of the job, but on the steps and decisions they make to achieve that outcome. When working in a team, the person with high metacognitive skills will be the one to say: "Wait—let's stop and see if we are making progress. Will our individual efforts work well together?" When working on a problem alone they might say: "This approach is not really getting me anywhere—what else might I consider?" In other words, they are mindful of their mental work. When they don't see progress toward a goal, they shift gears and try another approach.

Can metacognitive skills be trained? If so, what training methods are needed? In what ways can technology support the learning of metacognitive skills? Can practice on solving general problems like the puzzle problem in Figure 13.1 be used to make workers better thinkers? These are some of the issues you need to consider when selecting e-learning products to support effective problem-solving. Based on empirical evidence, we offer four guidelines to apply when reviewing or designing e-learning to support problem-solving on the job:

- Use real job contexts to build work-specific problem-solving skills.

- Provide expert models of problem-solving actions and thoughts.

- Promote learner awareness of their problem-solving actions and thoughts.

- Base the lesson on a detailed analysis of job expert problem-solving processes.

Problem-Solving Principle One: Use Job Contexts to Teach Problem-Solving Processes

A number of educational programs have tried to build general problem-solving or thinking skills through the use of puzzle problems like the one in Figure 13.1 or by training students in analytic skills such as Logo programming. The hope was that such training would build mental problem-solving muscle—muscle that could be applied to other kinds of problems. If learners could get good at the analysis required by Logo, it was reasoned, they should be more analytic when tackling other kinds of tasks as well. What was found, however, was that problem-solving skills are dependent on very specific job knowledge and metacognitive skills. Unless problem-solving is built using the environment, the tools, and the problem-solving processes of a specific job, there is little transfer of learning.

In Chapter One we defined three types of instruction for e-learning courses: teaching by show-and-tell (*receptive*), teaching by show-and-do (*directive*), and teaching by problem-solving (*guided discovery*). The guided discovery approach is a popular modern design used for courses that build job-specific problem-solving skills and related technical knowledge. To illustrate this approach, we describe two multimedia programs: Surgical Intensive Care Unit for Nurses (SICUN), for building problem-solving skills in surgical intensive care nurses, and Accelerate Expertise, designed to train bank loan agents how to evaluate a loan applicant.

SICUN

The student nurse begins the lesson with a case problem to solve. Figure 13.2 shows the case introduction. In this lesson student nurses are given background on a twenty-seven-year-old male involved in a motor vehicle accident who has suffered severe chest and facial injuries. Many of the technical terms in the case such as "flail" are in hypertext. When selected, their meanings appear in the lower left corner of the screen. The clock records when a learner begins and

Figure 13.2. Guided Discovery Training for Nurses.

Adapted from Lajoie, Azevedo, and Fleiszer, 1998.

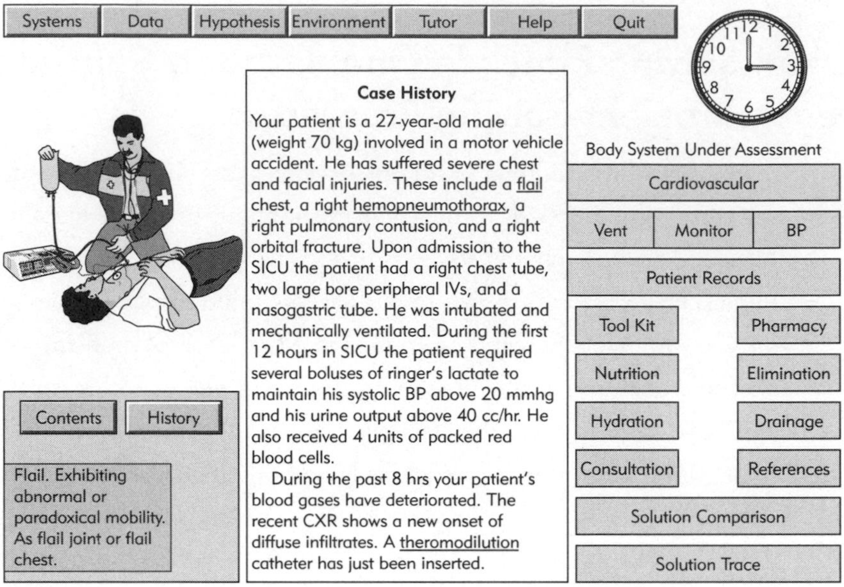

ends problem-solving, which is one metric that is used to assess problem-solving effectiveness. In intensive care situations, time can mean the difference between life and death. The student first selects a body system to evaluate from the upper left *systems button*. After selecting a body system, the program asks the nurse to type in his goals for assessing the system selected. To achieve his goal, buttons in the lower right-hand side provide a variety of actions, such as using various monitoring devices to collect patient data or a pharmacy for ordering medications. At any time the student may formulate up to three hypotheses by selecting the hypothesis button and choosing from a list of conditions. They both select a possible condition and indicate their degree of confidence in each diagnosis. The hypotheses can be changed as the nurse continues to assess and evaluate the patient (Lajoie, Azevedo, and Fleiszer, 1998).

Accelerate Expertise

In this program, the learner is asked to evaluate a new client applying to the bank for a business loan. As illustrated in Figure 13.3, she has a number of resources at her disposal in the office, including a fax machine for requesting

Figure 13.3. An Office Interface Offers Many Tools for Solving a Case Problem.

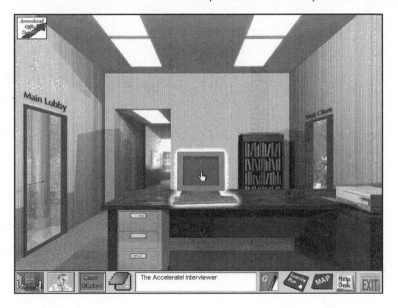

credit checks, a book shelf with literature on the client's industry, and a telephone for checking references. The office computer includes a program that the loan agent would use on the job to guide her through the loan analysis process. When the learner is ready, she completes the loan transmittal form, making a loan recommendation along with a justification statement.

Both these lessons follow a guided discovery instructional design. The lesson begins with a job-realistic case problem. Tools, data, and techniques specific to the career field are available for learners to apply to solve the case. Learners are free to explore the various resources in any sequence they wish. Support in the way of tutor advice and examples is available.

Psychological Reasons for Job-Specific Training

It seems reasonable that training on solving a series of generic problems could build a broad set of critical thinking skills that would apply to diverse job problems. Likewise it seems reasonable that training to solve problems in an analytic field like programming would transfer to solving other problems requiring a systematic approach. Based on this rationale, we could propose that metacognitive skills that underlie problem-solving are general, with applicability to many different career fields. The general thinking skills training approach would be quite efficient since one training course on a set of generic problems would suffice for all employees in all jobs. The thinking guidelines would be general problem-solving hints such as, "*Think outside the box,*" "*Consider all aspects of the problem,*" and "*Make a graphic representation.*"

What's wrong with this approach? We know that for training to be successful, it must transfer back to the job after the learning event, and transfer has proven to be a thorny problem. Our goal in improving worker thinking skills is to enable them to solve nonroutine problems, that is, novel problems for which they do not have a standardized response. We know that work-related problems are encountered in a specific job context, such as management, patient care, or commercial bank lending. It is unlikely that the general skills derived from solving puzzle problems will transfer effectively to these diverse settings. Good thinking skills courses will need to include the unique skills that underlie effective problem solving in a specific domain. According to Mayer (1998), "An important instructional implication of the focus on metacognition is that problem solving skills should be learned within the context of realistic problem-solving situation" (p. 53).

Think of metacognitive skills like a hand. A hand is a useful and flexible tool, but without something to grasp, a hand can't accomplish much. Further, the way a hand grasps a baby will differ from how a hand picks up a basket of laundry (Perkins and Salomon, 1989). Similarly, metacognitive skills must be wedded to job-specific knowledge to be useful. And metacognitive skills must be shaped to the type of work involved. In other words, highly generalizable guidelines such as "set your goal," "plan your approach," "monitor your progress" are fine as far as they go; but how they apply to specific jobs will differ. Unfortunately, there is no one generic set of thinking skills that all workers can apply successfully to their skill fields. Each job domain requires its own customized set of metacognitive strategies to be applied to specific and unique job cognitive knowledge. These skills need to be taught in the context of authentic work problems.

Evidence for Job-Specific Problem-Solving Training

Many thinking skills programs and courses have been developed. A comparison of successful and unsuccessful programs shows that the most successful approaches focus on skills that apply to a specific domain, rather than on building general mental muscle. The strategies taught in effective training are based on the thinking processes experts use to tackle problems in a specific career field. These programs will demonstrate expert thinking patterns and ask learners to reflect on their own problem approaches. In an extensive review of research on problem-solving transfer Mayer and Wittrock (1996) conclude that "in spite of claims for thinking skills programs aimed at general improvement in intellectual ability, classroom studies often fail to test for or to reveal convincing evidence that such programs result in general transfer to new kinds of problems" (p. 51).

Sherlock and the Acceleration of Expertise

Although a number of problem-solving courses like the ones described previously for nurses or bank loan agents have been produced, few have been systematically evaluated. One exception is Sherlock, an intelligent multimedia course designed to train Air Force technicians how to troubleshoot the F-15 test station (Lesgold, Eggan, Katz, and Rao, 1993). Sherlock provides learners with many simulated test station failures to resolve, accompanied by tutorial help as learners work through the problems. Thirty-two newly assigned airmen along with sixteen experts were included in an evaluation study, for a total of forty-eight participants. The thirty-two new technicians were divided into two groups of sixteen—one of which took Sherlock training for twenty-five hours and the other served as a comparison group. The skills of all thirty-two were evaluated through pre- and post-tests that required them to solve simulated test station diagnosis problems—problems that were different from those in the training. The sixteen expert technicians also took the post-test. Figure 13.4 shows the average test scores. Note that the average skill level of the sixteen who took Sherlock training was equivalent to that of the advanced technicians. The researchers conclude that "the bottom line is that 20 to 25 hours of Sherlock practice time produced average improvements that were, in many respects, equivalent to the effects of four years on the job" (p. 54).

Figure 13.4. Acceleration of Expertise Using Sherlock.
Lesgold, Eggan, Katz, and Rao, 1993.

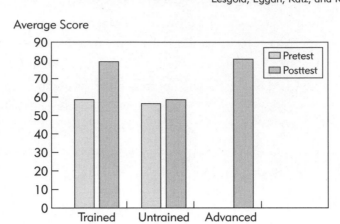

While this outcome seems almost magical, it points to the power of technology to compress experience. In essence, the Sherlock learners got the equivalent of four years of on-the-job experience in twenty-five hours. This reflects the acceleration of expertise that can be gained by exposing learners to a systematic series of job-specific problems to solve, along with tutoring to help them solve the problems. The Sherlock results suggest that the guided discovery types of training delivered via multimedia can effectively use simulation to compress experience and build skills that would take many months to build in the actual work setting.

Problem-Solving Principle Two: Focus Training on Thinking Processes Versus Job Knowledge

For effective problem-solving training, the focus must broaden from the cognitive skills to include the metacognitive skills of the job. Most job training today concentrates on knowledge of job facts, concepts, and procedures. This job knowledge is typically taught using a teaching by telling (receptive) or show-and-do (directive) type of training. Whether in the classroom or through multimedia, learners generally listen to lectures or read text, complete short exercises, and follow the steps to practice performing a task. The training emphasis is on direct job knowledge. Rarely are the processes, especially the invisible mental processes involved in solving job problems, explicitly trained. For example, in many mathematics classes, the focus is on the calculation procedures needed to solve a problem. Rarely has it been on the mental processes—especially the metacognitive processes underlying problem solution. The outcome is learners who can get the right answer, but fail to assess its relevance, as in the Army bus problem described previously.

In the last twenty years educators have designed programs with the explicit goal of building metacognitive skills in their learners. Alan Schoenfeld, a mathematics professor, has developed one such classroom program (1987). He noted that his graduate students were quite adept at specific mathematical techniques taught in their classes, but they lacked problem-solving skills. In studying the thinking processes of students, he noted that about 60 percent would read a problem, start down a solution path, and continue down that path, whether it was productive or not. Schoenfeld characterizes this as the "read the problem, make a decision to do something, and then pursue it come hell or high water" approach (p. 207). In contrast, experts solving the same problem were more reflective. Schoenfeld compared the problem-solving thinking processes of experts with students by graphing the thinking patterns of expert and novice problem-solvers who talked aloud while they solved problems. The results are shown in Figure 13.5. Unlike the

Figure 13.5. A Comparison of Novice and Expert Thinking Patterns During Problem Solution.

From Schoenfeld, 1987.

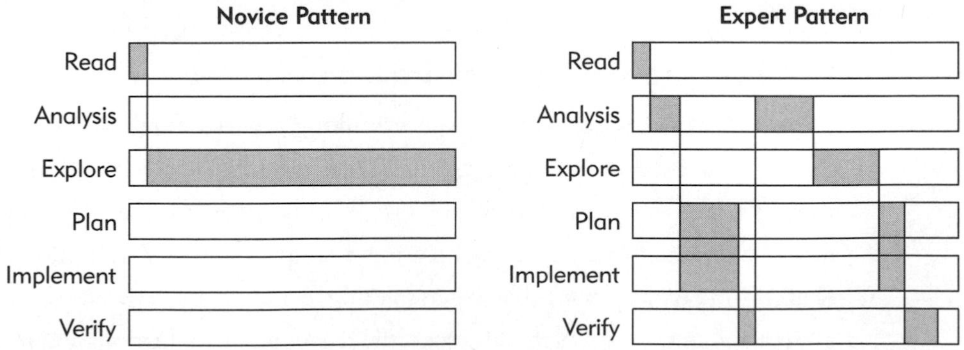

students who stuck to one approach, the expert thinking processes moved iteratively among planning, implementing, and evaluating problem-solving actions.

Schoenfeld designed and taught a course to make student problem-solving skills more like those of experts. He used worked examples and practice as his main instructional methods. To provide models of expert-like metacognitive processes, he would solve demonstration problems in class during which he would voice aloud his thoughts—including his monitoring and adjusting thoughts. On occasion he might deliberately go down an unproductive path during the demonstration. After a bit he would stop and say something like, "Wait—is this getting me anywhere? What other alternatives might I consider?" In this way he provided demonstrations not only of problem solutions but also of the thinking processes behind them. Second, he assigned problems to small student groups. As they worked together, he would visit the groups and ask "metacognitive questions" such as, "What are you doing now?" "Why are you trying that approach?" "What other approaches might you consider?" By first demonstrating and then holding learners responsible for these problem-solving process skills, they soon learned to incorporate this kind of thinking in their problem-solving sessions.

Based on these teaching methods, we suggest two guidelines for building problem-solving processes through e-learning:

- Provide examples of expert problem-solving actions and thinking.

- Promote learner awareness of and reflection on their problem-solving. process by making learners document their plans and by showing maps of student and expert problem-solving paths.

Adapting Problem-Solving Process Training to e-Learning

E-learning can be used to reveal expert thinking processes during problem-solving. For example, in a program designed to teach LISP programming, worked examples presented in video showed a LISP programming expert solving problems and then reflecting on and revising his solution (Lin, Hmelo, Kinzer, and Secules, 1999). The expert solution focuses on the cognitive aspects of the programming problem. However, the retrospective evaluations and revisions focus on the typically invisible monitoring and revising processes. As a second example, students learn geometry principles by designing a child's swing set. As they plan their designs, they can access designs of prior students that have been evaluated and annotated by experts. This technique is especially easy to apply in Web-based e-learning. Projects completed by individuals or by teams and annotated by the instructor or experts can be placed on a Web page gallery for future or current learner review. A third example, shown in Figure 13.6 appears in a program designed to teach reading comprehension strategies at a fourth to sixth grade level. On this screen, the expert is demonstrating how to comprehend the meaning of a story by answering key questions such as, "What is the story about?" A learning agent, Jim, serves as the expert. Jim's thinking process during reading is captured in the narration. As he starts to read, he writes down a first idea. Then, as he reads further, he changes his mind, scratches out his first answer and writes a more accurate sentence about the topic of the story. The learner sees the expert's

Figure 13.6. Audio Relays the Agent's Thoughts as He Analyzes the Story.
With permission from Plato Educational Software.

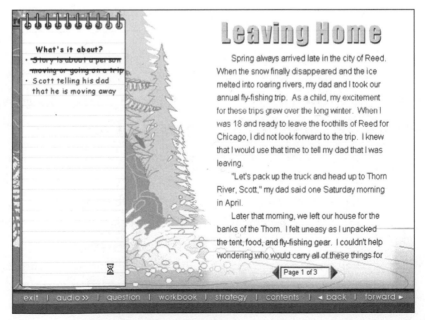

activities but also hears the mental processes behind them. In all of the above examples, invisible problem-solving thoughts of experts are made explicit through worked examples that model how to solve sample problems.

Psychological Reasons to Provide Metacognitive Worked Examples

In Chapter Ten we summarized the power of worked examples as training methods useful for building new knowledge in long-term memory. However, our focus in that chapter was on building direct knowledge and procedures needed to solve problems. Here we shift the emphasis from job skill knowledge to job problem-solving metaknowledge. But the principles remain the same. In these worked examples we are teaching metacognitive skills rather than job cognitive skills.

We also saw in Chapter Ten that, for far transfer job tasks that require judgment, the learner needs a flexible mental model—one that can adapt to a variety of problem types. This is accomplished by providing several diverse worked examples. The same approach applies here. To build flexible metacognitive skills, worked examples that illustrate how several experts might tackle a specific problem or several related problems tackled by a single expert are needed.

Problem-Solving Principle Three: Make Learners Aware of Their Problem-Solving Processes

It is not sufficient to give examples of problem-solving thinking processes. Learners must be required to respond actively—to practice what they have seen. And they need feedback on what they have done. Recall that Schoenfeld, after giving think-aloud demonstrations of mathematical problem-solving, required learners to respond to metacognitive questions such as: "What are you doing now? Why are you doing that? What other approaches have you considered?" This forces the learners to be mindful and explicit about their metacognitive processes.

Several techniques can be used in e-learning to direct the learners' attention to their problem-solving processes. These techniques include:

- Assignments to perform activities on worked examples of expert problem-solving

- Assignments to write out problem-solving plans

- Visualizations of learners' problem-solving paths, which can be compared with the paths of experts.

Assign Activities to Worked Examples of Problem-Solving Processes

In Chapter Ten we noted that assigning learners an activity related to a worked example, ensured that they processed the example. A similar technique applies here. For example, in the LISP training course described previously, the developers found that just watching the video of experts thinking about their solutions did not get as good results as requiring learners to respond actively to the video models (Bielaczyc, Pirolli, and Brown, 1995). Students were instructed to watch the video, comment on the strategies used by the expert in the video, identify strategies that seemed to be effective, and then apply them to their own practice problems. In this way, learners were encouraged to actively process and apply the examples provided.

Ask Learners to Document Problem-Solving Plans

In the geometry training using swingset design projects, a window entitled "Things I will change" is part of the program (Figure 13.7). This assignment requires students to reflect on their designs and explicitly document how they might be improved. The students are encouraged to use the expert annotations of prior student designs as models for their own analysis. A screen (Figure 13.8) from the reading comprehension program described earlier shows an assignment in which the student is given a sample story and asked to write on the blackboard answers to the key comprehension self-questions such as, "What is the story about?" After the student has written her answers, she can compare them to an expert model and revise if she wishes. The first and the revised student versions are saved in a portfolio for later analysis by an

Figure 13.7. Geometry Lesson Requires Reflection on First Solutions.

Adapted from Lin, Hmelo, Kinzer, and Secules, 1999.

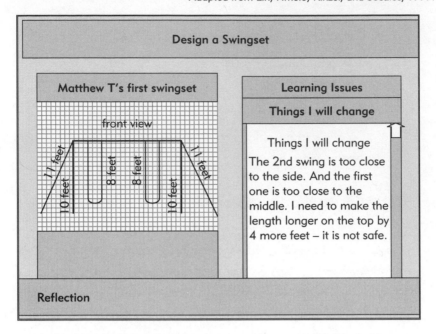

Figure 13.8. Learners Can Compare Their Analyses with the Analysis of an Expert.

With permission from Plato Educational Systems.

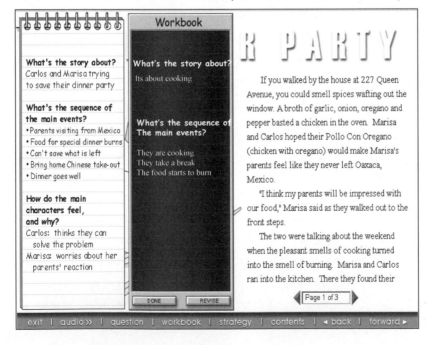

instructor. Note that in all of these lessons, the learner must document plans and then try them out in the context of actively solving problems. Meaningful feedback either from the program or from a mentor is an important element of these programs.

Make Problem-Solving Processes Visible

One of the most unique contributions of technology to problem-solving training is the ability to give the learner a visual map of her problem-solving steps and the opportunity to compare her path with that of an expert. For example, both the intensive care surgical nursing program and the bank lending training illustrated in Figures 13.2 and 13.3 track the actions the learner takes to solve the case problem. At any point in these programs, the learners can view the actions they have taken and compare them to the actions of the expert. Figure 13.9 illustrates the map of the expert nurse steps compared to the student steps in the SICU program.

Figure 13.9. Learners Can Compare Their Solutions with Those of Experts.
Adapted from LaJoie, Azevedo, and Fleiszer, 1998.

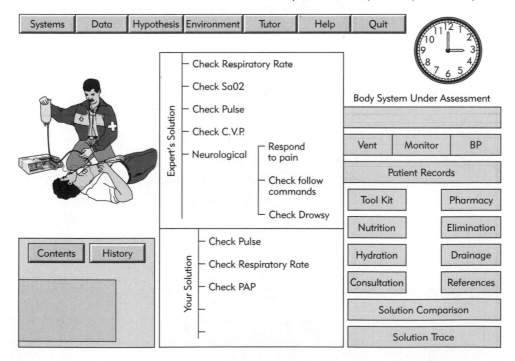

Psychological Reasons for Assigning Practice in Problem-Solving

While worked examples are a powerful supplement to practice problems, they cannot replace them altogether. We know that learning requires active processing in working memory that results in new mental models in long-term memory. We saw in Chapter Nine that practice exercises that require learners to explicitly apply new skills significantly improve learning. It is not surprising then that practice that requires learners to document and analyze their thinking processes will improve those processes.

Evidence for Guided Discovery Designs

Earlier in the chapter we summarized the evaluation showing that twenty-five hours on the Sherlock system resulted in the expertise of a four-year technician. While this research showed the effectiveness of the guided discovery design, it did not compare it to alternative teaching approaches. For example, might similar results be achieved from a more traditional "tell-and-do" directive teaching method? While there are a number of descriptive articles and conference presentations on the guided discovery designs to build problem-solving skills, few have been empirically validated. Until we have more research on these relatively recent problem-solving training programs, we cannot make any claims for their efficacy compared to more traditional instructional approaches. What we do know is that, all other things being equal, the guided discovery design is relatively complex and expensive to produce. Additional evaluation to demonstrate its return on investment is needed.

Whether a directive or a guided discovery approach is used, illustrating problem-solving processes through worked examples and encouraging learners to apply these in practice exercises using real-job contexts is likely to build transferable problem-solving skills.

Problem-Solving Principle Four: Incorporate Job-Specific Problem-Solving Processes

As you review e-lessons that claim to build problem-solving skills in your workforce, look for the tools, data sources, activities, and thinking processes that expert job performers would use in your organization. If the lessons incorporate these at least somewhat closely, you are more likely to get job improvement than a program that does not. These job-specific elements must be identified during the planning phases of the e-learning program. While some elements such as the tools and observable activities can be readily seen, others such as the thinking processes of experts cannot. Special techniques to define the problems to be solved in the training and the processes experts use to solve them must be applied during the design of the training.

For example, the developers of the intensive care nursing problem-solving (SICU) training documented their planning process in some detail. They started by interviewing three head nurses from the intensive care unit to determine the most difficult aspects of their jobs. These were used to define the job competencies that distinguish expert from beginning practitioners. Interviews with additional nurses were used to be sure that the types of problems built into the training would reflect the most difficult parts of the job a nurse would have to encounter.

Following the interviews, the team worked with expert nurses to identify specific case problems that would incorporate the key competencies identified earlier. Once some cases were developed on paper, the actions that experienced nurses would take to solve them were defined by asking three nurses unfamiliar with the case to talk aloud as they solved the problem. These problem-solving interviews followed a specific sequence. For every action that a nurse would mention, the interviewer would ask the reason for the action. Then the interviewer would state the outcome of the action and the nurse would state his or her interpretation of the outcome. An example from one interview is shown in Figure 13.10. The transcripts collected from these problem-solving sessions were coded into categories, including hypothesis generation, planning of medical interventions, actions performed, results of evidence gathering, and interpretation of results, along with overall solution paths. The goal of this phase was to define the problem-solving processes and actions experts used to provide the basis for the training program.

While all three nurses arrived at the same solution, each one used a different path to get there. Thus the program designers concluded that there is no one correct sequence of actions to assess a patient, but there are systematic approaches to clinical problem-solving that all three nurses used and that will improve novice nurse performance. The results of these analyses

Figure 13.10. Part of a Cognitive Task Analysis Interview.
From LaJoie, Azevedo, and Fleiszer, 1998.

Interviewer:	Which body system would you start with?
Expert:	Neurology system.
Interviewer:	Why?
Expert:	I want to see if the patient is conscious.
Interviewer:	What would you do first?
Expert:	I would use my flashlight to examine reaction of the pupils.
Interviewer:	The pupils both react equally to the light stimulus by contracting. What does this result imply or mean? How do you interpret this?
Expert:	There's no brain damage....

were used to design the interface shown in Figure 13.2 that included a patient, a patient case history, patient records, a pharmacy, a tool kit, and other medical treatment devices. In addition, the interviews provided the "expert" solution paths available for learner review shown in Figure 13.9.

This cognitive task analysis is a major project in itself that needs to be completed before starting to design the e-lessons. Initial interviews are used to define skills and competencies that distinguish expert practitioners from others. Based on these, specific cases are built that incorporate those competencies. Since expert job practitioners can rarely articulate their thinking process in a direct way, these must be inferred indirectly through a cognitive task analysis technique such as the one described here. Through a combination of interviews and cognitive task analysis, you should define target case problems, the normal tools and resources available to the worker, and expert solution paths. All of these elements should be used in the design of your e-lesson.

As you plan your analysis project, it will be important to define who is considered an expert, since it is their processes that will serve as the basis for your training. Ideally, you can identify experts based on metrics that objectively point them out as best practitioners. For example, sales records can be used to identify top sales practitioners. In other situations, you will need to use a combination of years of experience, job position, and/or practitioner consensus as indicators of expertise.

Cost-Benefit of Analysis

In summary, if problem-solving training is to pay off, the design of that training must be rooted in the tools, actions, and mental processes that underlie the competencies of expert practitioners. The analysis to define these components is labor intensive. Will there be a return on investment from this effort? To the extent that a large enough number of practitioners whose work has major and direct impact on organizational objectives can benefit from the training, these up-front costs can be regained. Also, to the extent that expertise can be accelerated, as in the Sherlock program, the costs of analysis and development can be justified. However, given the limited empirical evidence for the effectiveness of these programs, we advise you to pay special attention to the potential cost-benefit of these approaches to your situation.

DESIGN DILEMMA: RESOLUTION

Where does this leave you with your assignment to produce better thinkers in your company? You could take the easy way out and design a fun, creative, thinking skills course using the puzzle problem approach. It would be an enjoyable course for learners and you could show off a lot of the capabilities of multimedia, including animation and simulation. Alternatively, you could tell management that it will be necessary to teach job-relevant thinking skills in the context of real work problems to pay off on the job. Furthermore, it is likely that considerable effort will be needed to define cases and specific critical-thinking skills experts use to solve those cases. Which road should you take? Here is what you say to your team leader:

"Sure, we could develop a critical-thinking skills program based on solving generic problems that would be a lot of fun for workers to take at their desktops. Unfortunately, research on similar types of programs shows limited job impact. That means the company would spend money on the design of the program and even more money on the time people need to take it and there would not be much change in their thinking skills. However, I would be remiss if I did not recommend a plan with greater payoff. We know from research that problem-solving skills are job specific. What works well in one job often has limited application to another. We also know that thinking skills are best learned while solving authentic job problems. Therefore, we need to produce training based on job-specific problem-solving processes. One way we might save time is to embed thinking strategies into existing courses or extend existing courses with thinking skills modules. We would begin with those jobs in which effective problem-solving is most likely to have a direct and tangible impact on the company bottom line."

WHAT TO LOOK FOR IN e-LEARNING

☐ E-lessons based on job-realistic case problems and the thinking processes needed to solve them.

☐ Worked examples of expert problem-solving actions and thinking processes.

☐ Opportunities for learners to document their problem-solving plans.

☐ Opportunities for learners to try out job-realistic problem-solving actions to collect data, analyze results, and derive solutions.

☐ Opportunities for learners to view their problem-solving paths and compare them with the paths of experts.

☐ Opportunities to collaborate with other learners during problem-solving and/or to learn from the products of previous learners.

☐ Inclusion of the tools, data sources, actions, thinking processes, and cases that reflect real-world job-expert problem-solving.

☐ Feedback on the *process* as well as the *products* of learner problem-solving.

☐ Agents used to provide examples and coaching of problem-solving processes.

COMING NEXT

In each chapter of this book we have summarized a variety of guidelines derived from empirical studies related to specific aspects of e-learning, such as use of text, narration, and graphics, or design of instructional elements, such as practice and examples. To consolidate the many guidelines in the book, in the next and final chapter, we summarize all these guidelines and demonstrate how we apply them to a few sample e-lessons.

Suggested Readings

Lajoie, S.P., Azevedo, R., and Fleiszer, D.M. (1998). Cognitive Tools for Assessment and Learning in a High Information Flow Environment. *Journal of Educational Computing Research, 18*(3), 205–235.

Lin, Z., Hmelo, C., Kinzer, C.K., and Secules, T.J. (1999). Designing Technology to Support Reflection. *Educational Technology Research and Development, 47,* 43–62.

Mayer, R.E. (1998). Cognitive, Metacognitive, and Motivational Aspects of Problem Solving. *Instructional Science, 26,* 49–63.

Schoenfeld, A.H. (1987). What's All the Fuss About Metacognition? In A. Schoenfeld, (Ed.), *Cognitive Science and Mathematics Education.* Hillsdale, NJ: Lawrence Erlbaum Associates.

CHAPTER OUTLINE

Applying Our Guidelines to Evaluate e-Courseware

    Integrating the Guidelines

e-Lesson Reviews

Sample One: Ammunition Safety

    Description of the Sample

    Application of Guidelines

Sample Two: Creating Links in Dreamweaver

    Description of Sample

    Application of Guidelines

Sample Three: Accelerate Expertise—Researching Commercial Bank Loans

    Description of Sample

    Application of Guidelines

Sample Four: Identifying Hazardous Materials

    Description of Sample

    Application of Guidelines

The Next Generation of e-Learning

    Prediction One: e-Learning for Job Payoff

    Prediction Two: e-Learning to Build Problem-Solving Skills

14

Applying the Guidelines

CHAPTER PREVIEW

THIS CHAPTER consolidates all the guidelines we have discussed along with some illustrations of how we would apply them to some actual e-lessons. As mentioned in the Introduction, if you are not interested in the details of the earlier chapters, you can get a summary of the guidelines presented throughout the book here. If you have read the earlier chapters, you can look at how we apply all the guidelines in concert to some sample e-lessons. We also make some predictions about the future directions of e-learning for business and industry training.

Applying Our Guidelines to Evaluate e-Courseware

The goal of our book is to help consumers and designers make e-learning decisions based on empirical research and on the psychological processes of learning. In an ideal world, e-courseware effectiveness should be based on measurement of how well and how efficiently learners achieve the learning objectives. This measurement requires a validation process in which learners are formally tested on their skills after completing the training. In our experience, formal course validation is rare. More often, consumers and designers look at the features of an e-learning course to make an assessment of its effectiveness. We recommend that, among the features that are assessed, you include the research-based guidelines we have presented. We recognize that decisions about e-learning alternatives will not be based on learning theory alone. A variety of factors, including the desired outcome of the training, the culture of the organization sponsoring the training, the technological constraints of the platforms and networks available to the learners, and pragmatic issues related to politics, time, and budget, will shape e-learning decisions. That is why you will need to adapt our guidelines to your individual training situations.

In Chapter One we described three common purposes for e-learning: to inform workers, to teach procedural tasks, and to teach far transfer or principle tasks. Your technological constraints will determine whether you can only deliver courseware with low-memory intensive media elements like text and simple graphics or whether you can include media elements that require greater memory such as video, audio, and animation. If you are planning for an Internet or intranet delivery, you can use collaborative facilities, including e-mail, chats, and message boards.

Integrating the Guidelines

Taken together, we can make a general statement about the best use of media elements to present content and learning methods in e-learning. In situations that support audio, *best learning will result from concise informal narration of relevant graphics*. In situations that rely on visual elements only such as text and simple graphics, *best learning will result from concise informal textual explanations of relevant graphics in which the text and graphic are integrated on the screen*.

Table 14.1 compares the median gains and effect sizes for the media elements principles described in Chapters Three through Eight. While all had considerable impact, some had a greater effect on learning than others. For example, using relevant pictures and words compared to using words alone resulted in an 89 percent gain in learning. Eliminating irrelevant

Table 14.1. Summary of Research Results from the Six Media Elements Principles.
From Mayer, 2001.

Principle	Percent Gain	Effect Size	Number of Tests
Multimedia	89	1.50	9 of 9
Contiguity	68	1.12	5 of 5
Coherence	82	1.17	10 of 11
Modality	80	1.17	4 of 4
Redundancy	79	1.24	2 of 2
Personalization	67	1.24	5 of 5

graphics, music, and extraneous words resulted in an 82 percent gain in learning. Narrating graphics with audio as well as not presenting words with both text and narration yielded gains of about 80 percent each. Finally, writing in an informal style using first- and second-person constructions yielded gains of around 67 percent.

Because the research underlying the media elements principles was conducted in the same laboratory and used similar instructional materials (Mayer, 2001a), we can make these comparisons among the results. Regarding the other principles, however, we do not have data that can tell us of their relative impact on learning or how they might interact with each other. At this point we don't know.

e-Lesson Reviews

In this chapter we offer four brief examples of how the guidelines might be applied to e-learning alternatives. We do not offer these guidelines as a "rating system." We don't claim to have included all the important variables you should consider when evaluating e-learning alternatives. Furthermore, which guidelines you will apply will depend on the goal of your training and the environmental considerations mentioned previously. Instead of a rating system, we offer these guidelines as a checklist of research-based indicators of some of the psychological factors you should consider in your e-learning design and selection decisions.

We have organized the guidelines in a checklist in Exhibit 14.1 according to the three types of training listed below and indicated the chapters that describe them in detail. The commentaries to follow make reference to the guidelines by number so we recommend you refer to Exhibit 14.1 throughout this chapter. We suggest that you make a copy of Exhibit 14.1 to make the reference process easier as you read the rest of this chapter. We will discuss the following four e-lesson samples: Ammunition Safety, How to Create Links in a software tool called Dreamweaver, How to Analyze a Commercial Bank Loan Applicant, and How to Identify Correct Labeling of Hazardous Materials.

Exhibit 14.1. A Summary of e-Learning Guidelines.

Three Types of e-Learning:

Type	Best Used for Training Goals	Examples
Show-and-Tell—Receptive	Inform	New hire orientation Product updates
Tell-and-Do—Directive	Procedural Performance	Computer end-user training
Problem-Solving— Guided Discovery	Far Transfer or Problem-Solving Performance	Bank loan application analysis Sales skills

Chapters 3 through 8. Media Elements Guidelines for All Types of e-Learning:

If Using Visual Mode Only:

1. Use relevant graphics and text to communicate content—Multimedia Principle
2. Integrate the text into the graphic on the screen—Contiguity Principle
3. Avoid covering or separating information that must be integrated for learning—Contiguity Principle
4. Avoid irrelevant graphics, stories, and lengthy text—Coherence Principle
5. Write in a conversational style using first and second person—Personalization Principle
6. Use virtual coaches (agents) to deliver instructional content such as examples and hints—Personalization Principle

---

Exhibit 14.1. (Continued).

If Using Audio and Visual Modes:

7. Use relevant graphics explained by audio narration to communicate content—Multimedia Principle
8. Maintain information the learner needs time to process in text on the screen, for example, directions to tasks, new terminology—Exception to Modality Principle
9. Avoid covering or separating information that must be integrated for learning—Contiguity Principle
10. Do not present words as both onscreen text and narration when there are graphics on the screen—Redundancy Principle
11. Avoid irrelevant videos, animations, music, stories, and lengthy narrations—Coherence Principle
12. Script audio in a conversational style using first and second person—Personalization Principle
13. Script virtual coaches to present instructional content such as examples and hints via audio—Personalization Principle

Chapters 9 and 10—Guidelines for e-Learning with Performance Goal Outcomes
In addition to the above guidelines:

14. Provide job-relevant practice questions interspersed throughout the lessons—Practice/Encoding Specificity Principles
15. For more critical skills and knowledge, include more practice questions—Practice Principle
16. Design space for feedback to be visible close to practice answers—Contiguity Principle
17. Provide training in self-questioning when learning from receptive e-lessons—Practice Principle
18. Provide a worked example using realistic job tools and situations in the form of demonstrations for procedural skills—Encoding Specificity Principle
19. Provide several diverse worked examples for far transfer skills—Varied Context for Far Transfer Principle
20. Provide training in effective ways to study worked examples—Practice Principle

(Continued)

Exhibit 14.1. A Summary of e-Learning Guidelines. (Continued)

Chapter 11—Guidelines for Use of Collaboration in Internet/Intranet e-Learning

If your learning environment has high to moderate levels of concurrency:

21. Assign collaborative projects or problem discussions to heterogeneous small groups or pairs
22. Use e-mail, chats, message boards, and conferencing facilities for collaborative assignments
23. Use message boards for learner exchanges related to course topics

If your learning environment has low levels of concurrency:

24. Use e-mail and discussion boards for collaborative assignments modified for individual learners
25. Use e-mail for learners to contact instructors
26. Use message boards for learner exchanges related to course topics

Chapter 12—Guidelines for Navigational Options—Learner Control Principles

Allow learners choices over topics and instructional methods such as practice when:

27. They have related prior knowledge and skills and/or good self-regulatory learning skills
28. Courses are designed primarily to be informational rather than skill-building
29. Courses are advanced rather than introductory
30. The default option leads to important instructional methods such as practice

Limit learner choices over topics and instructional options when:

31. Learners are novice to the content, skill outcomes are important, and learners lack good self-regulatory skills

Use advisement diagnostic testing strategies when:

32. Learners lack good self-regulation skills and the instructional outcomes are important
33. Learners are heterogeneous regarding background and needs and the cost to produce tests pays off in learner time saved
34. Always give learners options to progress at their own pace, review prior topics/lessons, and quit the program

Exhibit 14.1. (Continued)

Chapter 13—Guidelines for Training Problem-Solving Skills
35. Use real job tools and cases to teach work-specific problem-solving processes—Encoding Specificity Principle
36. Provide worked examples of experts' problem-solving actions and thoughts—Worked Examples Principle
37. Assign learners to write out their problem-solving plans—Practice Principle
38. Provide learners with a map of their problem-solving steps to compare with an expert map—Feedback Principle
39. Base lessons on analysis of actions and thoughts of expert practitioners—Encoding Specificity Principle

Sample One: Ammunition Safety
Description of the Sample

Figures 14.1 through 14.4 are screen captures from a training course on ammunition safety. It is delivered on CD-ROM and uses audio and visual media elements. Module 1 titled "Explosives, Propellants, and Chemical Ammunition Fillers" focuses primarily on physical and chemical properties of explosives to provide background knowledge for military personnel working with ammunition. Some of the lesson objectives are:

- To identify characteristics of high and low explosive trains
- To identify components of high and low explosives
- To identify standard terminology used in ammunition handling

We would categorize this module as a tutorial on background information that is related to the tasks that military personnel might perform with ammunition. The module begins with the historical timeline illustrated in Figure 14.1. By clicking on the timeline at the bottom of the screen, the learner can access instruction that includes video, narration, background music from the historical period, and sounds such as explosions and gunfire from the siege of Normandy. The learner can exit from the history section at any time and begin the technical content of the lesson. Figure 14.2 is typical

Figure 14.1. Historical Timeline in Ammunition Safety Course.

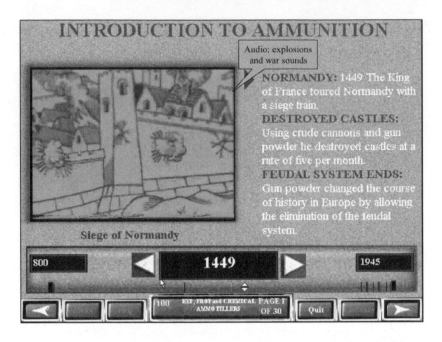

Figure 14.2. Explanation of Energy in Ammunition Safety Course.

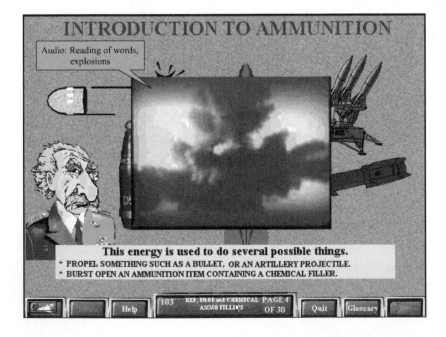

Figure 14.3. Exercise in Ammunition Safety Course.

Figure 14.4. Feedback in Ammunition Safety Course.

of screens that present the concepts of energy in explosives. The onscreen text is narrated. Animations and related sounds of bullets and a video of an ammunition explosion follow the narration. Figure 14.3 illustrates a drag and drop practice question that is placed approximately twenty-five screens into the program. The audio directions ask the learners to drag the bottom boxes that say "most brisant" and "most sensitive" to the relevant portions of the ammunition shell. Figure 14.4 shows incorrect answer feedback to this question.

Application of Guidelines

This sample violates many of the media elements guidelines summarized in Exhibit 14.1. For example, many of the content screens such as Figure 14.2 present words in text and in audio narration in violation of Guideline 10. There are numerous violations of Guideline 11. First, there are many distracting sounds and visuals such as the animation of the bullets and the videos of bursting ammunition in Figures 14.1 and 14.2. Second, the graphic of the general seen in Figure 14.2 is used throughout the program and is an irrelevant visual serving no instructional purpose. Third, the historical timeline at the introduction to the program is a seductive detail tangential to the goal of the training. Guideline 8 states that information that learners need time to process (such as directions to exercises) should remain on the screen in text. However, in Figure 14.3 the directions are in audio only. After completing the exercise, the feedback shown in Figure 14.4 appears on a separate screen from the question and thus violates Guideline 9. Instead, the feedback should appear on the same screen as the question, allowing the learner to easily integrate the question, her response, and the feedback.

Guideline 14 calls for frequent job-relevant practice integrated throughout the training. In this program there are approximately twenty-five screens of technical information presented prior to the first practice question. Cognitive overload from the amount of technical information presented prior to practice will likely depress learning. Guidelines 14 and 18 focus on the need for examples and practice presented in the context of how they would be used on the job. In this lesson, much background information is presented, but it is not related to job tasks or decisions. In evaluating this module, we would ask which topics are truly job relevant and whether they might be more effectively taught in conjunction with job tasks and decisions. Since they are presented out of context of the job, transfer may be at risk.

Sample Two: Creating Links in Dreamweaver
Description of Sample

Figures 14.5 through 14.8 are taken from a course on how to use the Dreamweaver software to build Web pages. The course was built using MacroMedia's Director/Authorware tools and is "shocked" for Internet delivery. Learners need the MacroMedia plug-in Shockwave on their computers to view the graphic and audio media elements. The goal of the course is to teach end-user computer procedures and related concepts. It is designed in a directive style. These screens are from a lesson on creating links. The lesson objective is, "You will create a relative link and an absolute link."

Figure 14.5. Use of Mouse-Over to Illustrate Concept of URL.

With permission from Element K.

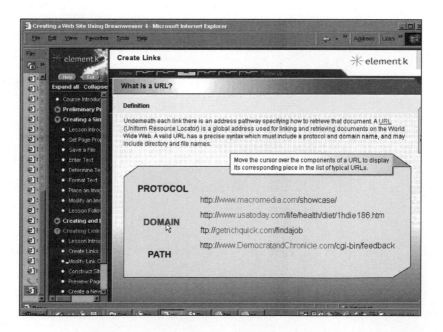

Figure 14.6. Guidelines for Constructing Links.

With permission from Element K.

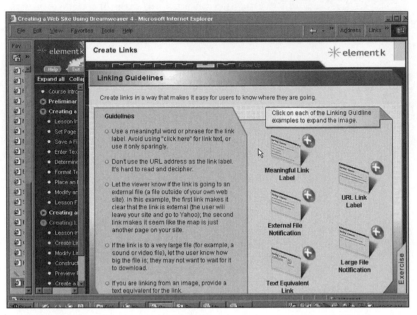

Figure 14.7. Steps for Creating Link in Dreamweaver Software.

With permission from Element K.

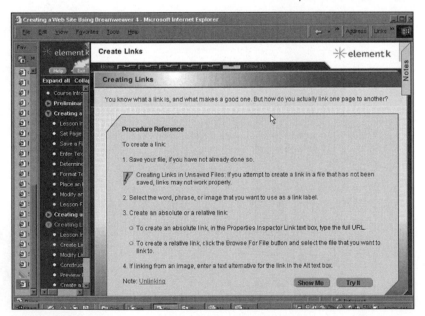

Figure 14.8. Exercise to Create Links. Audio Narrates the Text.

Courtesy of Element K.

A short motivational introductory exercise on the efficiency of links (not shown) is followed by a topic menu and several concepts related to links. One concept—URL—uses rollovers that change the text colors to illustrate the three parts of the URL, as shown in Figure 14.5. When you place the cursor on DOMAIN, it turns blue along with the domain portions of the three URL samples shown. In Figure 14.6 guidelines for how to construct links are presented along with an example of each guideline, which can be seen by enlarging the baby screens. A practice exercise can be accessed by clicking the *Exercise* tab in the lower right corner of this screen. It is a multiple choice question asking you to select the best link for a given purpose. Steps for how to create links in Dreamweaver are presented in Figure 14.7. From here you can access an animated narrated demonstration by clicking the *Show Me* button or go to a practice exercise by clicking the *Try It* button in the lower right-hand corner. If you click *Try It,* you go to a scenario that uses text and audio to present information about the kind of link you need to create (Figure 14.8). You then end the lesson by paging forward to a simulation of the Dreamweaver software to create the link.

Application of Guidelines

Overall, we found the lesson structure job relevant and well-organized. The short motivational demonstration of link effectiveness is to the point and involves the learner from the beginning of the lesson. Prior to learning the procedure for creating a link, related concepts such as URLs, absolute versus relative links, and guidelines for creating links are presented. This lesson effectively applies many of the guidelines in the checklist. Nearly every screen includes a relevant graphic described by text, per Guideline 1. The text is effectively integrated into the graphics as suggested by Guideline 2. Two noteworthy examples are the use of rollovers in Figure 14.5 and the use of baby screens in Figure 14.6. Regarding Guideline 11, there were no distracting graphics, sounds, or stories. Practice exercises such as those following Figures 14.6 and 14.7 were job relevant and were interspersed throughout the lesson. A worked example in the form of a demonstration, was an effective implementation of Guideline 18.

In a couple of places Guideline 9 was violated. For example, when you enlarge the baby screens in Figure 14.6, the guidelines are covered, making it difficult to mentally integrate the example with the guideline it illustrated. We would recommend a different placement of the baby screen enlargements or a rollover that brought up a different example when each guideline was touched by the cursor. Also, when attempting to complete the hands-on practice in the simulated Dreamweaver screen, neither the procedural steps nor the information in the scenario, both presented on prior screens, was visible. Although these could be accessed by requesting a hint on the simulation screen, we would prefer more direct access to the information needed to complete the exercise.

Learner choice over topics is available by way of the course map in the left frame and the horizontal topic tabs at the top of the lesson page. This gave us a good orientation to our location in the course and lesson. However, a deliberate choice by the learner is needed to access important instructional methods such as the examples of the link guidelines as well as the related practice exercise (Figures 14.6 and 14.7). Applying Guideline 30, we would recommend that the navigation be reworked to make examples and practice exercises the default option.

We did not see any use of collaborative facilities. Since the course is procedural and the number of concurrent learners is unpredictable, we would recommend the application of Guidelines 25 and 26, for example, use of e-mail for instructor questions and a message board for users to post questions and lessons learned about Dreamweaver.

Finally, we would suggest a different use of audio. Audio was used in two places: on the demonstration screen (not shown), where the procedural steps in text at the bottom of the screen were narrated, and on the scenario screen (Figure 14.8), where the onscreen text was narrated. For the demonstration, to implement Guideline 10, we would recommend removing the onscreen text. Since there was no important graphic on the scenario screen, reading of the text would not detract from learning. We would further suggest the use of audio on some of the more complex topics that relied on text and visuals to explain concepts.

Sample Three: Accelerate Expertise—Researching Commercial Bank Loans

Description of Sample

Figures 14.9 through 14.12 are from a guided discovery course designed to teach bank loan officers how to use a structured process to research and evaluate commercial loan applicants. The course is presented on CD-ROM and includes video, text, and various other graphic elements. You begin the case in your office with an assignment from your boss (Figure 14.9) presented on a brief video. You then are free to use various resources in your office, including a credit report request (Figure 14.10), interviews of the applicant, industry publications, applicant references and to gather information. An agent coach is available for advice and offers links to structured lessons related to the loan review process shown in Figure 14.11. At the end of your research, you make your recommendation to the loan committee and get feedback from your coach. You also have the opportunity to view the steps you took to solve the case (Figure 14.12) and compare them to expert steps.

Figure 14.9. Boss Introducing Case Study.

Courtesy of Moody's Financial Services.

Figure 14.10. Learner Reviews Credit Report.

Courtesy of Moody's Financial Services.

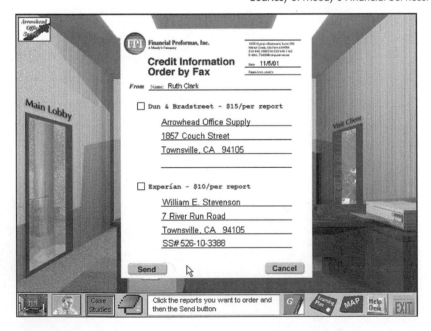

Figure 14.11. Coach Offers Access to Lesson.

Courtesy of Moody's Financial Services.

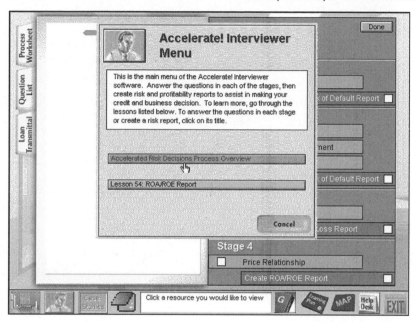

Figure 14.12. Learner Review of Steps.

Courtesy of Moody's Financial Services.

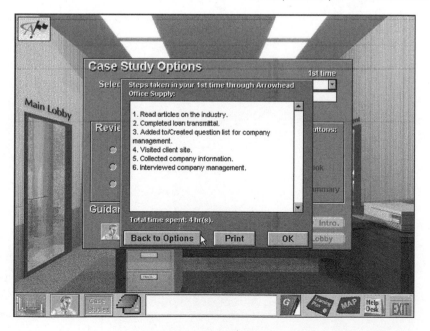

Application of Guidelines

The lesson effectively applies the media element Guidelines 7 through 13. The lesson is situated in a graphic interface using an office with various job-relevant tools illustrated visually. A file cabinet by your desk provides memory support by storing all the data you collect during your research. Other than paper documents, there is no onscreen text. Human interactions such as your boss's assignment are presented in video. A virtual coach is used to give hints and provide access to structured lessons on related topics. Although we do not show them here, another phase to the course provides a series of tutorial lessons that can be used prior to or during work on the case study.

Since the structure of the case study is guided discovery, it emphasizes learning during problem-solving. Regarding navigation, there was a high level of learner control in the case study segment. However, in the tutorial part of the course (not shown) a pretest is used to give advice regarding which lessons to study. Most of the guidelines relating to teaching of problem-solving skills are reflected throughout the case.

Sample Four: Identifying Hazardous Materials

Description of Sample

Figures 14.13 through 14.16 illustrate some screens from a course delivered on CD-ROM for individuals who are involved with the transportation of hazardous materials. The lesson objectives are:

- Identify the markings on packages that designate them as hazardous.
- Identify the information on a shipping paper that designates material as hazardous.
- Cite how vehicles carrying hazardous materials are identified.

The lesson starts with a review of labeling requirements presented in prior lessons, followed by the practice exercise shown in Figure 14.14. The narration that accompanies the visual shown in Figure 14.15 explains which identifiers from the hazardous materials government regulations table must appear on the shipping papers. As a specific identifier is mentioned, it is animated from the table to the shipping paper. In a similar way additional

Figure 14.13. Lesson Title Screen.

Courtesy of Defense Ammunition Center.

Figure 14.14. Introductory Exercise with Feedback.

Courtesy of Defense Ammunition Center.

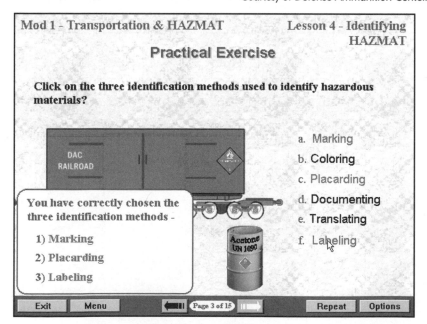

Figure 14.15. Audio and Animation Used to Explain the Elements That Must Be on Shipping Paper.

Courtesy of Defense Ammunition Center.

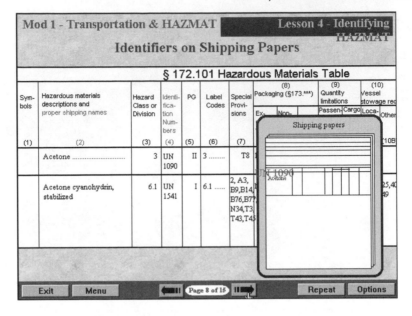

Figure 14.16. Practice on Hazardous Material Identifiers.

Courtesy of Defense Ammunition Center.

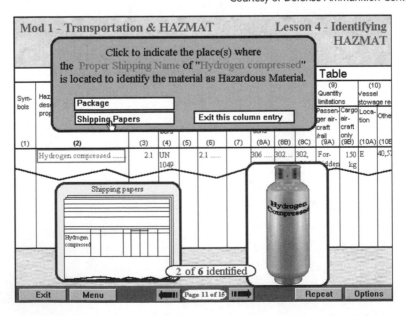

screens summarize the legal requirement for marking, labeling, and placarding containers and transportation vehicles transporting hazardous materials. Figure 14.16 is part of the practice exercise that asks the learner to select a hazardous material from the table and indicate what elements need to be included on the shipping paper and container. As a correct identifier is selected from the table and specified for shipping paper and/or container, it animates from the table onto the shipping paper and container.

Application of Guidelines

This lesson applies all of the media elements in Guidelines 7 through 12. Since the lesson goal is an accurate visual discrimination, illustrations of markings are used throughout. Audio is particularly effective in describing the graphics and animations on the screen. There are no violations of Guideline 11 since the information provided is relevant, the narrations are succinct, there are no irrelevant background sounds, and there are no extraneous stories. Onscreen text is not narrated except on screens with no graphics, thus supporting Guideline 10. Guidelines 8 and 9 are supported in several ways. For example, exercise directions remain as onscreen text and thus are accessible to the learner throughout the exercise. Also, after completion of an exercise, the feedback appears on the question screen so the learner can easily integrate it.

The learning objectives and content are directly related to job-relevant skills. For example, hazardous materials are appropriately labeled. Practice questions are placed throughout the lesson per Guideline 15. Prior to an exercise, examples such as those shown in Figure 14.14 have clearly illustrated the HAZMAT marking rules, supporting Guideline 18. In summary, this course provides a good illustration of a concise, informally narrated series of relevant graphics supported by effective practice and worked examples.

The Next Generation of e-Learning

What differences will we see in e-learning developed for organizational training in the next few years? Here we make some predictions.

Prediction One: e-Learning for Job Payoff

Because e-learning developed for workers in organizations is an expensive commitment, we predict more examples of online training that apply guidelines proven to lead to return on investment. Specifically, we believe that there will be:

- Fewer Las Vegas-style courses that depress learning by over-use of glitz and games. Instead, the power of technology will be leveraged more effectively to support acquisition and transfer of job-related skills.

- More problem-centered designs that use job-realistic problems in the start of a lesson or course to establish relevance, in the body of the lesson to drive the selection and organization of related knowledge and skills, and at the end of the lesson to provide practice and assessment opportunities.

- More creative ways to blend computer technology with other delivery media so that the features of a given media are best used to support ongoing job-relevant skill requirements.

Prediction Two: e-Learning to Build Problem-Solving Skills

The majority of e-learning currently on the business and industry market is designed to build near transfer or procedural skills such as end-user software training. However, the increasing economic dependence on knowledge workers, coupled with a shrinking workforce, will drive more courses that focus on building problem-solving skills in specific work domains. Specifically, we believe that

- E-learning will increasingly make use of the unique technological features that can support simulations and guided opportunites to learn from them. The current lesson designs that use text, audio, and graphics to describe content will survive. However, these will be supplemented by lessons that encourage the building of mental models and problem-solving skills.

- E-learning will increasingly be used to make invisible processes and events visible. Learners will be able to see maps of their own problem-solving activities and compare them to expert maps. Additionally, learners will be able to "see" invisible processes, such as how equipment works internally, or how to know what a customer is thinking.

- Alternative representations will be used to help to see dynamic relationships in ways that can only be described in other media. For example, in training of food professionals, a "germ meter" can be used to illustrate the effects of various methods of preparation and handling of food. The relationship between germ density and heat can be illustrated by a dynamic chart that graphs the number of germs as a function of temperature and time of cooking.

- Collaborative e-learning features will be used more extensively and more effectively. Teams of learners will work asynchronously to solve case problems and contribute to ongoing corporate lessons learned about issues relevant to a specific industry or cross-industry profession.

In summary, the courseware designers of the future will get better at finding cost-effective ways to exploit features unique to technology in ways that can make learning more effective and efficient. We hope that this book will play a role in helping those in business and industry to make good decisions about design and selection of e-learning now and in the future.

REFERENCES

Anderson, J.R., Farrell, R., and Sauers, R. (1984). How subject matter knowledge affects recall and interest. *American Educational Research Journal, 31,* 313–337.

Atkinson, R.K. (2002). Optimizing learning from examples using animated pedagogical agents. *Journal of Educational Psychology, 94,* 416–427.

Atkinson, R.K., Derry, S.J., Renkl, A., and Wortham, D. (2000). Learning from examples: Instructional principles from the worked examples research. *Review of Educational Research, 70*(2), 181–214.

Bahrick, H.P. (1987). Retention of Spanish vocabulary over 8 years. *Journal of Experimental Psychology: Learning, Memory, and Cognition, 13,* 344–349.

Beck, I., McKeown, M.G., Sandora, C., Kucan, L., and Worthy, J. (1996). Questioning the author: A year long classroom implementation to engage students in text. *Elementary School Journal, 96,* 385–414.

Bielaczyc, K., Pirolli, P., and Brown, A.L. (1995). Training in self-explanation and self-regulation strategies: Investigating the effects of knowledge acquisition activities on problem solving. *Cognition and Instruction, 13,* 221–253.

Bransford, J.D., Brown, A.L.O., and Cocking, R.R. (1999). *How people learn.* Washington, DC: National Academy Press.

Cassell, J., Bickmore, T., Campbell, L., Vilhjalmsson, H., and Yan, H. (2000). Human conversation as a system framework: Designing embodied conversational agents. In J. Cassell, J. Sullivan, S. Prevost, and E. Churchill (Eds.), *Embodied Conversational Agents* (pp. 29–63). Cambridge, MA: MIT Press.

Cassell, J., Sullivan, J., Prevost, S., and Churchill, E. (2000). *Embodied conversational agents.* Cambridge, MA: MIT Press.

Catrambone, R. (1996). Generalizing solution procedures learned from examples. *Journal of Experimental Psychology: Learning, Memory, and Cognition, 22*(4), 1020–1031.

Catrambone, R. (1998). The subgoal learning model: Creating better examples so that students can solve novel problems. *Journal of Experimental Psychology: General, 127*(4), 355–376.

Chandler, P., and Sweller, J. (1991). Cognitive load theory and the format of instruction. *Cognition and Instruction, 8,* 293–332.

Chi, M.T.H. (2000). Self-explaining expository texts: The dual processes of generating inferences and repairing mental models. In R. Glaser (Ed.). *Advances in instructional psychology: educational design and cognitive science.* Hillsdale, NJ: Lawrence Erlbaum Associates.

Chi, M.T.H., Bassok, M., Lewis, M.W., Reimann, P., and Glaser, R. (1989). Self-explanations: How students study and use examples in learning to solve problems. *Cognitive Science, 13,* 145–182.

Chi, M.T.H., De Leeuw, N., Chiu, M., and LaVancher, C. (1994). Eliciting self-explanations improves understanding. *Cognitive Science, 18,* 439–477.

Clark, R.E. (1994). Media will never influence learning. *Educational Technology Research and Development, 42*(2), 21–30.

Clark, R.C. (1998). *Building expertise: Cognitive methods for training and performance improvement.* Silver Spring, MD: International Society for Performance Improvement.

Clark, R.C. (1999). *Developing technical training.* Silver Spring, MD: International Society for Performance Improvement.

Clark, R.C. (2000). Four architectures of learning. *Performance Improvement, 39*(10), 31–37.

Cohen, E.G. (1994). Restructuring the classroom: Conditions for productive small groups. *Review of Educational Research, 64*(1), 1–35.

Crossman, E.R.F.W. (1959). A theory of the acquisition of speed skill. *Ergonomics, 2,* 153–166.

Cuban, L. (1986). *Teachers and machines: The classroom use of technology since 1920.* New York: Teachers College Press.

Dewey, J. (1913). *Interest and effort in education.* Cambridge, MA: Houghton Mifflin.

Dillon, A., and Gabbard, R. (1998). Hypermedia as an educational technology: A review of the quantitative research literature on learner comprehension, control, and style. *Educational Psychology, 81,* 240–246.

Dixon, N.M. (1990). The relationship between training responses on participant reaction forms and posttest scores. *Human Resource Development Quarterly, 1*(2), 129–137.

Duncker, K. (1945). On problem solving. *Psychological Monographs, 58,* 270.

Ebbinghaus, N. (1913). *Memory* (N.R. Ruger and C.E. Bussenius, Trans.). New York: Teacher's College. (Original work published 1885)

Ericsson, K.A. (1990). Theoretical issues in the study of exceptional performance. In K.J. Gilhooly, M.T.G. Keane, R.H. Logie, and G. Erdos (Eds.). *Lines of thinking: Reflections on the psychology of thought.* New York: John Wiley & Sons.

Fantuzzo, J.W., Riggio, R.E., Connelly, S., and Dimeff, L.A. (1989). Effects of reciprocal peer tutoring on academic achievement and psychological adjustment: A component analysis. *Journal of Educational Psychology, 81*(2), 173–177.

Galvin, T. (2001). Industry 2001 report. *Training, 38*(10), 40–75.

Garner, R., Gillingham, M., and White, C. (1989). Effects of seductive details on macroprocessing and microprocessing in adults and children. *Cognition and Instruction, 6,* 41–57.

Ge, X., and Land, S.M. (2002, April). *The effects of question prompts and peer interactions in scaffolding students' problem-solving processes on an ill-structured task.* Paper presented at the Annual Meeting of the American Educational Research Association Conference. New Orleans, LA.

Gick, M.L., and Holyoak, K.J. (1980). Analogical problem solving. *Cognitive Psychology, 12,* 306–355.

Glenberg, A.M., Sanocki, T., Epstein, W., and Morris, C. (1987). Enhancing calibration of comprehension. *Journal of Experimental Psychology: General, 116*(2), 119–136.

Glenberg, A.M., Wilkinson, A.C., and Epstein, W. (1992). The illusion of knowing: Failure in the self-assessment of comprehension. In T.O. Nelson (Ed.), *Metacognition: Core readings.* Boston, MA: Allyn & Bacon.

Graesser, A.C., Bowers, C., Olde, B., and Pomeroy, V. (1999). Who said what? Source memory for narrative and character agents in literary short stories. *Journal of Educational Psychology, 91,* 284–300.

Hall, W.E., and Cushing, J.R. (1947). The relative value of three methods of presenting learning material. *Journal of Psychology, 24,* 57–62.

Harp, S.F., and Mayer, R.E. (1997). The role of interest in learning from scientific text and illustrations: On the distinction between emotional interest and cognitive interest. *Journal of Educational Psychology, 89,* 92–102.

Harp, S.F., and Mayer, R.E. (1998). How seductive details do their damage: A theory of cognitive interest in science learning. *Journal of Educational Psychology, 90,* 414–434.

Hegarty. M., Carpenter, P. A., and Just, M.A. (1996). Diagrams in the comprehension of scientific texts. In R. Barr, M. L. Kamil, P. Mosenthal, and P. D. Pearson (Eds.), *Handbook of reading research. Vol. II* (pp. 641–668). Mahwah, NJ: Lawrence Erlbaum Associates.

Jeung, H., Chandler, P., and Sweller, J. (1997). The role of visual indicators in dual sensory mode instruction. *Educational Psychology, 17*(3), 329–343.

Johnson, D.W., and Johnson, R.T. (1990). Cooperative learning and achievement. In S. Sharan (Ed.), *Cooperative learning: Theory and practice* (pp. 23–37). New York: Praeger.

Johnson, D.W., and Johnson, R.T. (1992). *Creative controversy: Intellectual challenge in the classroom.* Edina, MN.: Interaction Book Company.

Jonassen, D.H., and Kwon, H.I. (2001). Communication Patterns in Computer Mediated Versus Face-to-Face Group Problem Solving. *Educational Technology Research and Development 49*(1), 35–51.

Kalyuga, S., Chandler, P., and Sweller, J. (1999). Managing split attention and redundancy in multimedia instruction. *Applied Cognitive Psychology, 13,* 351–372.

Kalyuga, S., Chandler, P., Tuovinen, J., and Sweller, J. (2001). When problem solving is superior to studying worked examples. *Journal of Educational Psychology, 93,* 579–588.

Kamin, C.S., O'Sullivan, P.S., and Deterdin, R.R. (2002). *Does case modality impact critical thinking in PBL groups?* Paper presented at the American Educational Research Association Annual Meeting, New Orleans, LA.

King, A. (1992). Facilitating elaborative learning through guided student-generated questioning. *Educational Psychologist, 27,* 111–126.

Lajoie, S.P., Azevedo, R., and Fleiszer, D.M. (1998). Cognitive tools for assessment and learning in a high information flow environment. *Journal of Educational Computing Research, 18*, 205–235.

Lee, S., and Lee, Y.H.K. (1991). Effects of learner-control versus program control strategies on computer-aided learning of chemistry problems: For acquision or review? *Journal of Educational Psychology, 83*, 491–498.

LeFevre, J.A., and Dixon, P. (1986). Do written instructions need examples? *Cognition and Instruction, 3*, 1–30.

Lesgold, A., Eggan, G., Katz, S., and Rao, G. (1993). Possibilities for assessment using computer-based apprenticeship environments. In M. Rabinowitz (Ed.). *Cognitive science foundations of instruction.* Mahwah, NJ: Lawrence Erlbaum Associates.

Lester, J.C., Towns, S.G., Callaway, C.B., Voerman, J.L., and Fitzgerald, P. J. (2000). Deictic and emotive communication in animated pedagogical agents. In J. Cassell, J. Sullivan, S. Prevost, and E. Churchill (Eds.). *Embodied conversational agents* (pp. 123–154). Cambridge, MA: MIT Press.

Lin, Z., Hmelo, C., Kinzer, C.K., and Secules, T.J. (1999). Designing technology to support reflection. *Educational Technology Research and Development, 47*, 43–62.

Lou, Y., Abrami, P.C., and d'Apollonia, S. (2001). Small group and individual learning with technology: A meta-analysis. *Review of Educational Research, 71*, 449–521.

Mandl, H., Weinberger, A., and Fischer, F. (2002). *Fostering individual transfer and knowledge convergence with scripts in computer-mediated communication.* Paper presented at the American Educational Research Association Annual Meeting, New Orleans, LA.

Mayer, R.E. (1983). Can you repeat that? Qualitative effects of repetition and advance organizers on learning from visual and verbal summaries of science textbook lessons. *Journal of Educational Psychology, 75,* 40–49.

Mayer, R.E. (1989a). Models for understanding. *Review of Educational Research, 59,* 43–64.

Mayer, R.E. (1989b). Systematic thinking fostered by illustrations in scientific text. *Journal of Educational Psychology, 81,* 240–246.

Mayer, R.E. (1993). Illustrations that instruct. In R. Glaser (Ed.). *Advances in instructional psychology* (Vol. 4, pp. 253–284). Hillsdale, NJ: Lawrence Erlbaum Associates.

Mayer, R.E. (1998). Cognitive, metacognitive, and motivational aspects of problem solving. *Instructional Science, 26,* 49–63.

Mayer, R.E. (2001a). *Multimedia learning.* New York: Cambridge University Press.

Mayer, R.E. (2001b). Cognitive constraints on multimedia learning: When presenting more material results in less learning. *Journal of Educational Psychology, 93,* 187–198.

Mayer, R.E., and Anderson, R.B. (1991). Animations need narrations: An experimental test of a dual-processing systems in working memory. *Journal of Educational Psychology, 90,* 312–320.

Mayer, R.E., Bove, W., Bryman, A., Mars, R., and Tapangco, L. (1996). When less is more: Meaningful learning from visual and verbal summaries of science textbook lessons. *Journal of Educational Psychology, 88,* 64–73.

Mayer, R.E., and Chandler, P. (2001). When learning is just a click away: Does simple user interaction foster deeper understanding of multimedia messages? *Journal of Educational Psychology, 93,* 390–397.

Mayer, R.E., and Gallini, J.K. (1990). When is an illustration worth ten thousand words? *Journal of Educational Psychology, 88,* 64–73.

Mayer, R.E., Heiser, J., and Lonn, S. (2001). Cognitive constraints on multimedia learning: When presenting more material results in less understanding. *Journal of Educational Psychology, 93,* 187–198.

Mayer, R.E., and Moreno, R. (1998). A split-attention effect in multimedia learning: Evidence for dual coding hypothesis. *Journal of Educational Psychology, 83,* 484–490.

Mayer, R.E., Sims. V., and Tajika, H. (1995). A comparison of how textbooks teach mathematical problem solving in Japan and the United States. *American Educational Research Journal, 32,* 443–460.

Mayer, R.E., Sobko, K., and Mautone, P.D. (in press). Social cues in multimedia learning: Role of speaker's voice. *Journal of Educational Psychology, 94.*

Mayer, R.E., Steinhoff, K., Bower, G., and Mars, R. (1995). A generative theory of textbook design: Using annotated illustrations to foster meaningful learning of science text. *Educational Technology Research and Development, 43,* 31–43.

Mayer, R.E., and Wittrock, M.C. (1996). Problem-Solving Transfer. In D.C. Berliner, and R.C. Calfee (Eds.). *Handbook of Educational Psychology.* New York: Macmillan.

McDaniel, M.A., and Donnelly, C.M. (1996). Learning with analogy and elaborative interrogation. *Journal of Educational Psychology, 88,* 508–519.

Moreno, R., and Mayer, R.E. (1999a). Cognitive principles of multimedia learning: The role of modality and contiguity. *Journal of Educational Psychology, 91,* 358–368.

Moreno, R., and Mayer, R.E. (1999b). Multimedia-supported metaphors for meaning making in mathematics. *Cognition and Instruction, 17,* 215–248.

Moreno, R., and Mayer, R.E. (2000a). A coherence effect in multimedia learning: The case for minimizing irrelevant sounds in the design of multimedia instructional messages. *Journal of Educational Psychology, 92,* 117–125.

Moreno, R., and Mayer, R.E. (2000b). Engaging students in active learning: The case for personalized multimedia messages. *Journal of Educational Psychology, 93,* 724–733.

Moreno, R., and Mayer, R.E. (2002). Verbal redundancy in multimedia learning: When reading helps listening. *Journal of Educational Psychology, 94,* 156–163.

Moreno, R., and Mayer, R.E. (in press). Learning science in virtual reality environments: Do multimedia design principles still apply? *Journal of Educational Psychology, 94.*

Moreno, R., Mayer, R.E., Spires, H., and Lester, J. (2001). The case for social agency in computer-based teaching: Do students learn more deeply when they interact with animated pedagogical agents? *Cognition and Instruction, 19,* 177–214.

Mousavi, S., Low, R., and Sweller, J. (1995). Reducing cognitive load by mixing auditory and visual presentation modes. *Journal of Educational Psychology, 87,* 319–334.

Muller, H. (2000). Stanford's Casper. *Fortune, 142*(9), 275–288.

National Research Council. (1991). In D. Druckman and R.A. Bjork (Eds.), *In the mind's eye: Enhancing human performance.* Washington DC: National Academy Press.

National Research Council. (1994a). Cooperative learning. In D. Druckman and R.A. Bjork (Eds.), *Learning, remembering, believing.* Washington, DC: National Academy Press.

National Research Council. (1994b). Illusions of comprehension, competence, and remembering. In D. Druckman and R.A. Bjork (Eds.), *Learning, remembering, believing.* Washington, DC: National Academy Press.

Niederhauser, D.S., Reynolds, R.E., Salmen, D.J., and Skolmoski, P. (2000). The influence of cognitive load on learning from hypertext. *Journal of Educational Computing Research, 23,* 237–255.

Norman, D.A. (1993). *Things that make us smart.* Reading, MA: Addison-Wesley.

O'Donnell, A.M., and Dansereau, D.F. (1992). Scripted cooperation in student dyads: A method for analyzing and enhancing academic learning and performance. In R. Hertz-Lazarowitz and N. Miller (Eds.), *Interaction in cooperative groups.* New York: Cambridge University Press.

O'Neil, H.F., Mayer, R.E., Herl, H.E., Niemi, C., Olin, K., and Thurman, R.A. (2000). Instructional strategies for virtual aviation training environments. In H.F. O'Neil and D.H. Andrews (Eds.), *Aircrew training and assessment* (pp. 105–130). Mahwah, NJ: Lawrence Erlbaum Associates.

Paas, F.G.W.C. (1992). Training strategies for attaining transfer of problem-solving skill in statistics: A cognitive load approach. *Journal of Educational Psychology, 84,* 429–434.

Paas, F.G.W.C., and van Merrienboer, J.J.G. (1994b). Instructional control of cognitive load in the training of complex cognitive tasks. *Educational Psychology Review, 6,* 351–371.

Perkins, D.N., and Salomon, G. (1989). Are cognitive skills context-bound? *Educational Researcher, 18*(1), 16–25.

Pressley, M., Wood, E., Woloshyn, V.E., Martin, V., King, A., and Menke, D. (1992). Encouraging mindful use of prior knowledge: Attempting to construct explanatory answers facilitates learning. *Educational Psychologist, 27,* 91–109.

Reeves, B., and Nass, C. (1996). *The media equation: How people treat computers, television, and new media like real people and places.* New York: Cambridge University Press.

Renkl, A., Stark, R., Gruber, H., and Mandl, H. (1998). Learning from worked-out examples: The efects of example variability and elicited self-explanations. *Contemporary Educational Psychology, 23,* 90–108.

Renninger, K.A., Hidi, S., and Krapp. A. (1992). *The role of interest in learning and development.* Hillsdale, NJ: Lawrence Erlbaum Associates.

Rickel, J., and Johnson, L.W. (2000). Task-oriented collaboration with embodied agents in virtual worlds.

Robinson, D.H. (2002). Spatial text adjuncts and learning: An introduction to the special issue. *Educational Psychology Review, 14,* 1–3.

Rosenbaum, D.A., Carlson, R.A., and Gilmore, R.O. (2001). Acquisition of intellectual and perceptual motor skills. *Annual Review of Psychology, 52,* 453–470.

Rosenshine, B., Meister, C., and Chapman, S. (1996). Teaching students to generate questions: A review of the intervention studies. *Review of Educational Research, 66*(2), 181–221.

Schmidt, H.E., and Moust, J.H.C. (2000). Factors affecting small-group tutorial learning: A review of research. In D.H. Evensen and C.E. Hmelo (Eds.), *Problem Based Learning.* Mahwah, NJ: Lawrence Erlbaum Associates.

Schnackenberg, H.L., Sullivan, H.J., Leader, L.R., and Jones, E.E.K. (1998). Learner preferences and achievement under differing amounts of learner practice. *Educational Technology Research and Development, 46,* 5–15.

Schnackenberg, H.L., and Sullivan, H.J. (2000). Learner control over full and lean computer based instruction under differing ability levels. *Educational Technology Research and Development, 48,* 19–35.

Schoenfeld, A.H. (1987). What's all the fuss about metacognition? In A. Schoenfeld (Ed.), *Cognitive Science and Mathematics Education.* Hillsdale, NJ: Lawrence Erlbaum Associates.

Slavin, R. (1983). Why does cooperative learning increase student achievement? *Psychological Bulletin, 94,* 429–445.

Steinberg, E.R. (1989). Cognition and learner control: A literature review, 1977–1988. *Journal of Computer-Based Instruction, 16*(4), 117–121.

Stone, N.J. (2000). Exploring the relationship between calibration and self-regulated learning. *Educational Psychology Review, 4,* 437–475.

Svetcov, D. (2000). The virtual classroom vs. the real one. *Forbes, 166,* 50–54.

Sweller, J. (1999). *Instructional design in technical areas.* Camberwell, Australia: ACER Press.

Sweller, J., and Chandler, P. (1994). Why some material is difficult to learn. *Cognition and Instruction, 12,* 185–233.

Sweller, J., Chandler, P., Tierney, P., and Cooper, M. (1990). Cognitive load and selective attention as factors in the structuring of technical material. *Journal of Experimental Psychology: General, 119,* 176–192.

Sweller, J., van Merrienboer, J.J.G., and Paas, F. (1998). Cognitive architecture and instructional design. *Educational Psychology Review, 10,* 251–296.

Tennyson, R.D. (1980). Instructional control strategies and content structure as design varibles in concept acquisition using computer-assisted instruction. *Journal of Educational Psychology, 72,* 525–532.

Tennyson, C.L., Tennyson, R.D., and Rothen, W. (1980). Content structure and instructional control strategies as design variables in computer assisted instruction. *Educational Communication and Technology Journal, 28,* 169–176.

Trafton, J.G., and Reiser, B.J. (1993). The contributions of studying examples and solving problems to skill acquisition. In M. Polson (Ed.), *Proceedings of the Fifteenth annual conference of the Cognitive Science Society (1017–1022).* Hillsdale, N.J.: Erlbaum.

Walczyk, J.J., and Hall, V.C. (1989). Effects of examples and embedded questions on the accuracy of comprehension self-assessments. *Journal of Educational Psychology, 81,* 435–437.

Wiley, J., and Voss, J.F. (1999). Constructing arguments from multiple sources: Tasks that promote understanding and not just memory for text. *Journal of Educational Psychology, 91,* 301–311.

Young, J.D. (1996). The effect of self-regulated learning strategies on performance in learner controlled computer-based instruction. *Educational Technology Research and Development, 44,* 17–27.

Zhu, X., and Simon, H.A. (1987). Learning mathematics from examples and by doing. *Cognition and Instruction, 4,* 137–166.

GLOSSARY

Adaptive Control	A process in which learners are directed or branched to different instructional materials in a lesson based on the program's evaluation of their responses to lesson exercises.
Advisement	A process in which learners are given advice as to what actions they should take in a lesson based on the program's evaluation of their responses to lesson exercises.
Agents	Onscreen characters who help guide the learning process during an e-learning episode. Also called called *pedagogical agents.*
Arousal Theory	The idea that adding entertaining and interesting material to lessons stimulates emotional engagement that promotes learning.
Asynchronous Interactions	Opportunities for learners and/or instructors to interact with each other via computer at different times.

Auditory Channel	Part of the human memory system that processes information that enters through the ears and is mentally represented in the form of word sounds.
Clinical Trials	Research comparing the learning outcomes and/or processes of people who learn in a target e-learning course versus people who learn in another venue such as a competing e-learning course. Also called *controlled field testing*.
Cognitive Learning Theory	An explanation of how people learn based on the idea of dual channels (information is processed in visual and auditory channels), limited capacity (only a small amount of information can be processed in each channel at one time), and active learning (meaningful learning occurs when learners pay attention to relevant information, organize it into a coherent structure, and integrate it with what they already know. Also called *cognitive theory* and *cognitive theory of multimedia learning*.
Cognitive Load	The amount of mental resource in working memory required by a task.
Collaborative Learning	A structured instructional interaction among two or more learners to achieve a learning goal or complete an assignment.
Concept	Lesson content that refers to a category that includes multiple instances.
Content Analysis	Research to define content and content relationships to be included in an educational course. See also *Task Analysis*.
Coherence Principle	People learn more deeply from multimedia lessons when distracting stories, graphics, and sounds are eliminated.
Contiguity Principle	People learn more deeply when corresponding printed words and graphics are placed close to one another on

the screen or when spoken words and graphics are presented at the same time.

Control — A comparison lesson that does not include the variable being studied in the treatment lesson.

Controlled Studies — Research comparing the learning outcomes and/or processes of two or more groups of learners; the groups are the same except for the variable(s) being studied. Also called *experimental studies.*

Dependent Variable — The outcome measures in an experimental study.

Directive Instruction — Training that primarily asks the learner to make a response or perform a task and then provides feedback. Also called *show-and-do method.*

Distributed Practice — Practice exercises that are placed throughout a lesson rather than all in one location. Compare to *Massed Practice.*

Drag and Drop — A facility that allows the user to move objects from one part of the screen to another. Often used in e-learning practice exercises.

Effect Size — A statistic indicating how many standard deviations difference there is between the mean score of the experimental group and the mean score of the control group.

e-Learning — A combination of content and instructional methods delivered by media elements such as words and graphics on a computer intended to build job-transferable knowledge and skills linked to individual learning goals or organizational performance.

Encoding — Integration of new information in working memory into long-term memory for permanent storage.

Encoding Specificity — A principle of memory stating that people are better able to retrieve information if the conditions at the time of original learning are similar to the conditions at the time of retrieval.

Experimental Studies	See *controlled studies*.
Exploratory Lessons	Lessons that are high in learner control and rely on the learner to select instructional materials they need.
Extraneous Load	The amount of mental work in a lesson that results from the instructional design of the lesson.
Fact	Lesson content that is unique and specific information.
Far Transfer Tasks	Tasks that require learners to use what they have learned in a novel situation, such as adjusting a general principle for a new problem.
Feedback	Information concerning the correctness of one's performance on a learning task or question.
Formative Evaluation	The evaluation of courseware based on learner responses (test results or feedback) during the development and initial trials of the courseware.
Graphic	Any pictorial representation, including illustrations, drawings, charts, maps, photos, organizational visuals, animation, and video. Also called *picture*.
Guided Discovery Instruction	Training in which the learner tries to accomplish an authentic job task, along with guidance from the instructor about how to process the incoming information.
Independent Variable	The feature that is studied in an experiment.
Inform Programs	Lessons designed primarily to communicate information rather than build skills.
Informal Studies	Research in which conclusions are based on observing people as they learn or asking them about their learning. Also called *observational studies*.
Information Delivery Theory	An explanation of how people learn based on the idea that learners directly absorb new information presented in the instructional environment. Also called the *transmission view* or the *information acquisition view*.

Instructional Method	A technique in a lesson intended to facilitate cognitive processing that underlies learning.
Integration Process	A cognitive process in which visual information and auditory information are connected with each other and with relevant memories from long-term memory.
Interaction	See *Practice*.
Intrinsic Load	The amount of work load in a lesson based on the complexity of the content. Compare to *Extraneous Load*.
Jigsaw	A structured collaborative process that requires the integration of sub-team research to a home team project.
Learner Control	Allowing the learner to control the presentation of the lesson, such as the pacing, topics, and instructional elements, practice or examples.
Link	An object on a screen (text or graphic) that when double clicked leads to additional information on the same or on different Web pages.
Long-Term Memory	Part of the cognitive system that stores memories in a permanent form.
Massed Practice	Practice exercises that are placed all in one location in a lesson. Compare to *Distributed Practice*.
Media Element	Text, graphics, or sounds used to convey lesson content.
Metacognition	Awareness and control of one's cognitive processing, including setting goals, monitoring progress, and adjusting strategies as needed. Also called *metacognitive skill* and *metaskill*.
Modality Principle	People learn more deeply from multimedia lessons when graphics are explained by audio narration rather than onscreen text.
Mouse-Over	A technique in which new information appears on the screen when the user places his or her mouse over a designed screen area. Also called *rollover*.

Multimedia Presentation	Any presentation containing words (such as narration or onscreen text) and graphics (such as illustrations, photos, animation, or video).
Multimedia Principle	People learn more deeply from words and graphics than from words alone.
Near Transfer Tasks	Tasks that require the learner to apply a well-known procedure in the same way as it was learned.
Performance Analysis	Research to determine that training will support organizational goals and that e-learning is the best delivery solution.
Perform Programs	Lessons designed primarily to build job-specific skills.
Personalization Principle	People learn more deeply from multimedia lessons when the speaker uses conversational style rather than formal style.
Practice	Structured opportunities for the learner to engage with the content by responding to a question or taking an action to solve a problem. Also called *interaction.*
Principle-Based Lessons	Lessons based on guidelines that must be adapted to various job situations. See also *Far Transfer.*
Procedural Lessons	Lessons designed to teach step-by-step skills that are performed the same way each time. See also *Near Transfer).*
Process	Lesson content that refers to a flow of events such as in a business or scientific process.
Probability	A statistic indicating the chances that we would be incorrect in concluding that there is a difference between the mean scores of the experimental and control groups.
Problem-Based Learning	A type of collaborative process in which groups define and research learning issues based on their discussion of a case problem.
Receptive Instruction	Training that primarily presents information without explicit guidance to the learner for how to process it.

Also called the *show-and-tell method.* See also *Inform Programs.*

Redundant Onscreen Text	Onscreen text that contains the same words as corresponding audio narration.
Redundancy Principle	People learn more deeply from a multimedia lesson when graphics are explained by audio narration alone rather than audio narration and onscreen text.
Rehearsal	Active processing of information in working memory, including mentally organizing the material.
Retrieval	Transferring information stored in long-term memory to working memory. Also called *Retrieving Process.*
Scripted Cooperation	A type of collaborative process in which pairs of learners work in a structured manner to learn course materials.
Seductive Detail	Text or graphics added to a lesson in order to increase the learner's interest but which is not essential to the learning objective.
Selecting Process	A cognitive process in which the learner pays attention to relevant material in the lesson.
Self-Questioning	The process of asking oneself questions about the presented material during learning.
Sensory Memory	Part of the cognitive system that briefly stores visual information received by the eyes and auditory information received by the ears.
Seven-Jump Method	A structured collaborative process that specifies a series of group interactions for discussion of a problem and research on learning issues. See *Problem-Based Learning.*
Simulation	An interactive environment in which features in the environment behave similarly to real-world events.
Statistical Significance	A measure of the probability that the differences in the dependent variables in the test and control groups are real and are not a chance difference.

Storyboard	A layout that outlines the content and instructional methods of a lesson, typically used for preview purposes before programming.
Summative Evaluation	Evaluation of the impact of the courseware conducted at the end of the project; may include cost-benefit analysis.
Synchronous Interactions	Opportunities for learners and/or instructors to interact with each other via computer at the same time.
Task Analysis	Research to define the knowledge and skills to be included in training, based on observations of performance and interviews of performers.
Transfer	Application of previously learned knowledge and skills to new situations encountered after the learning event.
Transfer Appropriate Interactions	Activities that require the learner to perform during training as they would on the job.
Treatment	A variable or factor incorporated in a lesson to determine its impact on learners.
Visual Channel	Part of the human memory system that processes information received through the eyes and mentally represented in pictorial form.
Worked Example	Step-by-step demonstration of how to solve a problem.
Working Memory	Part of the cognitive system in which the learner actively (consciously) processes incoming information from the environment and retrieved information from long-term memory. Working memory has two channels (visual and auditory) and is limited in capacity.

INDEX